REALITY IN A LOOKING-GLASS

INTERNATIONAL LIBRARY OF SOCIOLOGY

Founded by Karl Mannheim

Editor: John Rex, University of Aston in Birmingham

Arbor Scientiae

Arbor Vitae

A catalogue of the books available in the INTERNATIONAL
LIBRARY OF SOCIOLOGY and other series of Social Science
books published by Routledge & Kegan Paul will be found
at the end of this volume.

REALITY IN A LOOKING-GLASS:

rationality through an analysis of traditional folly

Anton C. Zijderveld
University of Tilburg

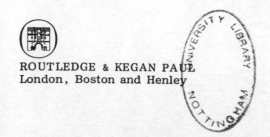
ROUTLEDGE & KEGAN PAUL
London, Boston and Henley

To the memory of Peppi, who
lived and recently died in Vienna
as a traditional fool

First published in 1982
by Routledge & Kegan Paul Ltd
39 Store Street, London WC1E 7DD,
9 Park Street, Boston, Mass. 02108, USA and
Broadway House, Newtown Road,
Henley-on-Thames, Oxon RG9 1EN
Printed in Great Britain by
Billing & Sons Ltd, Guildford and London
© Anton C. Zijderveld, 1982

Library of Congress Cataloging in Publication Data

Zijderveld, Anton C., 1937
Reality in a looking-glass

(International library of sociology)
Includes bibliographical references and index.
1. Fools and jesters - Social aspects. 2. Folly -
Social aspects. 3. Reality - Social aspects.

I. Title. II. Series.

GT3670.Z54   305.5'6   81-19882
ISBN 0-7100-0949-6   AACR2

CONTENTS

PREFACE:
encounter with a fool

In the late 1960s I met in the Viennese apartment of my parents-
in-law a genuine fool, and it is to his memory that I dedicate this
book. Although he did not properly function as the traditional
household fool to be described and discussed in this study, he
had many of his characteristics. He was not an entertainer and
not part of the prestige-promoting appendage of a noble or influential bourgeois family, like his fellow domestic fools were in the
sixteenth and seventeenth centuries. He rather functioned as a
factotum in the household of a medieval specialist, cleaning the
rooms of the large, old-fashioned apartment, located in the centre
of Vienna's ersten Bezirk, scrubbing the floors, dusting the furniture, carrying heavy bins of coals up several flights of old
staircases, from the cellar of the building up to the heating stoves
in the apartment, running errands in the Kärntnerstrasse, etc.
But the tricks he would play on others, for which he was always
excused beforehand due to the state of his mind, the grin on his
face - stupid and cunning at once - and his unremitting loyalty
to the masters of the house, were doubtlessly the main ingred-
ients out of which the great court and household fools were made
in former days, when European societies were still traditional and
not yet modernized to today's extent. In this respect, Peppi was
a relic of a bygone age, the social and cultural vestiges of which
are still observable in the upper-middle classes of this sometimes
melancholy town. Peppi died a few years ago, mourned first and
remembered later as a friend yet a stranger, a human being yet
not a real person. He is missed as one misses a dog which has
died after having loyally shared one's life for many years.

However, I have to admit in all honesty that my encounter with
this fool was a rather painful one. Being confronted as a supposedly rational 'man of science' and 'intellectual' with this
supposedly non-rational 'simpleton' and 'fool' was an utterly irritating experience which, as I found out later in my research on
folly, was not at all unique in history. When fools still functioned
in society, they made it a habit to confront intellectuals with their
folly, and thus to render them quite helpless. Indeed, Peppi
always made me feel ill at ease in his presence, and I am quite
confident that he realized this with a considerable measure of joy
and pride. For instance, while he would address my wife by her
first name, as he had always done since her childhood, he would
insist on addressing me with a reverential 'Herr Professor'. Often
he would even bow in addition, and then, getting up slowly, he
would show me his eerie and devastatingly mocking grin, as if he

said: 'who is the fool now?' He would also play little silly tricks
on me, like hiding my shoes in a dark closet, or repeating my
words when I spoke to him, or complaining loudly about the
quantities of dust he found each day under the bed of the 'Herr
Professor'. At first I thought he hated me for the Dutch accent
in my German speech, but that was not the case at all. He confronted me on a much more sophisticated level. It was the very
ancient, well-nigh archetypal confrontation of one person, socially
defined as being foolish, and another person, socially defined as
being wise. Meanwhile, I began to realize, with inward anger,
that I grew afraid of him. He reminded me of a dog that would
wag its tail and suddenly, without any warning, bite. I found
myself avoiding him, and I knew for sure that he enjoyed this
victory of his! What else can I do now but dedicate this book to
his eerie memory?

Next to supposedly wise men, traditional fools have always
(ab)used supposedly holy men as the targets of their folly. Also
in this respect Peppi belonged to their ilk. He would go to church
on Sundays and recite the Mass in Latin and by heart, just one
line ahead of the celebrating priest. In fact, as idiotic as he was,
or pretended to be, he had unmistakably some remarkable mental
capacities. When, for example, his favourite chicken had died -
a pet he would fondle and carry around on his broad shoulder -
he composed a pompous paean in rhymed German verses. In this
ballad he praised the great qualities of this only friend he ever
had. He could recite it by heart on request.

My encounter with Peppi - a truly historical-sociological
experience - gave rise to the age-old question many people have
asked themselves, before they modernized into supposedly rational men and women: what is folly and what is wisdom; and what
are the criteria by which we can declare one person to be a fool,
and the next to be wise? Ecclesiastes was already puzzled by this
problem. Like our predecessors, I certainly have not found a sat-
isfactory answer. But I have at least found the question again!
Modern man lost sight of it because, ever since the Enlightenment
model of 'Rational Man', imbued as it is with the austerity of
Puritanism and the arrogance of Rationalism, became predominant,
serving the process of modernization exceptionally well, folly has
been removed from the centre of life to the peripheries of our
consciousness and social structure. In some societies people will
still indulge in folly once a year, when they celebrate carnival
(mardi gras), but, apart from such rather isolated vestiges, folly
is now defined as either childish and irresponsible silliness, or -
which is infinitely more fatal - as a symptom of psychiatric disturbance. As a result, contemporary fools, who make a habit of
their folly, are eliminated from social life, and either delivered to
the understanding care of case workers and other welfare professionals, or institutionalized in psychiatric asylums. Just as the
God of pre-modern life has been institutionalized into the church,
forced to retreat from the centre of daily social life, the fool has
been declared to be dysfunctional and similarly forced to retreat

to life's peripheries. But at the very same time that God and
everything that stands for this word is being relegated to these
outlying areas, a vague and indetermined religiosity has spread
throughout modern society, like an oil spot on the water. As I
shall argue later, a similar vague and indetermined kind of folly
has spread throughout modernity - while we still believe firmly
to have superseded folly by our scientific wisdom, or confined it
professionally to psychiatric institutions.

What was the nature of folly? Can we still reconstruct its specific characteristics, its spirit, its 'Geist', analysing and interpreting it sociologically in order to arrive eventually at a better
understanding of modernity? What was folly's socio-cultural role
in life? What were its social functions, when it still occupied the
very centres of consciousness and social structure? Why and how
did it retreat from these centres to the peripheries of consciousness and social structure, evaporating into the cultural air which
modern individuals breathe? Is folly really superseded by modern
scientific wisdom, by the rationality of technology and bureaucracy?

We are back at the initial question again. What is wisdom, what
is folly? But this time we have reformulated the question in contemporary, sociological terms.

Then I dreamt a marvellous dream;
suddenly, as I stood there, I was
wafted away by the goddess Fortune,
who brought me all alone into the land
of longing and made me look into a
mirror - the Mirror of the World -
saying, 'Here you can see untold
wonders - all the things you most long
for - and reach them too, perhaps.'

William Langland, 'Piers the
Ploughman', c. 1377

How nice it would be if we could only
get through into Looking-Glass House!
I'm sure it's got, oh!, such beautiful
things in it! Let's pretend there's a
way of getting through into it somehow...
Oh, what fun it'll be, when they see me
through the glass in here and can't get
at me!

Lewis Carroll, 'Through the
Looking-Glass', 1871

INTRODUCTION:
innocents in an enchanted garden

If traditional society is viewed as an enchanted garden, as Max
Weber did in his study of Ancient China,(1) folly should be
seen as the main component of its flora. When human societies
were not yet ruled by bureaucracy, technology, and the
sciences, when human minds were leavened with metaphysical
notions and associative patterns of thought, when reality was
experienced as a vast field of contingencies, structured mainly
by fictitious and magical connections between cause and effect,
the world was still full of surprises and miracles - a true
'Zaubergarten'. Omnipresent folly overgrew this garden of wonders like a tenacious weed which would at times strangle delicate
flowers, but sometimes also produce itself remarkable blossoms.
As is natural for a weed, folly grew wildly, spreading out over
the yard like an unmanageable contamination. Its many-faceted
appearance contributed to the inscrutability, the mystery of
alternating shades and colours, the wildness of the garden.
    Folly gave traditional society a fascinating quality, and this
very fascination was magical by nature, namely attractive and
repulsive at once. To the traditional women, men and children
who observed his antics and felt the irresistible itch to participate, the fool presented a truly magical 'fascinans'.(2) Since we
have left this enchanted garden on our way to modernity - Max
Weber called modernization 'the disenchantment of the world' -
we find it difficult to understand this fascination and its inherent ambiguity of attraction and repulsion. Our children, not
fully socialized yet into the rational worldview of modernity, still
possess this rapport with the magical ambiguity of folly. The
circus clown, for example, is to them still a truly magical 'fascinans' - attractive and repulsive at once, like many heroes in their
fairy tales. Recently my five-year-old son asked me if there
were a world in which 'everything is the other way about'. When
asked to be more specific, he said, with a faraway look in his
eyes, 'a world in which animals go to the zoo to look at people',
and he added immediately: 'I would not like to live there!'
    In the process of modernization we have crossed a cultural
threshold, to use a simile of Arnold Gehlen.(3) Compared to
traditional man, as well as to the modern child, the adult in
modern society experiences reality differently, and he acts upon
it in a different manner. Not only the content of our knowledge
differs, but also the ways in which we observe, experience and
know reality have changed during the transition from traditional
to modern society. This is very apparent when we try to under-

stand the phenomenon of magical fascination. It became ever
more residual in the process of modernization. As a result it is
very hard for us to understand the nature and functions of
folly, since it requires a reconstruction of the enchanted garden we have left so long ago - as individuals since our childhood, as a collective species ('modern man') ever since roughly
the Renaissance and the Enlightenment. Understanding traditional folly requires a mental re-enactment of innocence and
naivety, bracketing as it were the acquired thought habits of
modernity. Yet, to be communicable and scientifically relevant,
this reconstruction of the enchanted garden and this re-enactment of pre-modern innocence should remain a reflexive thought-
experiment, a rational and ideal-typical construction. One does
not have to become Caesar in order to understand Caesar in a
rational and scientific manner, Max Weber once said.(4) Likewise, one does not have to become a fool in order to understand traditional fools sociologically, as we shall try do do in
this book. Incidentally, this rational reconstruction of the
non-rational, this reflexive re-enactment of traditional folly is
only feasible and possible after one has become aware of the
limits of modernity. It is in any case imperative that one wear
the garments of modernity loosely, if one wants to understand
such a phenomenon as traditional folly. For the duration of their
mirthful performances traditional fools rejected the established
patterns of thought and emotion, the norms, values and meanings of daily routine, the roles and habits of everyday life - in
short, the structures of the taken-for-granted lifeworld. During
their foolish acts these nitwits would live beyond 'good' and
'evil', like Nietzschean immoralists. They would exert a reign of
anarchy in the structureless no-man's-land between the regions
of meaning which have been given names like 'human' and
'animal', 'female' and 'male', 'sane' and 'insane', 'old' and 'new',
etc. Indeed, fools would govern between 'life' and 'death',
'hope' and 'despair', always brushing aside the tensions by
raucous laughter or just a silly grin. They were strangers in
the most original sense of the word - in this world but not of
this world. Traditional fools played erratic games with the primary foundations of human existence, with the basic structures
of the lifeworld, with the essential criteria by which human
beings manage to experience meaning at all. Turning reality upside down, they rendered it, for the duration of their performance, to chaos, to the forces of unstructured primeval energy.
Indeed, these fools were, throughout their silly activities,
irresponsible, rude, uncivilized 'anarchists' - highly irritating,
yet endearing children in an enchanted garden. They possessed
a magico-religious surplus value.

Why did these fools exist at all? What was the nature of their
folly? What were its functions in traditional societies? Why and
how did traditional folly disappear from the orbit of modern
society? Did it really disappear? Did the disenchantment of our
world cause the eradication of folly - its destruction by the

roots - or have its roots been spared, ready to sprout again
under favourable socio-cultural circumstances? Did perhaps folly
itself modernize, spreading out over modern society in a highly
generalized and thoroughly secularized manner?

These are the leading questions this study sets out to answer. They might help us to gain a better understanding of the
world we are presently living in because, if rationalization is
one of the main hallmarks of modernization, we shall be able to
understand modernity better by looking, as it were, 'a contrario'
at the very counterpart of rationalization, namely the reign of
traditional folly. That is, folly was not only a mirror of traditional society, but it is as much a looking-glass of our own
modern world. Reflecting traditional society reversedly, we shall
discover in this looking-glass some very basic, often deeply
hidden components of our own reality. In the traditional fool -
in his reversal and relativization of traditional values and meanings, in his individualism and lack of stern principles, in his
transcendence of primary bonds of solidarity, in his easily
switching loyalties - we shall encounter characteristics which
must strike us as being 'typically modern' despite the fool's lack
of rationality.

There are several cliché interpretations of traditional fools and
folly. As is in the nature of clichés,(5) these interpretations
are never totally wrong nor intellectually satisfying. Two of
them are particularly tenacious and it will be the task of this
study to render them less apodictic and heuristically more fruitful. The first cliché about traditional folly is the notion that it
presents a phenomenon within the history of psychiatry. Fools
were, according to this interpretation, 'mental patients' who were
not recognized as such by their pre-modern contemporaries and
thus badly treated. This is a typically modern bias which the
present study must try to avoid. I do not argue that there were
no cases of mental illness in pre-modern society (although I
realize that in general the definition of 'mental disease' has
become a questionable one), but I merely argue that most traditional fools were not at all 'mentally ill' but the mirthful performers of social roles which were grounded in ancient magico-
religious sentiments. A 'mental patient' who physically endangered
himself or his fellow human beings was viewed as a fool who got
out of hand, who went berserk, and had to be contained by
force. Contrary to unsubstantiated views, medieval contemporaries were quite humane in their treatment of such fools who had
lost touch with reality. It was in early-modern times, when
bourgeois notions of 'normal' behaviour became firmly institutionalized, that the maltreatment of the mentally ill began.

The second cliché and biased interpretation of traditional folly
is of a semi-political nature. Pre-modern society is often described as highly repressive, and the fool seen as an outlet of
democratic feelings within an undemocratic system. One step
further still and the fool is seen as rebel who, under the disguise

of his seemingly innocent folly, criticizes 'the system' or 'the status quo'. If he is not a potential rebel or revolutionary, he is at least the only one who could freely criticize the established hierarchies of power and prestige by simply turning them up- side down. Again, this interpretation is not completely false but it certainly is not completely correct either. For a start, the Freudian notion of psychological outlet in a repressive civilization and the Marxian notion of political critique in an authoritarian society may easily cause a biased view on the culture of pre- modern societies and on the position of fools therein. The pres- ent study tries to operate conceptually in a more circumspect manner. The concept of ambiguity is crucial in this approach. Ambiguity is the essence of traditional folly. Every time we affix one definite characteristic to it, we must discover its con- ceptual inadequacy.

Fools, to begin with an essential ambiguity, operate in this world. They interact, they communicate, they play social roles. But the moment one tries to pin them down with the help of sociological categories, like 'status group', 'social class', or 'formal organization', one experiences their sociological effusive- ness: they are in social reality but, in a strange way, they do not belong to it - in this world, but not of it. They are never clearly male or female, but engage happily in transvestism. They are somehow human, but may suddenly act like animals. They are usually sane, but may at any time behave like lunatics.

Ambiguity should also be taken into consideration with regard to their alleged social and political criticism. It is at this point that I must briefly explain a conceptual distinction which will function as a guiding interpretive notion in the following chapters - the distinction, namely, between the 'regressive' and the 'pro- gressive' thrust in traditional folly. Although there are some profound differences which cannot be expounded here, this dis- tinction is similar to Karl Mannheim's well-known distinction between 'ideology' and 'utopia'.(6) In the regressive thrust the fool takes his audience away from the reality of everyday life to the mythological time prior to the emergence of any kind of civilization and order. He is an anomic monster, partly god, partly demon, partly human, partly animal. He has no knowledge yet of 'good' and 'evil' and is ignorant of the dominant values and norms and meanings. He is crudely materialistic, vitalistic, and brutal, yet innocent, naive and generally non-aggressive - symbol of an as yet undifferentiated energy. He thus reminds his fellow human beings, as in a mythopoeic performance, of what they once have been, prior to the creation of the cosmos, and also what could become of them if they would chance to abandon tradition and forsake the established norms and values of their society. That is, in their regression fools engage in mythological mimesis. This regressive thrust is, of course, strongly magical by nature and the notion of fertility is, as we shall see, essential. This regression, finally, is sometimes mani- fest, as in the 'ceremonial fools' discussed in chapter 4, sometimes

latent, as in the case of medieval folly discussed in chapter 2.
   In this regressive thrust, traditional folly was not at all rebellious or revolutionary. On the contrary, this regression contributed to the rooting of tradition in the consciousness of men,
women and children, shielding society against the threat of
anomie: by demonstrating as in a mirror what happens if the
cultural dictates are forsaken, these fools drive their audiences
closer to the existing status quo. In fact, the distinction between performer and audience is not even right: everybody
could and often would participate in the antics of fools. In any
case, such foolish performances were part of an imperative,
meant to ground tradition - its norms, values and meanings - in
the life experiences of human beings. The activities of fools
were magico-religious exercises in reality-maintenance.(7)
   However, as becomes particularly apparent in the development
of Western-European folly from the high Middle Ages on, folly
bore a progressive thrust also. For example, from a functionally
undifferentiated host of medieval entertainers professional fools
began to emerge after roughly the thirteenth century. They
settled at courts or in influential homes, not merely as entertainers but also, and ever more primarily, as appendages of
their master's social prestige and influence. Thus functions were
acquired which reached beyond the original entertainment function. They gradually crystallized into a specific institution and
profession: the household fool and the court fool. The latter
gradually developed into a rather influential courtier with specific rights and duties. Meanwhile, this process of structural
differentiation was paired to a gradual generalization of meaning,
because folly began to lose its distinctly medieval, raucous, and
naive quality. Above all, it began to lose its magico-religious
essence - it began to secularize. To the degree that the officially appointed court fool's influence grew, his folly faded into
taken-for-granted, saltless remarks and routine acts. As will be
demonstrated in chapter 3, the modernization of folly was first
and most clearly observable in the case of the sixteenth- and
seventeenth-century court fools.
   If the regressive thrust could be viewed as a 'conservative'
or 'reactionary' component of traditional folly, we could indeed
adjudicate a certain measure of social and political criticism to
this progressive thrust. However, such an argument should be
put forth with more care and circumspection than usually happens. Some officially appointed court fools would indeed at times
engage in rather sharp critiques about their sovereigns, but I
shall argue that even then they were still instruments in the
hands of their masters. They were progressive, I shall argue,
not so much because they would rebel against feudalism or absolutism, but rather because they became willy-nilly engulfed in
the modernizing processes of differentiation and generalization
that is, before they knew it, they were normal courtiers and
their folly had lost all meaning and heuristic pith. Indeed, the
famous virtuosos among them in the sixteenth and seventeenth

centuries were no longer innocent flower children in an enchanted garden, but canny courtiers in a steadily modernizing society. Their success as courtiers was their end as fools.

However, fools never die, they just fade away. If the sociocultural circumstances allow it, they may arise again, grinning whatever establishment there is, in its stern face. The further modern society advances into the direction of a pluriform and abstract society, the greater the chance will be that regressive reactions against an ever-growing sense of alienation will occur. Doubtlessly, folly will constitute an essential ingredient of such reactions, as could be witnessed in various parts of the so-called 'counter culture' during the 1960s and early 1970s. But as is in the nature of reaction, these fools remained alien to the sociological nature of modernity. They were typically part of modern society but refused to live in it.

We hear much these days about the quantitative limits of modernization. The doctrine of economic growth, for example, can no longer be preached unhampered. Yet, relatively little is heard about the qualitative limits of modernity, except in exercises of journalistic social philosophy. Such limits have been reached, when the complexities of modern life begin to hinder basic forms of communication and solidarity, when fundamental social bonds lose their authority and legitimacy, when consequently a disquieting sense of anomie spreads out. Such qualitative limits of modernity have also been reached when the generalization of values and meanings have reached a stage on which society can but be experienced as an abstract society which apparently controls one's life and limits one's freedom, albeit in a vague and indeterminate manner. This causes an equally disquieting sense of alienation.(8)

The guiding idea of this book is that traditional folly was not destroyed but has modernized: it became structurally differentiated into professions and roles (cf. the circus clown, the comedian, but also the mental patient) while its original values and meanings generalized simultaneously. As to the latter, folly has now spread out over modern societies in an inflationary manner, losing its original strength and pith. Above all, however it has secularized radically and consequently lost its enchanting power.(9)

But once again, the more abstract a society grows, the larger the chance will be that various groups of people begin to long for re-enchantment. The question is, indeed, whether human beings can live at all, for a prolonged period of time, without any kind of enchantment. In any case, in a highly abstract society traditional folly may recurrently emerge and provide people with an enchantment they have gradually come to long for. This infantilization, this return to the innocent stage of flower children, as artificial as it may be in a radically disenchanted world, is only possible because during the modernization of the enchanted garden the weed of folly was never really destroyed by the roots. However, contrary to popular ideas about the greening of modern culture through the follies of an alleged counter-culture,(10) it must be seriously doubted whether such a re-enchantment will manage to diminish, let alone take away, the typically modern threats of anomie and alienation.

In contrast to what its contemporary adherents want us to believe, any resurgence of traditional folly in modernity is doomed to remain regressive instead of progressive.

1   INTO THE LOOKING-GLASS:
the spectrum of traditional folly

INTRODUCTION

During the research for and the writing of this book, I ran into
two major problems. In the case of studies of folly, it is apparently very seductive to digress constantly into philosophical
reflections and considerations. Several books I consulted indulged in sometimes profound, sometimes trivial, and all the time
elaborate philosophical discussions. This lies, admittedly, in the
nature of the subject, because speaking and writing about folly,
one is bound to touch such metaphysical issues as 'wisdom' and
'truth'. Ironically, the fool seems to trigger philosophical
thoughts more readily than the wise person. In any case, I
made a conscious attempt to keep such metaphysical digressions
which usually do not lead up to much - the tragic hallmark of all
metaphysics - to a minimum.

   Whenever I felt the need to make a few philosophical remarks,
in which I indulged because I do not belong to the present-day
'cultured despisers' of metaphysics,(1) I kept them brief and
allusive, leaving it to the readers to further reflect upon them,
if they feel the need of it. The main focus of the book is not
philosophical but sociological and thus empirical. This should be
said particularly at the beginning of the present chapter in
which I shall transcend the empirical facts and details that are
so crucial in the other chapters, in order to arrive at a general
theoretical picture of traditional folly - i.e. a 'phenomenology of
folly'.

   This leads to a second major problem. The present study lies
in the field of European 'Kultursoziologie' which is essentially
historical and comparative by methodological nature.(2) This
approach, developed and applied in an exemplary manner by Max
Weber, was adopted because it fits my intellectual nature best -
probably the only solid reason why one adopts a certain method.
It also seemed most adequate for the realization of the main
objective of this book. The present study makes an attempt to
give further insight into the process of modernization - a process which Weber labelled poetically 'the disenchantment of the
world'. Despite several important differences of national tradition and political structure, modernity based on the rational
infra-structure of science, technology and bureaucracy, has
spread out over the world as a general worldview and ethos,
causing the last remnants of traditional society to cave in. Folly
was essential to traditional society but no longer exists in modern

society as a distinct phenomenon. By focusing on it, we shall receive a better understanding of the 'disenchantment of the world'.

'Kultursoziologie' presents, I am confident, the best intellectual tools to subject this process of modernization to sociological scrutiny, as the accomplishments of such diverse theorists like de Tocqueville and Durkheim, Weber, Simmel and Mannheim have demonstrated. However, comparative and historical sociology carries its own methodological problems which cannot be discussed here. I mention only one issue, since it has caused me the most headache. It is difficult in any kind of science to keep a balance between empirical precision and theoretical adequacy, but I find this exceptionally hard in the case of 'Kultursoziologie'. (The neo-Kantian methodology of Heinrich Rickert and Max Weber tried to solve it. However, this approach may easily end up in formalistic rationalism which was realized by such diverse theorists as Georg Simmel, Georg Lukács and Karl Mannheim.)(3) In any case, after I had completed the historical and anthropological research - which, naturally, had the character of a thorough secondary analysis of the available data - it turned out to be difficult to find my way between the Scylla of empirical precision and the Charybdis of sociological theory. I wanted to do justice to the wealth of minute data, much of which belongs to the sociologically relevant 'petite histoire' but I had to remind myself constantly also that I was not a historian writing a historical study or an ethnographer gathering anthropological facts. This was the more pressing since I knew more or less precisely at which points of my argument the professional historian or anthropologist would frown, or even worse, smile ironically. These were always the points at which I ventured to draw general, sociological conclusions from the available data. Yet, my main objective was not a historical or anthropological monograph on traditional fools and folly, but a sociological contribution to the interpretation of modernization, as was initiated in particular by Max Weber. The phenomenon of traditional folly, which Weber as far as I know never noticed, was to my mind of great importance for any interpretation of the transition from traditional to modern society. Meanwhile, heeding the facts gathered by many historians and anthropologists, I had to be very careful not to construct a theoretical strait-jacket. It probably needs the intellectual stature of a Max Weber to master this dilemma and if one is aware of the limits of one's own intellect and mind, this consideration alone suffices to abandon the project altogether - which, in fact, I have done many times. Due to my foolhardy nature, I have yet completed the book which begins in this chapter with a theoretically constructed 'phenomenology of traditional folly'.

Actually, this chapter should present a substitute for a concise and formal definition of traditional folly. Each time I tried to construct such a definition the result seemed to have been doomed to be basically and essentially foolish.

Traditional folly is a distinct historical phenomenon. Therefore, it should be possible to define it more or less succinctly, one is inclined to object. That is, of course, true. Yet my research led me to the conviction that this phenomenon is ambiguous and multi-faceted to such a degree that it defies any sensible definition. It is like defining religion at the start of a treatise on the sociology of religion.(4) It can be done, of course, but the heuristic yield is really minimal

Luckily, it is not necessarily unscientific to refrain from such a definition at the start of a scientific treatise. Nor is it necessarily a sign of intellectual weakness, if one admits after due research that the phenomenon under scrutiny exhibits a degree of complexity which defies a heuristically fruitful definition. But in this case there is a dual condition to be met: after the total study has been read, the reader should (a) be convinced that the subject discussed and analysed is indeed a historically distinct phenomenon, and (b) have received a convincing exposition and interpretation of the nature and functions of this particular phenomenon. As is in the nature of any cultural science, I have of course no foolproof guarantee that this dual condition will be met in the present study. However, it has been my continuous concern to realize this objective.

FOLLY AS WORLDVIEW AND ETHOS - BEYOND GOOD AND EVIL

Medieval and early-modern monarchs in Europe, emperors of the Aztecs, shoguns in ancient Japan, khalifs in the ancient Near-East employed court fools.(5) The awe-inspiring and often revolting exploits of ceremonial clowns in traditional African tribes and among several American Indian tribes were in many respects similar to the often sacrilegious activities of the participants of the medieval Festival of Fools in Europe. The license of these fools was similar again to the bold inversion of hierarchies during the Roman Saturnalia. Moreover, in the literary tradition of many civilizations we find the legendary trickster, acting like a kind of folk hero who ridicules the values and violates the norms of his society in playful banter. 'Foolery, sir, does walk about the orb like the sun: it shines everywhere.' ('Twelfth Night', III, 1) Despite many differences due to specific material and immaterial circumstances, traditional folly seems to represent a universal phenomenon whose basic characteristics transcend these circumstantial particularities. By reflecting everyday-life reality in a looking-glass, and so reversing everything that exists, folly presented a curious reality, a chimeric reality, and even a very peculiar kind of ethos and worldview.

A worldview is a system of thought which explains to its adherents why reality is not chaotic but structured, why time does not just float on meaninglessly but tends to form recognizable patterns which constitute 'history', why birth and death are not mere biological contingencies but points in man's biography which are couched in some sort of design. A worldview, says Clifford Geertz appositely, verbalizes the 'assumed structure of reality'.(6) Such a worldview contains, of course, also moral and aesthetic precepts. They spell out, not just what reality is all about 'objectively', but also how human individuals and groups ought to behave, how life and reality are to be experienced cognitively and emotively, what the style of existence should be morally and aesthetically. Geertz calls these dimensions the 'approved style of life' - i.e. the ethos of a particular worldview.(7) In sum, the assumed order of reality is brought to expression in a worldview, while the intrinsically related ethos contains the moral and aesthetic precepts which make for a distinct and coherent mode of existence.

Traditional folly carries, in this sense, the characteristics of a worldview and ethos, but does so in a very peculiar manner. Traditional fools, namely, play mirthful games with their contemporaries' assumptions about reality and happily violate the precepts of their ethos. That is, these fools do not possess values, norms and meanings of their own, making for an autonomous kind of worldview, but they attach themselves parasitically to existing worldviews and next turn the values, norms and meanings of these worldviews upside down, inside out, or backward. Accordingly, their ethos lacks any firm set of principles but is highly opportunistic, if not immoralistic - it lies, to quote Nietzsche, 'beyond good and evil'.

As to the problem of good and evil, we may in general distinguish three (analytic, or 'ideal') types of ethos and worldview, namely 'monotheistic monism', 'gnostic dualism', and 'nihilistic immoralism'. By juxtaposing traditional folly with these constructed types, one will receive a first characterization of traditional folly as parasitical worldview and ethos. I shall first briefly discuss the three types of ethos and worldview. If the reader, as in a thought experiment, reflect these types in a looking-glass, reversing all their constitutive elements, he or she will automatically receive a first impression of traditional folly as a parasitical ethos and worldview.

The reality into which the human individual is born, has been viewed by Judaeo-Christian monotheism as the result of a divine 'creatio ex nihilo' - i.e. a creation from nothingness.(8) This doctrine had a defensive purpose, as it could avert both natural religion and dualism. Since God created the world from nothing, he had to be absolutely transcendent, not belonging to nature, not immanent in cultural institutions (cf. notions like sacred trees or divine monarchies). In fact, the doctrine meant to emphasize that nothing was sacred in reality - only the Creator and his actions with his chosen people, with Israel, with the Christian church were sacred. These actions constituted history - a history of salvation. The same doctrine meant to prevent dualism also, because it stated emphatically that reality did not originate in a cosmic clash between the good forces of light and the evil forces of darkness, as gnosticism did. This

dualistic and metaphysical myth of creation was rejected by
monotheistic monism in favour of the idea of a historical beginning of reality: the creation of heaven and earth by an omni-
potent and absolute God. Prior to this creation there was mere
nothingness - 'tohuwabohu'. Even the forces of evil did not
exist yet. What is, is historical, and thus relative. Only God
the creator is eternal, and thus absolute.

Due to this rejection of dualism, theologians were confronted
with the problem of explaining why and how evil - the devil,
human sin, human suffering, and, above all, death - could have
invaded this divine creation.(9) That is, a justifying explanation -
a theodicy - was urgently needed.(10) Such a theodicy was the
more pressing, since it could in principle clarify also the other
problematic ambiguities of life: opposites like nature and culture,
order and chaos, female and male, past and future, etc. -
various contrary phenomena, in mutual tension, yet inextricably
tied together. They suggested that God's creation was plagued
by ruptures which stood in need of a reconciling explanation.

These and similar contrary forces have preoccupied human
beings throughout all ages in many different cultural contexts,
far beyond the Judaeo-Christian, monotheistic tradition. Yet,
they were rarely elevated to the level of morality, to the level
of good and evil, conceptualized in ethical terms. Only when
this happened, have they been very hard to deal with theologically. Within the monotheistic and anti-dualistic tradition
theologians have tried generally to found their theodicies on the
idea of human sin ('the fall of man') which was linked again to
the notion of man's free will and inherent moral responsibility.
The notion of freedom and responsibility, and of man's abuse of
these - the fall of man, not as a mythological and metaphysical
event, as in gnosticism, but as a historical event, as in Genesis -
originated from the notion of God creating man after his own
image and thus with a great measure of autonomy.

Needless to add that this piece of theodicy placed a heavy
moral burden on the shoulders of the individual believer. It
penetrated deeply into the consciousness of Western human
beings, even in its modern, post-Christian appearance. Many of
us, to give a simple example, will still ask 'what have I done to
deserve this?' when struck unexpectedly by some disaster or
other. Rather than admitting the absurdity of the event in res-
ignation, we still tend to search for some sort of meaning and
for a moral explanation - the vague and highly secularized remnant of an ancient, monotheistic theodicy.

This theodicy was radicalized in Puritanism, particularly in
its well-known doctrines of original sin and predestination. The
latter, as Weber argued cogently, contributed to the rationalization of the modern world.(11) There is no need to repeat his
argument here. However, it should be pointed out that Puritanism, if carried out to its extreme consequences, could lead up
to irrationality and even absurdity. This is important to the
present discussion because here we find a link between the first

type of worldview and ethos (monotheistic monism) and the third
one (nihilistic immoralism).

The emphasis upon original sin, for instance, was indeed a
rational answer to the problem of theodicy, but, elaborated radically, this very same doctrine entailed the seeds of the irresponsible and the immoral because it took away from the individual his sense of responsibility and his notion of his own free will.
Radical Puritans tended to become moral zombies. Meanwhile, the
God of radical Puritanism was very far removed from experienced
reality and alien to the emotions of piety and mystical love. He
was strange and abstract to such an extent that the thin line
between the sacred and the secular, between God and believer,
could easily be severed. The result was a kind of Puritanic
atheism. Gnostic dualism has been the great adversary of monotheistic monism.(12) According to this type of worldview and
ethos reality should be seen in terms of an ongoing metaphysical
struggle between the good forces of light and the evil forces
of darkness, between spiritual and material forces, between
subjective-creative and objective-alienating forces. From this
universal clash reality emerged. If it was created at all, it was
the evil work of a demiurge who stole the divine, absolute and
pure light and threw it into the dungeon of matter, where it has
been kept in bondage and alienation (a concept, incidentally,
that originated in Hellenistic gnosticism and still seems to satisfy
modern, gnostic yearnings). However, a spark of this original
and absolute light has been preserved in the inner soul of man,
where it is held captive by the body, and frustrated by objective forces of social control, exerted by the institutions. The
gnostic has always been a subjectivist who rebels against the
institutions of his societal surroundings. The original, authentic
spark yearns for liberation which can be brought about by a
special kind of consciousness, by an esoteric kind of knowledge -
by 'gnosis'.

Subjectivism, anti-institutionalism, the search for esoteric
knowledge, the longing for 'authentic' experiences have been the
hallmarks of any kind of gnosticism. Needless to add that it has
assumed a complex array of historical appearances to which the
present discussion can do no justice.

Gnostic dualism is a worldview which was probably derived
from ancient Eastern philosophies (Iran) and merged with notions
of Platonism when it came to Europe. It penetrated deeply into
Judaism, and had a strong impact on Western philosophical
thought ever since the days of Hellenism. It functioned as a
perfect ideology for religious and political sectarian movements
(cf. Thomas Münzer, the Albigenses of Languedoc, etc.),(13)
but was also put to aesthetic use because of its strongly sub-
jective thrust (cf. German Romantics like Hölderlin and Goethe).
It had a particularly strong impact on German philosophy (cf.
Hegel, Marx, Heidegger, etc.), whereas much of the contemporary revolt against tradition and traditional institutions carries
ancient, rather irrational gnostic connotations (cf. the ongoing

lament about alienation and the subjectivist search for 'pure'
experiences, if necessary artificially triggered by drugs).(14)
As to the issue of good and evil, gnostic dualism designed a
relatively simple schema of explanation. Reality is to be considered as a vast field on which all kinds of opposites tend to
clash. The world is indeed a miserable place in which the demiurge, whatever shape or appearance he may assume (the state,
the monarch, the pope, the capitalist, the enemy, etc.) plays
his sadistic games. Reality is nothing but the scene of metaphysical conflicts and of a universal alienation. But finally, the
gnostic believes, the forces of light will win a cosmic victory.
The illuminated, the knowledgeable, the people with correct
consciousness (i.e. with 'gnosis') will be gathered and carried
to the pure, unalienated, absolutely free community.

A peculiar and seemingly rational logic was designed by
gnostics in order to explain the progress of mankind towards
this final, apocalyptic destiny. It is called 'dialectics'. Hegel
and Marx, as is well known, have tried to elevate it to a
scientific and modern method with considerable theoretical and
political consequences. This was admittedly a gigantic attempt
to give gnosticism, which was often simplistic and irrational, a
modern scientific status. Dialectics seem to satisfy strongly
romantic-gnostic minds which desire to remain both rational and
irrational - as is, for example, clearly illustrated by Georg
Lukács, the noted Hegelian Marxist. His famous and influential
'Geschichte und Klassenbewusstsein' (1923) was indeed a prime
example of a twentieth-century gnostic treatise.(15)

In nihilistic immoralism both these mutually exclusive worldviews met a common adversary. In this third type of worldview
and ethos reality is envisioned as an essentially absurd chaos
in the midst of which human beings entertain and maintain,
rather pathetically, the illusion of some kind of meaningful order.
It lingered in Eastern philosophies, particularly in ancient India,
but gained momentum in Europe when for various reasons evan-
gelical hope and rationalist faith in progress began to wane -
roughly since the eighteenth century. According to the vision
of the world, reality constitutes a meaningless mess. It is consequently an absurd illusion to believe in objective meaning (cf.
'the meaning of history'), in objective order (cf. 'the social
structure'), and in objective moral and ethical standards (cf.
'the normal rule of behaviour'). Therefore, it is senseless and
silly to toil with the problem of theodicy: one should learn to
live 'beyond good and evil', facing absurdity without fear,
approaching death with one's head up, heeding the supreme
values of dignity and honour. Such values are indeed of a higher
order than moral righteousness and ethical humaneness.

Nietzsche, of course, has most contributed to this worldview
and ethos, but a name like Schopenhauer should certainly be
added, while within the sociological tradition Max Weber came
close to it (as far as he could come close to any worldview, of
course). Needless to add that this tragic vision of the world had

many ancient predecessors (cf. Ecclesiastes, stoicism) but it
seems as if modernity has provided it with its most fertile
soil.(16)

Meanwhile, the problem of theodicy is, of course, solved by
declaring it to be a senseless problem. The opposites of existence, those of good and evil in the first place, are to be
viewed as tragic ruptures, the absurdity of which cannot be
alleviated but has to be accepted as the consequences of fate.
However, this absurdity can be transcended by the force of a
strong character, grounded on the values of dignity and honour. Nietzsche called this 'Herrenmoral'.(17)

This is, of course, not the place to elaborate these three types
of worldview and ethos in further details, discussing their res-
pective socio-economic 'Sitz im Leben', as well as their socio-
political consequences. As to the latter, it should be briefly
mentioned that such worldviews have exerted a heavy impact on,
respectively, social democracy, communism, and fascism. I could
only indicate their bare outlines in order to juxtapose them with
traditional folly which carried the characteristics of a worldview
(certainly in its Wester-European crystallization), yet deviated
on various points from these three dominant types. In fact, as
I said before, if one tries to reconstruct the worldview and
ethos of folly one discovers a vast array of elements from these
three types of worldview, albeit in a reversed manner, as if
reflected in a looking-glass. As a result there is no logical con-
sistence in this foolish worldview - which, of course, stands to
reason!

Whereas monotheistic monism, particularly in its Puritanic
form, laid heavy emphasis on the responsibility of the individual,
shaping the individualism characteristic of Western civilization,
traditional fools would also appear as true individualists but
without any sense of responsibility. In fact, their individualism
was a mocking image of Puritanic individualism. They were
immoralists and opportunists. Similarly, whereas monotheistic
monism, particularly its Calvinist brand, caused the emergence
of rationalism, contemporary fools continued to play the role of
magical enchanters who escaped any predictability and calculability - not for ever, though, as we shall see when we discuss
the modernization of folly. But prior to this modernization, these
foolish individualists were consistently inconsistent, coherently
incoherent, consciously eerie, unpredictable, hard to grasp.
Were they irrational? Did they then lack all reason? The opposite
was true, the members of Dijon's famous Fools' Society 'Mère
Folle' (sixteenth century) claimed. Theirs was a surplus of
reason:

> Tout par raison
> Raison par tout
> Par tout raison (18)

In monotheistic monism the individual believer bore responsibility for his behaviour. If he had any freedom (cf. the doctrine of 'free will' which was needed for theodicy reasons), it was always tied to the burden of this moral responsibility. The fool was also free – the well-known but usually ill-understood 'Narrenfreiheit'. But to this freedom there were no moral strings attached! On the contrary, the individual fool could engage in irreverent licence and insipid deviance, in real autonomy – because in his looking-glass reality nobody could get at him.

According to a widely spread belief in traditional societies, fools were able to relate secrets from the unseen world. Ibn Kaldun said in his 'Muqaddama' (fourteenth century): 'The mad have cast upon their tongues words from the Unseen and they tell them.'(19) In fact, they were allowed their freedom because it was believed that they were the harbingers of secret messages. Yet, theirs was not the 'gnosis' of the dualistic worldview and ethos, because they were simply too materialistic and down-to-earth. They were not prepared to tire themselves out with metaphysical issues, while the rather melancholic experience of alienation remained completely beyond them. Their gnosis was folly, and instead of brooding over alienation and man's deliverance from it, they propagated a superficial 'dolce far niente'. The gnostic notion of a cosmic clash between good and evil would meet with their silly laughter, and operating beyond good and evil, they would rather invite people to join their carefree and insipid ilk – an impish reflection of the unalienated community of delivered gnostics.

Indeed, these fools were immoralists and in a sense also nihilists, since they knew no moral bonds and precepts, while they also negated any kind of authority and social order – at least as far as their own realm of folly was concerned. However, in the case of the third type of worldview and ethos too, these nitwits presented an impish reflection. They lacked, for once, any trace of tragic awareness, while the values of honour and dignity, precious to the nihilistic immoralists as the last ground to stand on, were simply rendered ridiculous by them. The notion of honour, the notion of dignity – they were enough to make these fools snicker. The fool is, of course, not a hero. On the contrary, he is the mirror image of a hero. He is not even quixotic, because unlike Cervantes's endearing knight with his 'sad countenance', the fool lacks any trace of tragedy. Likewise, Nietzsche's famous fool who runs about wildly, warning fellow human beings that the cosmos has been reduced to a helter-skelter of debris after God has been murdered,(20) is far too involved and pathetic to be a traditional fool.

The traditional fool, in short, fools around in terms of all worldviews and all kinds of ethos. He juggles lightheartedly with all meanings, values and norms. Laughter, and silly laughter at that, seems to be the only sensible response to his performance. For the duration of his foolish act – and not much longer – reality changes into a floating mass in which there seems to be no solid distinctions left, no borderlines, no structures, no beacons for perception, cognition and emotion. Or, if any structures are still discernible, they happen to be the mocking images of the structures that provide everyday-life reality with its assumed stability and coherence. The fool renders his audience speechless. As a result, laughter assumes command.

The worldview and ethos of folly have always been parasitical and derivative. However, there is one element in folly which is truly genuine and the solid prerogative of fools. This is its technique of reversal. Like the discussed worldviews, folly would focus on the opposites of human existence, but unlike these worldviews it would play an irreverent game with them: male fools would dress up and behave like women, female fools would act like men and assume male roles and responsibilities; they would change into animals or undifferentiated, crassly materialistic and rudely erotic monsters. Left would be changed into right, right into left; sacred into secular, secular into sacred; high into low, low into high; etc. This technique remained original, because it could only be realized within the terms of folly itself. Whoever would venture to imitate this technique, would immediately join the ruleless ilk of fools. This also is the essence of the fool's freedom, of 'Narrenfreiheit': the fool is not just a parasite, he is an untouchable also. Everyone who lives within the structures of everyday life, can be fooled or made a fool and thereby lose authority and even authenticity. Meanwhile, there is no means of defence. Whoever ventures to castigate, or satirize, or fool a fool makes a fool of himself and thereby joins their silly ranks. Indeed, the fool lives in a looking-glass reality and can say with Carroll's Alice: 'they see me through the glass in here, and can't get at me!'(21)

THE MEMORY OF AN UNDIFFERENTIATED REALITY - THE REGRESSIVE THRUST

Traditional fools were never considered to be fully human. Their crass behaviour, their mad comments, their weird appearances, and their often meaningless gestures undergirded this conviction. The fool's nature, it was believed, lies on the borderline between man and animal where it is subjected to strange impulses which are not controlled by the mind and the traditional values and norms. The fool, in other words, is thoroughly uncivilized. He represents the chimeric no-man's-land between nature and culture, between meaninglessness and meaning. Compared to animals, human beings are the weaklings of nature. They miss, for example, a well-developed instinctive apparatus and must make out with some rather diffuse instinctive residues. Also unlike the animal which is tied to a specific natural environment by his instincts and general physical constitution, the human being is, as Max Scheler once said, 'weltoffen', i.e. open to the world, not tied to any specific natural environment.(22) That is, man is biologically not very well equipped to survive in nature. He is, as the eighteenth-

century German philosopher Herder claimed, basically a 'Mängel-
wesen', i.e. a deficient creature.(23) However, this disadvantage
is changed into an advantage the moment homo sapiens creates a
'second nature' around himself, namely culture. This point was
elaborated in many details, using a host of biological and etiolog-
ical research data, by the twentieth-century German philosopher
and sociologist Arnold Gehlen.(24)

Gehlen's main idea is that human beings can and must compen-
sate for their biological disadvantage by acting upon nature, by
constructing through an ongoing praxis a 'second nature', i.e.
culture which is adjusted to them. The bear is well adjusted biologically to his particular natural environment but would immediately die on the equator. Man, however, not adjusted to any
particular environment (world-open), is able to envelop himself,
through all kinds of activities, with culture - clothes, houses,
tools, and, above all, institutions which regulate behaviour in a
semi-instinctive manner. In sum, whereas the instincts provide
the animal with a regulatory system of behaviour, man commands
over a cultural regulatory behaviour system - the traditional
institutions. He is not organically tied to these institutions, like
the animal which is caught in the web of his instincts. On the
contrary, the institutions are historically 'achieved' not biologically 'ascribed', they can be modified, even overthrown in revolution. Yet, they are, as the substitutes of instincts, of supreme
biological relevance.(25) Therefore, man does wise, Gehlen warns,
to treat his institutions with much care and circumspection, because without them, or with institutions that function only mini-
mally, man would be delivered to the terror of biological chaos,
cf. biological disorientation. To Gehlen, anomie is in essence a
threat of nature which modern man has lost sight of, because he
has enveloped himself with thick layers of culture for so many
centuries. Outside the control of institutions, man would be delivered to the tensions of unstructured sense impressions which
try to pour into the individual, and of unstructured impulses
which try to pour out. In such a situation, the human individual
would be unable to orient himself towards reality in a sensible
manner, and he would be incapacitated to act upon it. Loss of
institutional control over man does not promote greater freedom,
as modern man tends to believe ever since Rousseau, but causes
a fundamental and fatal incapacity to act - Gehlen speaks of 'Hand-
lungsverlust' - which eventually would lead to a gradual, biological conditioned decline of the human species.

Maybe because he stays in closer touch with nature and experiences its threats and dangers daily, pre-modern man entertains
a far greater respect for tradition and the traditional institutions
than modern man. In traditional society, the institutions of religion, family, education, polity and community were never merely
means for the maintenance of a rational and meaningful order in
society. They were first and foremost sacred realities in which the
collective sense of life, the trans-individual experience of meaning,
and the ancient values and norms were 'stored up'. The institutions

staked out the safe social realm within nature, providing the
individual with a solid sense of (collective) identity. Without
tradition, without the institutions, one realized, man would be
delivered to the threats of nature and deteriorate to a senseless
monster. Indeed, he would become a fool!(26)

It was, of course, necessary to remind people of this fact constantly - a kind of mimesis, a grounding of tradition in the consciousness of the members of society. Learning and reciting the
myths and legends of the tribe, and above all participating in
the rituals and ceremonies, were the prime instruments of this
mimesis. The performance of fools which prior to modernization
was always ceremonialized, should be viewed as part of this ritual
mimesis.

If one reads the ethnological accounts of the so-called 'ceremonial clowns' in traditional Africa and among several Indian tribes
of North and Middle America, it becomes apparent that these fools
carried, among other functions, an instructive one. In a structured (i.e. ceremonial, ritual) manner, these fools were to act
contrary to the sacred values and norms of their society. Their
behaviour was surprisingly blasphemous and irreverent, over-
throwing for the duration of their performance all the rules of
good behaviour, all the tabooed precepts and all the established
hierarchies of power and prestige. Their speech was badly distorted, their faces were hidden behind hideous masks, their movements and gestures odd and weird. At times they would act and
chatter like small children, then again they would suddenly behave
like animals, then act like strange and outlandish monsters. In
fact, the established borderlines between men and women, adults
and children, nature and culture, human beings and animals were
blurred or even wiped out. It was as if they regressed to a stage
of human development prior to the primeval differentiation between
nature and culture, between man and animal. It was as I shall
argue later with more details, as if these fools enacted the raw
material of culture, the undifferentiated lava of civilization, the
primeval energy from which human reality emerged - not institutionalized yet, not civilized yet, not belonging yet to either
nature or culture. Their foolish exploits were a staged 'tohuwabohu' - awe-inspiring, yet majestic in its hideousness, fascinating
in its magical sense of the word, i.e. repulsive and attractive at
once. These ceremonial fools were to demonstrate the raw material
of socio-cultural reality - still meaningless, senseless, worthless;
pure energy and force without any structure yet. They represented aboriginal anomie. To everybody present, ceremonial fools
demonstrated vividly what would become of man, if he would forsake the burden of tradition.

Although hidden under a much thicker layer of civilization,
medieval folly shared this regressive feature. The famous Festival
of Fools, for instance, was a set of absurd festivities at the end
of the old and the beginning of the new year, celebrated in the
medieval churches of Western Europe up till roughly the seventeenth century. It was, as we shall see in chapter 2, an abundant

celebration of vitalism which carried several, rather obvious magical remnants of pre-Christian heathenism. In this festival the
garments of Roman Catholic civilization had been laid off to be
exchanged for weird vestments and hideous masks worn during
mummeries in church and blatantly magical rituals in front of the
altar. When theologians and prelates objected to these practices,
they did not reject their inherent folly so much as their hardly
disguised heathenism. Finally, in our modern society we may still
encounter this regressive vitalism in the circus clown whose magic,
incidentally, is usually only understood genuinely by our children.
Unlike our children, we have been disenchanted too much to
understand empathetically the blurring of borderlines and structures which occurs in the clown's act. He does not fascinate us,
acting upon us with attraction and repulsion both. He merely
amuses us.(27)

FOLLY AND MODERNIZATION - THE PROGRESSIVE THRUST

Although the regressive thrust predominates in traditional folly,
we can discern a progressive thrust too. In order to explain this,
I must deal briefly with some basic sociological notions about modernization. The intriguing issue of folly's modernization will be
discussed again at the end of this book, in the conclusion. This
book has departed from the admittedly debatable proposition that
modern man is quite different from his predecessor in history,
traditional man. To begin with, the concepts 'traditional man' and
'modern man' are, of course, sufficient to call forth strong irritations and objections on the part of historians and anthropologists,
since they seem far too simplistic to be of any scientific use. Yet,
in a cultural-sociological study like the present one, these and
similar conceptual constructions ('ideal-types') are indispensable,
since they help us to indicate and understand, as in a shorthand
manner, the most characteristic features of a process like modernization. Such concepts can be justified, I am convinced, as long
as one keeps in mind that they have been constructed for heuristic
purposes - i.e. as long as one uses them as heuristic tools which
indicate as in a shorthand manner the essential dimensions of
cultural phenomena. They certainly do not pretend to provide
empirically tested, 'correct' pictures of reality.(28)
     As to the alleged difference between traditional and modern
man, a few basic and by now common-sense, if not cliché, notions
have to be repeated first. We live in a world today which is predominantly conditioned by industrialization, advanced mechanization
of work, bureaucratization, urbanization, professionalization, etc. -
processes we usually lump together conveniently into the concept
of modernization. Traditional man, on the other hand, lives in a
world prior to these processes and therefore his whole style of
life, his outlook on reality, his mentality, his ways of feeling and
experiencing are different from ours and consequently hard for us
to understand.(29) His is a world ruled by religious doctrines and

magical rituals, a world explained in terms of myths and legends and metaphysical conceptions, a world with a different time structure and an altogether different notion of space. This world is still an enchanted garden, full of mysteries, contingencies and surprises.

Naturally, an ethnographer like Malinowski could discover quite easily provinces of meaning in the worldview of the Trobrianders which were not at all determined and conditioned by metaphysical and religious conceptions, but solidly and pragmatically entrenched in down-to-earth, technological and rational expertise and knowledge.(30) Likewise, it is not difficult to point at various premodern survivals or revivals of enchantment in our contemporary industrial society, evidence of which presents the recurrent interest in astrology precisely at a time in which man has landed on the moon, or the abiding fascination with paramedical therapies and medicines in a time in which medical research has won unprecedented victories.(31)

Yet, having taken these facts into due account, the cultural sociologist is still inclined to see essential differences in terms of social structure and of human consciousness between modern society and the traditional world. The process of disenchantment is the very essence of this difference. This becomes very apparent if one studies the phenomenon of traditional folly.

Various social theorists have described modernization as a twofold process, consisting of an expanding 'structural differentiation' and a gradually increasing 'generalization of meanings and values'.(32) As to differentiation, the prime focus of these theorists was generally on the division of labour (specialization) which caused social structures to grow ever more complex. Durkheim, for example, saw the division of labour as a crucial variable in the transition of mechanical (traditional) to organic (functional) solidarity (integration). Weber focused mainly on the ever-increasing process of rationalization which he observed in the capitalist mode of production, in the emergence of science and technology, and in the rise of legal-rational bureaucracy. Among other things, we find in the latter a strict (formal) division of powers and authorities by means of a structural differentiation of positions and tasks.

During modernization, various institutional sectors began to change their structural position. Sectors like the family, religion, and the law were still located in the very centre of social life under pre-modern conditions, but under the impact of industrialization these same sectors acquired a relative autonomy and functionally specific position within the social structure at large. Whereas, for example, the family under pre-modern conditions still carried a host of undifferentiated functions, in modern circumstances several of these functions have been distributed over various functionally specific institutional sectors, like those of the economy, the polity, religion, education and leisure, each harbouring their own professional specialists. In other words, structural differentiation is not only an increased division of labour in terms of professions but at the very same time an expanding division of functions in terms of institutional sectors.

The socio-structural position of the individual changes concurrently. As Georg Simmel argued cogently, due to structural differentiation the individual is forced to live in a complex web of affiliations which each impose on him their particular demands of loyalty and role performance, and thus mould his identity in a pluriform manner.(33) The modern individual plays indeed a plurality of roles which are not only constantly in danger of mutual conflict but also prevent the individual from living with a clear set of values, norms, meanings and motivations.

The bonds of kinship presented traditional man with a hierarchical structure within which he could occupy an ascribed position, moulding his experiences of reality in a subjectively as well as intersubjectively meaningful manner. The family or clan was, in other words, a heuristic niche which rendered life itself meaningful, understandable and thus bearable, despite the often unbearable material conditions of existence. Indeed, the family, the clan, the tribe, the rural community were circles of meaning around the individual, repressive to the taste of modern man and certainly struck with many conflicts and often nasty feuds. But these were the price to be paid for the experience of concrete and existentially real meanings. Family feuds are increasingly impossible in modern society, precisely because there are but few existentially relevant meanings left which family members share and over which they can get into a conflict. Within the small and relatively isolated modern nuclear family conflicts can still reach fever pitch (cf. the so-called generation gap), but they hardly grow into long-term feuds because it has become morally easy simply to walk out, either as teenaged child or as spouse. Loyalty and commitment have indeed become old-fashioned values.(34)

One can observe that meanings, values and related symbols, connected with the institutional sector of the family, begin to spread out over society far beyond their structural boundaries, when the nuclear family starts to occupy a particular and relatively isolated (autonomous) segment of the total social structure under the impact of modernization. A general, elusive, morally uncommitted ideology of 'familism' will penetrate into other institutional sectors and spread over society as a vague philosophy and worldview. This diffuse ideology with its inflated semantics is distributed by various media, in particular by the family-oriented women's magazines which inform the readers about the education of the children (with lots of vague, psychologistic theories), about children's clothes, about problems of marriage (with a vague counselling not founded on any clear-cut moral and religious standards), about decorations of rooms and dinner tables, about gardening, etc. Thus, while the nuclear family is segregated to the very corners of the modern social structure, due to the process of differentiation, familism as a vague worldview and ethos tends to spread out over the various institutional sectors of society (cf. such a generalized notion as 'the family of man').

The same can be observed in the case of the law or of religion. The more law differentiated into a specific and professionalized part of the social structure at large ('the rule of law'), the more 'legalism' as a vague and rationalistic ideology has spread out over society and modern social life - a transition indeed, as Maine argued, from a society based on 'status' to a society ruled by 'contract'. If it was a most serious threat in traditional society to be exiled from one's extended family and community, since it spelled social and sometimes even physical death, (35) modern man can be actually threatened seriously only by a law suit. The status of a medical doctor, for example, would defend a physician in traditional society, if he would chance to commit an error. Today, physicians have to invest great sums of money in insurances in order to be covered against medical malpractice suits. Similarly, while religion differentiated structurally from an encompassing 'sacred canopy' (P. L. Berger) to a rather remote corner of the total social structure, a 'vague religiosity', a 'civil religion' (R. Bellah), began to spread out over modern society, often reaching far beyond the proper sector of religion, the church. In fact, modern man might be secularized thoroughly in that he does not frequent the church anymore and forsakes the ecclesiastic observances of former days, yet he might well be infinitely more 'religious', albeit in a vague and indetermined manner, than his pre-modern predecessor who went to church and adhered to the doctrines of his faith because tradition had told him to do so. (36)

The list can be easily prolonged. Education, for instance, has been structurally differentiated thoroughly, emerging from the sectors of the family and of religion. Yet, while it developed into a functionally specific institutional sector, the call for a permanent education for all layers of society is heard ever stronger, reaching far beyond the proper boundaries of formal education, as if life itself is not worth living anymore without at least a bachelor's degree. Needless to add that contrary ideologies, arguing against religion, law, the family and education will also emerge, using various arguments and ideas which remain generally vague since they are not tied clearly to any particular institutional tradition - they are, as the clichés have it, 'interesting', 'relevant', 'creative' and even 'liberating': feminism versus familism, notions of 'responsive law' versus those of 'autonomous law', ideas about 'deschooling society' versus those of 'permanent education', etc. (37)

In such a cultural climate anything can be actually thought, said, experienced and believed - i.e. indeed, as modern lingo has it, 'everything goes'. This is one of the reasons why folly as a distinct configuration, establishing a counter-reality, can no longer exist today. In fact, in such a situation everything tends to become a token of folly which, of course, causes the disappearance of folly as a distinct phenomenon. I shall return to this point at the end of this book.

The structural differentiation of folly can be observed clearly in Europe since the sixteenth century when it gradually began to institutionalize and professionalize to a degree unknown to earlier centuries. Folly professionalized, for instance, in the institution of court jester to such an extent that it began to lose its traditional parasitical features - a development, as we shall see in more detail later, which has led to the disappearance of this curious courtly profession. At the very same time, the fool began to develop into a specific stage role to be played by specialized actors. Such a role did exist in ancient Roman theatre plays and can also be found in ancient Indian theatre (cf. the 'vidūsaka') and in the Indonesian 'wajang' play (cf. the role of Semar).(38) Yet, in the Renaissance theatre of Western Europe the role of fool or clown acquired a degree of specificity which was not found earlier within this particular orbit. This is demonstrated by various plays of Shakespeare and above all by the Italian 'commedia dell'arte'. Historians have argued, in fact, that after the court fool's disappearance, the medieval fool continued to exist exclusively as a literary figure on the stage, and as entertaining clown in the circus.(39) The modern commercialized comedian (Danny Kaye, Bob Hope, Peter Sellers, etc.) may thus be seen as representatives of the last phase in a long development in which the traditional fool gradually modernized - an evolution from the medieval folk fool, to the court fool of absolutism, to the stage role and literary figure of the Renaissance, to the circus clown and the film-television comedian of our days. It is one line from the fools of Dijon's 'Mère Folle' to Archibald Armstrong, to Scaramouche and 'dummer August', to Grock and Chaplin. At the end of this evolution, the highly uncivilized and magical features of the medieval fool are but faintly recognizable. The modernization of folly was its structural differentiation, its gradual generalization of meanings, its progressing civilization.(40) The meanings of traditional folly generalized and evaporized during this long process of evolution. This is, for instance, apparent in the modern conception of the fool which has lost all its original heuristic vigour and pith. Calling someone a fool today, one applies a concept which resembles only faintly the rich set of connotations it originally carried. In traditional society a fool was always more than a person behaving in a silly, childish and non-rational manner. A true fool performed an act of entertaining yet awe-inspiring relevance. He carried a magical aura with a metaphysical surplus value. Magical connotations were still operative in the medieval Festival of Fools, grew increasingly vague and indetermined in the early-modern court fools and bourgeois fools' societies, and evaporated radically in contemporary, modern society. To us, a fool is just a silly, somewhat childish, non-rational person, if not a lunatic.

Traditional folly was contagious. It was a popular pastime, a fundamental component of popular culture. This dimension has generalized into what we call humour and wit. In our jokes we juggle also with the established meanings and values of daily social life, inverting social hierarchies, perverting standard pieces of common-sense knowledge. In these our daily humorous endeavours we do indeed create a reality with its own 'logic' and 'order' - a kind of looking-glass reality which exists for the duration of our jokes and witticisms. Yet, they do not by far constitute the peculiar kind of worldview and ethos which traditional folly

incorporated and which gave to it its eminent functionality. Our
humour and wit are indeed a far cry from the wealth of boorish
meaning which folly possessed in a pre-modern context. They are,
in fact, too 'civilized' to be compared with traditional folly from
which they yet have emerged.(41)

TRANSITIONS AS THE MAIN FIELD OF OPERATION

Traditional folly always thrived in times and situations of transition.(42) In many different traditional societies people have
ceremonially reversed the existing order of things during periods
of time in which fundamental changes took place. The ancient
Roman Saturnalia, the medieval Festival of Fools, and the contemporary European carnival are examples of such foolish transition
ceremonies. During the transition from the old to the new year,
during Shrove Tide or Lent – a period in which nature regener-
ates and in which the Easter drama of death and resurrection is
commemorated – during marriage and funeral ceremonies, during
initiation rites, people throughout the ages and in culturally quite
different contexts have staged foolish performances, changed sex
roles, reversed social hierarchies, overthrown value patterns,
violated tabooed norms, and acted generally as in a mirror fashion.
In maritime history crossing the equator for the first time has
always been an event which called for a ritual initiation ruled by
folly.(43)
   Prior to the process of modernization, people of most societies
have been very sensitive to such periods of transition. They were
experienced with a certain measure of enchanting awe. It seemed
as if such transitional periods possessed an indeterminate kind of
power. The traditional and sacred values and norms were temporarily suspended, the structures of the social order in temporary
disarray, the routine securities and certainties in limbo. What was
'old' had passed away, what would be 'new' had not yet taken
over command. During such transitions, reality seemed to assume
a floating nature in which actually everything seemed possible. In
short, reality itself had lost its inner structure, its borderlines,
its order. Indeed, reality had turned, for the duration of the
transition, foolish.
   Traditional man dealt with this hazardous phenomenon as he
dealt with all contingencies, namely ceremonially and ritually. The
lack of structure was forged into a ceremonial mould, the floating
nature which reality assumed during the transition, was grounded
in a ritual performance. Van Gennep, for instance, demonstrated
in his well-known monography how traditional man tried to come to
grips with transitional situations and their inherent contingencies
by the performance of 'rites de passage', transition rites in which
three main stages were to be distinguished for heuristic purposes:
separation ('séparation'), transition ('marge'), and incorporation
('agrégation').(44) It stands to reason that folly has been particularly prominent in the second phase. When the novice has been

separated from the safe centre of reality, entering the chimeric
realm of reality's margins, prior to the incorporation, the return
to reality, he dwells in no-man's-land and is reduced to a fool.
During the transition the novice is subjected to the unpredictable
rule of folly which is yet not totally open and unstructured because it is forged into a ceremonial and ritual mould. However, the
'social structure' within this chimeric reality is a mocking mirror
image of the social structure of everyday-life reality: the lord of
misrule is a slave-crowned-master in the Saturnalia, is a man-
dressed-up-as-woman in the medieval Fools' Society, is a boy-
ordained-bishop in the Festival of Fools, is a weirdly disguised
god Neptune during the first crossing of the equator. In short,
the transition phase is not sheer 'tohuwabohu', but the order that
is present is a derived one - a mocking order, a looking-glass
image of everyday life, 'normal' order.

Marginality was the hallmark of traditional folly because fools
lived in society without really being part of it. Therefore, it was
quite natural that folly would strive in situations of transition and
in 'rites de passage'. In a way, folly was the 'logic' of transition,
the 'method' of structuring the unstructured, the 'language' by
means of which the unspeakable was verbalized.

As I said before, reality itself assumes foolish features, when it
passes from 'old' to 'new', from the past to the future, from the
known to the unknown. Since it is invested with many transitions,
'normal' reality seems to be full of folly: from the death of winter
to the life of summer during the spring, from the end of one year
to the start of the next at the end of the calendar, from the dependence of childhood to the independence of adulthood in puberty
and adolescence, and, above all, from life itself to the darkness
of the after-life in death. Indeed, these are periods of time and
moments of man's biography which lack taken-for-grantedness,
stability, certainty, order. They may well carry the seeds of a
better life, but they may as well carry the seeds of chaos and
destruction. They are situated in a kind of no-man's-land between
a promising order and a threatening anomie, between meaning and
meaninglessness. In the midst of a taken-for-granted, 'normal'
reality, these transitional periods of time in nature and society
and these points in a person's biography constitute phases of folly.
Unlike modern man, traditional man was very much aware of this
marginality inherent as it is to human existence, and he did realize the foolish nature of this marginality. In order to cope with it,
he ceremonialized it and held the fool in esteem. The fool was more
than just a simpleton or lunatic. He, in fact, represented the world
of transition, the chimeric reality of no-man's-land whose order
can but be fathomed in a looking-glass fashion. It was believed
that this inhabitant of the transitional world could convey messages
from beyond, from the yet unseen world to which all individuals
necessarily move through the passage of time.

If in the preceding discussion folly was perhaps too much set
apart conceptually when it was described as a counter-reality, we
are now able to correct this error. As much as death is part of life,

functioning as its time limit, folly belongs to reality, exhibiting
the very borders of its 'order', its 'normalcy', its 'rationality'.
Likewise, if folly was interpreted in the preceding discussion as
a force which would reinforce dialectically, as in a looking-glass
fashion, the dominant values and norms of traditional society
(particularly in its regressive thrust), we are now able to argue
in a much more subtle manner: folly is not merely a function of
the status quo, but manages to demonstrate its very contingency
by showing to people that reality as it is, could very well be
different, even contrariwise! The traditional fool contributed to
the grounding of tradition, - the values, norms and meanings of
society - in the consciousness of individuals, yet by his contrary
behaviour in which standard social roles and hierarchies of power
and authorities were reversed, he demonstrated to the members
of his audience that things as they are could just as well be quite
different, that reality as it is experienced in the routine of daily
life can be transcended to a level from which 'normal' reality suddenly looks 'abnormal'. That is, if one follows the fool into the
reality of his looking-glass, if one adapts to his 'language', his
'logic', his kind of 'reason', the routine and 'normal' reality of
everyday life, with its rules, structures and hierarchies, begins
to look genuinely foolish. Stepping out of the looking-glass again,
back into 'normal' reality, one will appreciate the security, the
certainty, the cognitive and emotional clarity of this reality again,
but one will also do so 'tongue in cheek' because one has received
a very deep insight in the contingency of this very reality.

This is hard to grasp for modern individuals, entrenched as
they are in the often simple-minded rationalism of modernity.
Rational man is too one-dimensional to be able really to understand
the fool.

POWER, AUTHORITY AND FOLLY

Power wants to be legitimated. Rarely does man try to realize his
will against the will of others merely by the use of physical force.
It is inherently human to search for the acceptance of one's power
on the part of the others on whom it is exerted. That is, one will
try to convince the others that one's power is legitimate. Legitimacy is the social cash value of power. We call legitimated power
'authority'.

The fool will accept power for what it is, but he is never impressed by authority. He has to accept the balance of power in
a certain status quo simply because he is not in any position to
counteract it effectively. Being in the system, yet never fully
part of it, the fool remains unable to form a party which one needs
if one wants to contest a given balance of power with effect. Moreover, combating power effectively needs a certain measure of planning, scheming, organizing - qualities, in short, which are alien
to the fool's nature. And indeed, as we shall see recurrently in
the following chapters, traditional fools would never act as rebels

or revolutionaries, combating a status quo in terms of power. On the contrary, fools are in general conservative in their attitudes towards the holders of power - if they entertain any opinionated ideas in these matters at all, which is very rare indeed.

In the later Middle Ages, as we shall see in the next chapter, peasant revolutionaries were decried as fools, but the notion of folly had then already acquired bourgeois connotations which were alien to the true nature of traditional folly. The remarkable peasant leader from the late fourteenth century, John Ball, described by Jean Froissart (c. 1337-c. 1410) as 'a crack-brained priest of Kent', could not by means of any description be called a fool. On Sundays, after Mass, he would wait for the poeple coming out of church and preach his 'social gospel':(45)

> Good people, things cannot go right in England and never will, untill goods are held in common and there are no more villeins and gentlefolk, but we are all one and the same. In what way are those whome we call lords greater masters than ourselves? How have they deserved it? Why do they hold us in bondage? ... They have the wines, the spices and the good bread: we have the rye, the husks and the straw, and we drink water. They have shelter and ease in their fine manors, and we have hardship and toil, the wind and the rain in the fields. And from us must come, from our labour, the things which keep them in luxury. ... Let us go to the King - he is young - and show him how we are oppressed, and tell him that we want things to be changed, or else we will change them ourselves.

This, of course, is not fool's talk!

However, it is authority which will always meet with their mocking remarks and irreverent antics. If power is respected by fools, any attempt to dress it up with justifications and legitimations must reckon with their mockery and derision. Throughout the evolution of mankind power has been dressed up, disguised, wrapped up with theories ('ideologies'), with symbolic gestures and acts, with garments, uniforms, etc. Power wants to be enacted, authority wants to be shown. If power calls forth fear, authority aims at impression. The authority of a powerful person shows in the speech, his manners, his clothes, the reverent ways in which others treat him, the admiring stories that are told about him. Power needs strength, authority needs decorum. In order to be accepted as legitimated power, i.e. as authority, power stands in need of 'impression management' (E. Goffman).

The fool now is never much impressed by the powerful. He is irreverent in the face of authority and tries his best to undermine the impression management that is staged by the powerful. The success of impression management and thus of authority depends, of course, wholly on social interaction between people in power and those that will have to follow it. Authority is dependent on a social game with a set of rules and agreements by which situations

are being defined as 'real'. The fool, however, is by definition
never part of the game and therefore in the position to disturb it
severely. He is prone to lift the veil of authority from the positions
of power by means of silly remarks, irreverent antics, devoid of
any decorum, showing as it were the unpleasant nakedness of
power. Incidentally, when people in power make too many mistakes
consistently, they will not only lose authority but also run the
risk of being defined as fools. 'Public figures who become classi-
fied as fools', Orrin E. Klapp once wrote, 'lose their chance of
leadership.'(46)

Meanwhile, the fool himself will be unable to destroy authority,
because after the laughter he elicited has died out and people
have returned to the reality of mundane facts and occurrences,
the affected authority is restored again. The veil was lifted for a
short while, the structures of authority had been relativized
momentarily, it was briefly demonstrated that power could well
have been justified and legitimated differently or maybe not at all.
But the power itself had not been really affected and its legitimation was only relativized for a moment. In fact, it is well possible that the latter is tolerated or perhaps even stimulated by
those in order to demonstrate that there is indeed power behind
the mask of authority! Is it possible that the fool's relativization
of authority which leads only to laughter anyhow, serves the purposes of those who want to hold a firm grip on power? If this
question is to be answered affirmatively, one may expect to find
debunking folly in highly authoritarian organizations.

There is indeed much historical evidence for this hypothesis
which admittedly deviates from the rather cliché and simplistic
interpretation of folly as a critical, if not rebellious, component of
the generally authoritarian structures of traditional society. Why
would the ancient Roman slave society institutionalize the foolish
reversal of its authority structures in the yearly Saturnalia - an
anarchistic happening which we shall discuss in more detail later?
On the level of local parishes in rural France and England, why
would the medieval and early-modern Catholic Church celebrate a
yearly Festival of Fools in which the lower clergy would reign and
in which a temporary bishop would be elected from amongst the
choir boys - a festival, as we shall see, which was primarily con-
tested by theologians and prelates because of its rather ostent-
atious paganistic content and not because of its inherent relativization of the ecclesiastic authorities? An utterly authoritarian,
well-nigh fascist organization like the French Foreign Legion, to
give a contemporary example, celebrates yearly Camerone Day
which commemorates a famous and victorious battle fought in
Mexico in 1863. 'The legion goes mad on Camerone Day,' a legionnaire writes in his diary. 'Officers and N.C.O.'s do all the *corvée*,
including serving the food. There will be side-shows and a parade
of floats through the town. There will even be a bullfight. It is
apparently a carnival of carnivals and frantic preparations are
under way for all the many events.'(47) Doubtlessly worked-up
aggression was vented in this celebration which, in 1963,

reportedly got completely out of hand. But even then the victims
of the drunken and berserk legionnaires, celebrating their cen-
tennial Camerone Day with true riots, were not their repressive
officers but the innocent inhabitants of the Algerian town in
which the barracks were located. It was 'a sight of total devast-
ation that was absolutely unbelievable.'(48) The stores were
ransacked, the town actually destroyed. Folly let loose within an
otherwise strictly hierarchical and authoritarian system can indeed
become violently explosive, as if the fragile bonds of civilization,
held together by too strict a social control, are being fractured,
giving free reign temporarily to corked-up impulses and irrational
instincts. Once again in this particular case the holders of repressive power, the officers, are significantly not at all harmed.

This interpretation of folly in terms of the safety-valve function
is rather old. As we shall see in the next chapter, the early-
modern participants of the Festival of Fools used it already in
defence of their folly against the attacks levelled against them by
Parisian theologians. Yet, as correct as this interpretation may be,
one should not lose sight of the important fact that such foolish
games with the paraphernalia of power remained at all times what
they really were: playing. The fool has always been primarily a
'homo ludens' who engaged in folly first and foremost for the sake
of playing. His primary aim has never been somehow to improve
humanity or society. If they relativized authority, lifting its
socially accepted masks, showing its real face of power, these
fools did so primarily because the discrepancy involved was funny,
because the disjunction of impressive authority and naked power,
if layed bare without concealment, elicits laughter. In fact, 'debunking' is much too strong a word for this kind of playing.
'Poking fun' at the holders of authority is a much more adequate
expression.

In sum, authority is a game in which the fool does not participate. On the contrary, he is constantly out to play a game with
authority, for the sake of fun. Holders of power benefit from this
playing with authority because it demonstrates what lies behind
the paraphernalia of authority: power. Particularly in an authoritarian system, holders of power are eager to drive this point
home. The more dictatorial they are, the more they need fools and
folly.

RATIONAL MAN VERSUS THE FOOL

When European modernization was still in its early stage of development, the Enlightenment designed a normative anthropological
model - an ideal human being who had to carry out the Promethean
programme of rationalism, namely the progress of mankind from
the darkness of tradition to the light of modernity. Rational Man
was thoroughly secularized, the first representative of modern
paganism.(49) Yet he bore the character vestiges of the Calvinist
Puritan, of whom he was the cocksure descendant. Puritan

rationalism was described by Max Weber in a masterful manner
and there is no need to repeat his account of the influence Puritanism exerted on the birth of modernity. Severed from its theological origins - which, as we saw before, was possible easily
since the God of Puritanism was rather far removed from existential reality - Puritan rationality could develop smoothly into
Enlightenment rationalism.(50) Naturally, the Puritan's secularized descendant, the Enlightenment's Rational Man, lacked prophetic zeal and moral grandeur, and when he tried to don such
qualities, as did Saint-Simon or Comte, he looked genuinely silly. Meanwhile, Rational Man inherited from his Puritan ancestors,
among other things, a deep-seated aversion against the Roman
Catholic Middle Ages. Apart from its rational organization which
he, in fact, admired, Rational Man hated the Roman Catholic faith
which had made of the Middle Ages a 'dark age',(51) founded on
superstition and misguided beliefs, ruled by corrupt ecclesiastic
and secular powers, politically shaped by the despicable system
of feudalism. Much of this indictment was similar to the condemnations levelled against 'Rome' by the 'Reformation', although one
should realize, with the cogent arguments of Ernst Troeltsch in
mind,(52) that Protestantism reasoned primarily theologically,
calling for a religious purification of Christianity, using the Bible
as the ultimate authority.(53) The Enlightenment, on the other
hand, fought for the purification of mankind and proposed to use
human reason as the ultimate authority. The latter turned out to
be fatal to traditional folly.

The model of Rational Man had its economic and socio-cultural
'Sitz im Leben' in the successful bourgeoisie which emerged from
feudal society through capitalistic trade and industry as the leading class of the modern era. In fact, this class was the initial
carrier of the Enlightenment also. If the world of traditional men
and women resembled an enchanted garden, full of saints, demons,
spirits, angels and fools - a strongly institutionalized reality surrounded by contingency - the world of the modern bourgeoisie
began to resemble ever more a functional factory in which life
itself could be produced. The German philosopher and sociologist
Hans Freyer once coined a very appropriate expression for this
expanding rationalization of modernity when he spoke of 'die
Machbarkeit', i.e. the constructibility of modern reality.(54)
Indeed, the idea that the world was not ruled by a non-rational,
'blind' fate but should rather be viewed as a field of exploration,
as a range of opportunities and possibilities to be calculated and
realized in a rational manner, became the leitmotiv of bourgeois
philosophy, the guiding notion of the bourgeois worldview and
ethos. Contrary to his own claims, Marx was both typically modern
and typically bourgeois when he defended the priority of 'Praxis'
over 'Anschauung' against Andreas Feuerbach who in this respect
remained rather traditional.(55) In the worldview of the bourgeoisie, reality was to be manipulated and if need be exploited -
i.e. nature, society and history were not to be left to their own
developments but were to be planned rationally. The reign of

contingency and the irrationality of seriousness typical for traditional society, where they were represented by the fool, were to
be diminished as much as possible by constantly calculating one's
chances and by rationally planning one's actions. Science and
technology, of course, were the instruments by which this aim
could be realized.(56)

In this fateful process which led eventually to the rise of the
welfare states most of us are presently living in, folly gradually
lost its impact and its reason for existence. It withered away
because Rational Man could no longer acknowledge the existence
and the relevance of contingency and spuriousness – this is what
he himself likes to call his 'realism'. In terms of personal biography, to take one example, he simply denies death by separat-
ing it rather artificially from life, just as he denies the intrinsic
contingencies of puberty and fails to institutionalize them in
appropriate 'rites de passage'. That is, life is no longer experienced in terms of transitional phases but instead structured in a
uniform, predominantly bureaucratic manner: one is dead after
the physician has filled out and signed the appropriate forms, as
one is no longer a child after one has reached the legally established age at which parents lose the children's allowance and one
may vote in political elections. Who needs fools and folly when
'rites de passage' have been superseded by rational (i.e. legal
and bureaucratic) rules and even the possibility of contingency is
being denied? Rationalization means that the margins of reality,
where the meanings, values and norms of daily life lose their
power, are progressively reduced while rational planning and calculability take over command. In the calculable world of Rational
Man there is no room left for the spuriousness of the fool. Certainly, whenever Rational Man stumbles or staggers, whenever
the rationality he has to offer seems to lack relevance and mean-
ingfulness, whenever in short society grows abstract, the fool
may arise from his ashes again, offering traditional enchantments
to culturally discontented modern individuals. During the 1960s
the hippies of America and the provos of the Netherlands re-
enacted the social roles of traditional fools.(57)

But such re-enactments of traditional folly are doomed to remain
interludes in an otherwise thoroughly disenchanted world. Rationalism will remain the heart of modernity and as long as society
remains modern, folly will be banished from its core, pushed aside
by forces which are outside its control.

What would have happened if Puritanism and Enlightenment had
not acquired their forceful preponderance in modernity, and if
the only dominant rationality existent consisted of the hierarchical
organization of the Roman Church, based on traditional rather
than legal-bureaucratic authority? What would have happened if
science and technology, the modern state and its bureaucratic
apparatus had, in one way or another, not been given the chance
to lay the foundations for a thoroughly disenchanted society and
culture? Folly, the answer to this imaginary question may be,
would have come to a grand domination over European culture and

would have rendered its society to a magically oriented chaos.
Under the totalitarian reign of folly, humanity would eventually
be defeated by nature, crushed between two contradictory forces:
without institutional control, sense impressions would incessantly
pour into the human organism without any internal coherence,
while uncoordinated impulses would simultaneously try to pour out
in an equally chaotic manner. Vitalism would rule rampantly, causing the destruction of any form of culture and society. Anomie
would be the rule until humanity vanished altogether.

This thought experiment neglects one basic fact. Reality needs
the looking-glass function of folly and this fact has been neglected
by Rational Man to his own detriment. But the reverse is also true:
folly needs reality, an existing institutional order which it can
reflect contrariwise. If one wants to know the limits of reality -
e.g. its inherent contingencies, its dimensions of spuriousness -
one ought to acknowledge the relevance of folly. In this respect
reality is parasitical vis-à-vis folly - something which is very hard
to understand in our post-Enlightenment age. But again, the
reverse is also true: without institutions, without tradition, without the status quo of established values, norms and meanings,
folly could not exist at all. In this respect folly is parasitical vis-
à-vis reality - something which most fools would refuse to acknowledge. If folly would venture to emancipate itself from an existing
status quo, erecting as it were its very own autonomous reality,
it would have to break the looking-glass which it is itself. This
would no longer be folly but lunacy, schizophrenia.

While writing this book, I have often seriously considered iden-
tifying myself completely with the reality behind the looking-glass,
to approach, as it were, socio-cultural reality from the mirror's
own perspective. This would have meant, among other things,
that reality should be described and interpreted as a parasite of
folly. However, I have decided to stay in reality, to operate as an
empirical sociologist, and thus to view folly as a parasite of reality.
This decision was not just inspired by the fear of lunacy, but as
much by the genuinely sociological desire to come to grips with
the process of modernization and the phenomenon of modernity,
both of which become better understandable if one studies historically and comparatively the various functions of folly in a traditional setting and their dramatic changes during the emergence of
the modern world.

Meanwhile, these reflections might suggest that traditional folly
ought to be viewed in terms of mental illness. Since that would be
a very erroneous interpretation, I shall discuss this point in more
detail in the next section.

BEYOND SANITY AND INSANITY

Under the pervasive influence of Renaissance humanism, Puritan
ethics, and Enlightenment rationalism, we today are inclined to
evaluate folly negatively as some kind of irrational behaviour and

state of mind. To call someone a fool has, admittedly, always been
a kind of indictment, even in medieval days when folly experienced
its heyday. Yet, in those days prior to the disenchantment of the
world, the fool still carried a magical aura and a heuristic surplus
value, as he was viewed as the representative of a counter-reality
who somehow had important things to say. This was the case in
particular, traditional man believed, when the fool happened to
be mentally deranged, genuinely mad. In contrast, when we call
a person a fool, we mean this in a very generalized manner without any magical connotations and without any heuristic intentions.
To us, a person is a fool who behaves in a silly, irrational, 'childish' manner. If we allot a specific meaning to the notion of folly,
we mean it exclusively in the sense of psychopathological behaviour.
In fact, we are strongly inclined to view fools as mentally deranged
patients, in need of being set apart and treated psychiatrically.
As a result, the history of folly has become primarily a chapter in
the history of psychiatry and of psychiatric care. This is a mis-
conception which was caused primarily by the Enlightenment and
its model of Rational Man. It is a biased view of one of the crucial
components of traditional society, comparable to the equally fallacious definition of shaminism in terms of psychopathological
behaviour.(58) Closer scrutiny of these pre-modern phenomena
must convince the serious student to be careful with such typi-
ically modern qualifications and their inherent value-judgments.
The main argument of this study is that traditional folly cannot at
all be understood adequately, if it is primarily defined in terms of
psychiatric disturbance.(59) In fact, the following chapters will
clearly demonstrate that most traditional fools were not at all 'disturbed', or 'deranged', or 'mentally sick', or however one wants
to conceptualize the phenomena of mental pathology. If these
concepts are even questionable with regard to mental deviance
nowadays,(60) they are certainly fallacious with regard to traditional fools. Most of these were the performers of culturally
established social roles.

   This is not to say, however, that there were no 'psychotic' fools
in traditional society. If measured by the standards of modern
psychiatry, some late-medieval court jesters may indeed have been
genuinely 'mad'. The stories told about the fool of France's Louis
XIV, the highly erratic L'Angéli, feared by friends and foes alike,
suggest strongly that he was far from 'sane'.(61) Likewise, the
royal masters of these jesters were in some cases equally disturbed.
The detailed information about France's Charles VI (1368-1422)
and his maladies seems to indicate that he was severely deranged.(62) The famous 'lettres de rémission' of the fourteenth
and fifteenth centuries in which the French crown was requested
to pardon convicted individuals for various reasons, refer often to
cases of psychotic behaviour. In medieval legislation such behaviour fell usually outside the realm of jurisdiction - an early notion
of forensic psychiatry.(63)

   Therefore, it cannot be denied that mental illness did occur in
medieval society - if one is willing, that is, to maintain the notion

of mental illness at all. Thus, a history of psychiatry is a legitimate and scientifically valuable enterprise. The point is, however,
that the history of folly does not at all concur with the history of
psychiatry, because traditional fools were in most cases not at all
mentally deranged. As we shall see, it was quite common in the
Middle Ages to distinguish between natural and artificial fools,
the former being half-witted simpletons or mentally deranged
psychotics by birth, the latter in full command of their mind but
performing skilfully the role of fool. In many cases, it was very
hard to draw a sharp dividing line between the two, as in the case
of Peppi described in the postscript of this book. However, even
if such natural fools were 'obviously' mentally disturbed in the
psychiatric sense of the word, their madness was not experienced
by their contemporaries as a rationally observable disease, to be
treated in a medical manner. The traditional fool carried a magical
aura and this aura was the more observable when he happened to
be psychotic.

In other words, traditional folly was located, as it were, on a
continuum which ranged from innocent and playful banter to physically dangerous psychotic behaviour. It was all folly, but when
the fool became physically violent, threatening the lives of others
as well as his own life, he had to be contained. In that case, folly
had gone rampant, and medieval men and women were quite helpless when this happened. Meanwhile, between these two poles of
playful banter and psychotic behaviour folly remained a very
multi-faceted phenomenon. This was demonstrated by the many
names it received in those days: a fool was first and foremost
'deviatus', but he was also 'ignarus', 'ineptus', 'stultus', 'fatuus',
'stolidus', 'exensis' and 'demens'.(64) He was 'insensatus', 'insap-
iens', 'garrulus', 'baburrus', 'idiotus', 'rabiaticus', 'maniacus',
'furiosus', 'demoniacus', 'lunaticus' and 'melancholicus'.(65)
Obviously, he could not be denominated by one single epithet, as
Rational Man would do: 'mental patient'. It is also obvious that all
these colourful names were but variations of one theme: the fool as
a looking-glass image of the 'normal' human being.

In his biography of the great humanist, Huizinga expressed his
surprise that Erasmus whose arguments in his 'Moriae Encomium'
('In Praise of Folly', 1509) were otherwise rather subtle, failed to
distinguish between unwise, innocent and mentally disturbed
individuals. He simply lumped these different types of human
beings together in one concept, that of 'fools'. This indicates,
Huizinga concludes as a true heir of Rational Man, how far removed
we moderns are mentally from the world of Erasmus.(66) It rather
indicates, I suggest, that Erasmus was still able to experience and
exercise folly in a traditional manner. In fact, the great humanist
was simply too close still to the medieval world to speak about folly
in terms of sanity and insanity. To him folly was a distinct phenomenon beyond sanity and insanity.(67)

The history of the hospitalization of psychotic fools is, in this
respect, quite remarkable and interesting. I can, of course, only
discuss a few main lines of development here. It is usually assumed

that psychiatric hospitalization began roughly in the twelfth century. However, one should realize first that initially only those who had become an obvious threat to their own life and to the lives of others were set apart for special treatment. Second, these segregated fools would not receive anything comparable to a therapeutic treatment. Obviously their medieval contemporaries simply did not know what to do with these rampant fools whom they really pitied. Confronted with such fools who had clearly gone 'off the rails', who willingly or not drove their folly to an unmanageable extreme, medieval men and women reacted in a helpless manner: as in a defensive and also prophylactic move, such violent fools were summarily set apart and locked up. This, of course, was not really a form of hospitalization and it is, consequently, better not to use this concept too readily.

The places in which such psychotic fools were locked up were structurally very undifferentiated, because they functioned simultaneously as havens for the physically ill, the utterly poor, the elderly without family support, and other outcasts, such as orphans and tramps. In other words, unmanageable fools were simply packed together with various sorts of social pariahs. For instance, the Sint Janshuis at Ghent, founded in 1191, and a similar outfit in Bruges,(68) functioned for several centuries as a repository of all kinds of social outsiders, including the mentally deranged. In these homes they would meet with the blessings of Christian charity. In sum, mentally deranged fools were treated as socially maladjusted and unadjustable individuals who had to be taken off the streets and segregated from the main streams of social life. Their folly had obviously gone too far and had become out of hand. But folly it still was nevertheless! At this point I must state emphatically that I have found no historical proof for Foucault's allegation (69) that psychotic fools were sent into the sea on little boats - 'ships of fools' - travelling from harbour to harbour, rejected by their contemporaries like lepers (comparable also, if I may continue the structuralist mode of analysis, to the boat-refugees of our own age). As we shall see later, the notion of a 'ship of fools' was merely a powerful metaphor which appealed strongly to the fancy of late-medieval men and women. Real ships in the course of real history, carrying mental patients from harbour to harbour, because they had been evicted from the orbit of social life by their fellow human beings, have not existed as far as my research indicates. As long as factual proof to the contrary is not provided, we may view these medieval boat-fools as the fanciful creatures of Mr Foucault's structuralist fantasies. Meanwhile, historical research, not mesmerized from the start by the lures of structuralism, will discover that medieval men and women were rather compassionate in their attitudes towards their deranged fools. They worried about them, they were also puzzled by them, and they tried by all possible means (which were very limited, of course) to prevent them from harming themselves and others. All they could think of, however, was to separate them from social life, together with other strangers. The reasons given for the foundation of Valencia's 'Hospital of the Innocents' - an institution often mentioned in the history of psychiatry as the first European mental asylum - present a splendid example. On Shrove Tuesday of 1408, (70) Fra Joffre Gelabert delivered a sermon in the cathedral of Valencia, the contents of which have been recorded in a manuscript, dated a few years later, called simply 'Memoria'. There is already a lot of commendable charity in our city, the priest said, but we still miss a home for the poor, the innocent, and the mentally disturbed. They suffer from hunger and cold, roam through the town aimlessly, without any place to go. Often they are maltreated, and in particular the women and girls among them chance to meet with sexual abuse. The sermon managed to impress ten rich citizens, who in a concerted action put up the money for the foundation of a home which would provide shelter to the city's pariahs. One of them, the author of the 'Memoria', and the first director of the asylum, petitioned the king for founding permission. In this request, he described once more the aim of the house: it should give shelter and food to those unable to care for themselves as they were, more often than not, physically and mentally incapable of living a decent life. Since they were innocent and mad they caused damage and inconvenience to fellow citizens, and thus presented a real threat to the community. (71) As in the 'Memoria', it becomes again clear in this request to the crown that the respectable citizens of Valencia wanted to found this asylum in order to clean the streets of the city from its 'clochards', its tramps and beggars, its social riff-raff. To these solid citizens these homeless deviants were in fact all 'mad', not in the psychiatric so much as in the sociological sense of the word.

The sociologically interesting case of the psychiatric care in the Belgian village of Geel should also be seen in the same light. From the early Middle Ages onwards this village was a place for pilgrims from different nations who came to adore the shrine of Dimphna, believed to be the saint of 'innocents', healing the mentally disturbed through miracles. According to the legend, Dimphna was the daughter of an Irish king of whom the devil had taken possession - i.e. who was considered 'mad'. After his wife had died, the devil inspired him to marry his beautiful daughter. She refused and fled to mainland Europe, accompanied by her confessor Gerebernus. They landed at Antwerp and then moved to Geel, where they were, however, eventually found by the wicked king. When she continued to refuse to yield to her father's incestuous desires, even after he had killed her confessor in front of her, he beheaded her summarily, being obviously out of his mind. Dimphna then became a saint of 'innocents' and Geel a pilgrims' resort to which sick people would come for what is called 'hagiotherapy' - i.e. treatment through the miracle of a saint. (72) In 1286 a hospital was founded which functioned initially as haven for poor and sick pilgrims who were either mentally or physically ill. Gradually, however, a specialization towards the hagiotherapy of mental patients developed, a process which was completed in the fifteenth

century.(73) Meanwhile, when too many pilgrims descended on
the village and the hospital could no longer take them all, private
homes would open their doors to them, lodging patients against
an officially established fee. This interesting practice was explicitly mentioned in official documents not earlier than the seventeenth century and has been continued allegedly to this very
day.(74) In sum, the village of Geel was a kind of psychiatric
centre from the Middle Ages on, yet one should realize that the
notion of mental illness remained very diffuse and indetermined
until approximately the seventeenth and eighteenth centuries.
Before the emergence of modernity, the 'innocents' were a strange
mixture of poor and physically sick pilgrims, psychotic patients,
natural fools, and social pariahs. They all flocked to Dimphna in
order to experience a miracle and receive charity from the hospit-
able villagers of Geel.

In such a cultural climate, the label 'fool' carried heavy social
connotations which can perhaps best be summarized by the concept of pariah.(75) Late medieval society itself preferred to
concept of vagabond. In fact, in the sixteenth century various
Western European cities treated vagabonds and the mentally deranged as one and the same category, and with the example of
Geel in mind one should realize that it was not always easy in
those days to distinguish properly between religiously motivated
mendicant friars, morally honest pilgrims and definitely asocial
tramps. In fact, they were often all viewed as fools, and fools
were considered to be vagabonds, either literally or metaphorically.
The whole lot of them was considered to be 'mad'. Only the officially appointed court fool, to be discussed in chapter 3, could
escape this kind of labelling - the label of social and legal infamy.(76) But then, as we shall see, the more he institutionalized
and professionalized, the less he remained a genuine fool.

Meanwhile, such asylums for pariahs were generally few in number during the Middle Ages. When an individual became unmanageable in his folly, he was usually locked up in either a small cell,
or a movable wooden box. Such boxes were called 'cista stoli-
dorum' in Latin, 'Narrenhäuschen' in German, 'dolhuisjes' in
Dutch.(77) Such a 'fools' house' was placed in a private home if
there was sufficient space in it, or in a church, a monastery, a
hospital, or the city jail. This shows once more that medieval
people were quite at a loss when confronted with someone whose
folly went out of bounds. He was simply locked up in a kind of
wooden strait-jacket and released again when he had quieted
down.(78) Significantly, such wooden movable boxes were also
used to keep other unruly persons under arrest. The city tower
of Dresden, for instance, harboured a 'Narrenhaus' in which citizens were kept in custody who had been arrested during the night
on the charge of drunkenness and bawdiness. Trier had one for
unruly beggars. In the sixteenth century, such 'fools' houses'
were even in use for the punishment of unruly children who by
their naughty behaviour had made fools of themselves. Thus, like
the pillory,(79) these 'fools' houses' functioned as forensic rather

than therapeutic instruments. If a fool was put in one of them,
this was done because of his unruly behaviour, not because he
had to be cared for therapeutically.(80)
  Finally, mention is regularly made of the surgical cutting of
stones as an alleged therapeutic measure against folly. Stone-
cutting, or as it was also called, cutting of fools ('Narrenschneiden'), was depicted by Jeroen Bosch and Jan Steen: a quack
physician cuts a stone from the head of a patient, or he cuts with
a knife in the patient's neck, producing little pebbles, supposedly
taken from the inside of the victim's cranium. The stones are next
demonstratively placed on a platter. On one of these funny paintings, Jan Steen shows us a little boy who passes the pebbles on
to the 'surgeon' behind the back of the visibly ailing victim.(81)
A similar scene occurs in a Shrove Tuesday play by Hans Sachs,
called 'Das Narrenschneiden' (1557): a quack doctor enters a pub,
accompanied by his 'assistant', shows his papers and asks if
there is any man or woman present who suffers from coughing,
stones, warts, longing or envy, toothache, etc. He then begins
to treat his patients by operating on them in a semi-professional
way, cutting out of their bodies many fools, such as avarice, un-
chastity, and similar moral diseases.(82) Interestingly, physical,
psychic and moral ailments (toothache, longing and avarice) were
simply put together under the general heading of folly.
  Throughout the Middle Ages, incidentally, the stone remained
the main symbol of folly - hard, impenetrable, stolid. Many Bible
manuscripts carry in the margin of Psalm 53, which starts by saying that only a fool denies the existence of God, an illumination
showing a fool with a stone either in his hand or in his mouth.(83)
A stone on one's head (maybe a boil, or a tumour?) was always
considered in the Middle Ages to be a sign of folly, just as horns
were the symbol of the devil.
  In sum, the cutting of stones might well have been a historical
attraction in pubs and on fairs and markets, performed by entertaining quack doctors on superstitious farmers and citizens, but
it was above all a metaphor which demonstrated well-nigh myth-
ologically the intrinsically foolish nature of human beings. It was
a moral metaphor which had nothing in common with the modern
medical model.

CONCLUSION

To their contemporaries fools were the harbingers of unseen
powers, the representatives of a reality which was linked in a
contrary manner to the paramount reality of daily routine. They
were the enchanters in a thoroughly enchanted garden. During
the process of modernization in the Western world, this notion of
divine or demonic inspiration and possession wore off gradually,
although magical connotations lingered on as long as traditional
folly existed in Europe. Outside the European cultural orbit traditional fools have always been felt to be awe-inspiring in the

magical sense of this word - i.e. both attractive and repulsive.
The traditional fool, to use the concept from Otto's phenomenology
of religion once more, was a 'fascinans'.

Albeit less manifestly, enchanting power was an essential ingredient of medieval European folly. Throughout the Middle Ages,
folly functioned as a disguise for ancient forms of magical paganism.(84) It was for this reason that the official hierarchy of the
Roman Church persisted in its attempts to ban folly from the orbit
of medieval social life, and in particular from its own ecclesiastic
institutions into which it had deeply penetrated, not in the least
because of the support folly received from the lower clergy. These
attempts, as we shall see in the next chapter, were largely unsuccessful. Like the often bizarre gargoyles of the Romanesque and
Gothic cathedrals,(85) the fools of medieval society testified of an
underground paganism which continued to move the fancy of medieval men and women until deep into the seventeenth century. It
was not the theologians and the higher prelates of the Church of
Rome who were able to crush this dormant and enchanting paganism which surfaced to life in foolish festivals and organizations.
That task was left to the representatives of their adversaries -
the Reformation and the Enlightenment - who won the definitive
victory over traditional folly and the remnants of ancient heathenism it covered up. Was this victory really definitive? Can folly
be eradicated from the orbit of human life? Or may we expect a
resurgence of it, when for various reasons modern paganism,
brought about by the Enlightenment,(86) has reached its limits
in an abstract society which itself seems to have reached its
quantitative and qualitative limits? We must still suspend such
intriguing questions because first we must gather more historical
and anthropological facts about traditional folly.

2 TWISTERS OF REALITY:
popular fools in medieval and early-modern Europe

INTRODUCTION

In many respects the Middle Ages were a dark and gloomy era.
Poverty, cruelty, physical and mental destitution, brought about
by warfare, plagues and ill-controlled natural disasters, could at
times reach unbelievable levels of human degradation. Huizinga's
famous 'The Waning of the Middle Ages' (1919) gave an impressive
picture of this side of medieval life. The atmosphere of a medieval
'Götterdämmerung', increasing its intensity the closer this era
approached the Renaissance, was perhaps as impressively evoked
by Ingmar Bergman in his motion picture 'The Seventh Seal' (1956).
Yet these and similar accounts of the Middle Ages were contributions to a tenacious and rather distorted image of this crucial
period in the development of Western civilization. It is the one-
sided and thus erroneaous image of 'the dark Middle Ages'.

This era was dark in terms of human degradation, and it was
admittedly so in almost all dimensions conceivable. Yet, at the
very same time, these centuries were also characterized by much
laughter and genuine pleasure and fun! To use a medieval metaphor, the fool danced hand in hand with death and it was believed
that this dyad constituted the inscrutable foundation of human
existence. Maybe ubiquitous death was acceptable to these people
because it was viewed in terms of folly?

In any case, one commits a grave error if one focuses only on
suffering and death when one tries to come to grips with this complex period of European history in which life, as short as it
usually was to almost everyone, had acquired a high degree of
intensity. Earthly pleasure, coarse laughter and fun, plain folly
were closely, and in fact inseparably, tied to these dark and
gloomy dimensions of medieval life. This duality of pleasure and
fun, laughter and pain, life and death was expressed beautifully
in the paintings of Pieter Brueghel (c. 1525-69).

Even when they were in an alleged stage of decline, radiating
the melancholic light of sombre autumn days, as Huizinga suggested, the Middle Ages were not merely a human nightmare, a
continuous dance of death. They were as much, and at the very
same time, a continuous festival in which the fool waved his silly
and irreverent sceptre, and became the master of enacted misrule
who played the role of sovereign of laughter.

Medieval humour often strikes us as coarse, boorish, primitive
and childish. It seems to be impulsive and gross, anti-rational and
uncivilized, as in the case of the court fool's antics or of the

practical jokes by folk fools like Till Eulenspiegel. This humour
was indeed sheer folly, and hard to understand or appreciate by
modern individuals. Indeed, a thorough 'process of civilization'(1)
separates us from these fools. What separates us from medieval
and early-modern folly in particular is one aspect of this process
which I propose to call 'intellectualization'. Before we meet the
popular fools of this era, we must first discuss this point in a
few details.

Whatever else they may have brought about, the Renaissance
and the Enlightenment have contributed to a pervasive 'intellectualization' of the Western world. This is the process by which
human impulses and emotions, such as the erotic drive, the play
'instinct', or love and hatred, are gradually and increasingly subjected to and controlled by man's cognitive capacities. It refers,
for example, to the modern prevalence of planning and calculability, two earlier discussed dimensions of the modern belief in the
constructibility of the world. The notion and practice of family
planning is yet another rather obvious example of intellectualization. Today, the birth of a child is no longer experienced as a
gift of God, or of Nature, or of Fate, but as the rational and
rather technical result of a planned action of two 'partners'. At
best, such traditional 'causes' as God, Nature, or Fate are but
referred to rhetorically.

The experience and practice of humour was likewise subjected
to intellectualization. Erasmus, for example, made a conscious
attempt to intellectualize folly when he wrote his 'Moriae Encomium'.
He personified folly, placing it on a stage as a rather silly goddess who delivered a lecture on folly to a baffled audience. The
whole treatise, composed incidentally for fun and distraction during a long and boring journey and written in the house of his
friend Thomas More, to whom it was dedicated, aimed at a target
beyond folly: it was a witty satire of Erasmus's contemporary
society.

Rabelais's humour was predominantly medieval, but even in his
case folly had acquired a dimension of calculation and thus of
reflective wit. Villon's ballads were aesthetically refined to such
a degree that they defy in many instances any comparison with the
often primitive songs of his fellow vagabonds, the goliards - a
specimen of folk literature which we will discuss shortly.

Naturally, this intellectualization was strongly reinforced by the
rationalism of the Enlightenment. Voltaire's wit comes to mind
readily. Compared to the mild, if not innocent humour of Erasmus,
Voltaire's wit bore a biting and sometimes even ferocious quality
and was thus far removed already from the silly and harmless folly
of the Middle Ages. Maybe Romanticism mitigated this biting wit
somewhat, as in the case of Oscar Wilde who gave to wit a distinct
aesthetic quality.(2) In fact, the dandy came rather close again to
the fool of pre-modern times.(3) Intellectualization was not the
exclusive prerogative of the Renaissance and the Enlightenment,
as it did occur prior to these harbingers of modernity. Obviously,
the philosophy of Aristotle, in particular as mediated in the twelfth

century by the Spanish Arab Averroës, had functioned as a rather
rationalistic strait-jacket of medieval minds, in particular of the
adherents of Scholasticism.(4) Busy as they were with their cas-
uistic logic and metaphysics, these medieval thinkers did of
course intellectualize their impulses and emotions. However, the
study of medieval folly as a massively distributed phenomenon
amongst the populace at large suggests that this intellectualization
remained restricted to a relatively small elite, to wit the clergy
and, within the clergy, to some specialists like the philosophically
trained scholars. Outside this elite, medieval minds and bodies
were unhampered by the intellect and by the norms and rules of
theological ethics, allowing instead an uninhibited indulgence of
instincts, impulses, emotions, free associations and fantasies,
mocking regularly the painful labours of the scholars who pursued
intellectual aims.(5)

In short, there was a reign of folly which had taken possession
of people in all walks of life, from monarchs to peasants, from
artisans to members of the (mainly lower) clergy. They adhered
to the doctrines and moral rules of their taken-for-granted religion in a superficial manner by fulfilling the ritual duties of the
church without much theological reflection, obeying the dictates
of Christian morality mechanically. Under this thin cloak of
Christian civilization folly could do its thing. As we shall see, not
surprisingly this folly happened to be an excellent medium for the
expression of ancient paganism. Under the disguise of innocent
folly heathenism could continue to exist in the centre of the medieval 'Corpus Christianum'.

The process of intellectualization was, of course, enhanced by
the Reformation. Folly was part of the traditional enchanted garden, of which Catholicism was an inherent component due to its
wealth of rituals and festivals, and its host of saints, angels and
archangels. As a result, there was indeed a rather strong 'elective
affinity' (M. Weber) between folly and Catholicism. In contrast,
the Reformation, particularly its Calvinist brand, stood squarely
opposed to the enchanting reign of folly, its licentious and immoral
penchants, and its ethos of loitering and 'dolce far niente'. The
Puritanic ethos with its emphasis on 'innerworldly asceticism'
(M. Weber), on a thoroughly rationalized style of life, stressing
frugality and relentless labour, dealt a serious blow to the medieval reign of folly. This was reinforced when it merged, though
unintentionally, with the 'spirit of capitalism' (M. Weber) - which
is, of course, generally opposed to folly due to the latter's unre-
liability and unpredictability.

Two elements in this Puritanic intellectualization should be
singled out. First, because of its emphasis upon the Scriptures
and the theological exegesis thereof, to be grasped reflectively by
the serious believer, the Reformation caused a spread of intellectualization to an extent unknown previously in the Roman Catholic
Church. That is, it was no longer sufficient to participate in the
weekly obligatory ceremonies of the church, leaving the difficult
theological questions of faith to the appropriate professionals. On

the contrary, the Protestant, in particular the Calvinist, confronted as he was with a remote God directly (i.e. without such intermediaries as the Virgin Mary, the saints, the sacraments and the clergy), had to reflect about this faith constantly. He had to read the Bible daily, and had to listen to elaborate sermons in the church weekly. He had to participate in theological debates in Bible-study groups, and had to attend as a representative of his congregation the synodical conferences, etc. 'Solus Christus', 'sola fides', 'sola Scriptura' - these slogans entailed a massive intellectualization among the common believers. More than ever before, Christianity had now become a true book-religion, thoroughly intellectualized and with very little room for direct impulses and emotions. Even if people could not themselves read the Bible and popularized theological tracts, they participated in a book-religion, based on continuous cognitive reflections. Second, the intellectualization of this book-religion could receive a wide and massive distribution due to the invention of book printing which had occurred in the fifteenth century, just before the Reformation. Prior to the Reformation, as I argued before, intellectualization remained restricted to a relatively small elite. The knowledge of this elite was not arcane, to be held secret and to be guarded within the confinements of a priestly caste. On the contrary, the scholars of medieval Scholasticism were quite eager to distribute their knowledge and wisdom, as they actually did in the universities of Bologna, Paris, Louvain, etc. Yet their audiences were relatively small and the manuscripts which carried their scholastic rationalizations had to be copied slowly and in small numbers by industrious monks in monasteries. These rare copies reached but a few of their fellow intellectuals in monasteries and universities. Beyond this small circle, the contents of these manuscripts would only reach the students in the universities to whom they were read 'ex cathedra'. Thus one should realize that the often vigorous debates among the scholars of Scholasticism (cf. Nominalism versus Realism) were actually carried out well-nigh privately. Compared to the impact of Protestant intellectualization on the minds of common believers after the sixteenth century, the intellectualization of the medieval scholars prior to the invention of book printing went over the heads of most of their contemporaries.

However, in contrast to these limits put on pre-Reformation intellectualization, folly could be distributed widely and intensively, acquiring very firm roots in the popular culture of its time.(6) The wandering entertainers discussed in the next section, harbouring fools of many shades and colours, were not dependent on the spoken or written word for the distribution of their anti-intellectual ideas. By singing their often bawdy songs and performing their funny sketches, these popular fools disseminated their anti-intellectual folly widely. It was not the Roman Catholic Church, rooted in the masses in a non-intellectualized manner, which posed a real threat to medieval folly, but it was the Reformation as a book-religion, intellectualizing its believers by its continuous emphasis on a conscious and morally reflected-upon faith, which

became folly's first adversary. It forged, as Weber argued, the
mental cast for bourgeois capitalism and laid the foundations for
the Enlightenment rationalism. It thus contributed, albeit unintentionally, to the emergence of modernity in which science,
technology, and bureaucracy would rule, and not folly.

THE FOLLY OF CLERICAL AND INTELLECTUAL MISFITS

As in the Roman empire, a host of entertainers roamed through
medieval Europe.(7) Trying to make a living, they wandered from
village to village, from city to city, from castle to castle, and
from country to country - always on the road, restless, ruleless,
given to foolish exploits. They had a life-style similar to that of
the gypsies, although they lacked their social, clan-based coherence and integration. They shared, however, something else: a
similar treatment by those who led settled lives. The treatment
was a mixture of attraction and rejection, of fame and infamy. The
gypsies who began an intensive invasion of Northern Europe in
the beginning of the fifteenth century, radiated an attractive
spell due to their mysterious, carefully preserved strangeness.
At the fringe of the society which they had entered, these gypsies
functioned as horse traders and tinkers while their women performed the mysterious art of fortune-telling. Very soon, however,
these nomads who were closely tied together and impenetrable as
a group, began to encounter feelings of hostility and racist reactions which seem to be typical of the fate of social pariahs. Ever
since roughly the sixteenth century gypsies have been persecuted
and deported. The problem is that they refuse to adjust to any
social system - they roam through a society, but never become
part of it.

The wandering entertainers, to be discussed in this section,
shared the gypsies' errant nature and met a similar fate, although
they never suffered the fierce persecution the gypsies had to
endure, mainly because they were not at all organized as an impenetrable group with its own laws and mores, and with its own
characteristic wall of mysteriousness. The gypsies were never
fools; the wandering entertainers, however, were very much so.
The general attitude towards them may be summed up simply as
follows: these fools were appreciated for the entertainment they
had to offer, but one would not want one's daughter to marry one
of them!

They carried various names such as 'scenici', 'mimi', 'pantomimi',
'histriones' and 'ioculatores' in Latin, and 'jongleurs', 'minstrels',
'troubadours' and 'bards' in the vernacular. It is quite impossible
to categorize them more or less precisely according to specific
branches of entertainment, because such a specialization did not
exist yet in those days when functional differentiation was in general still very underdeveloped. They were the singers of ballads,
celebrating virtues of honour and valour (if duly paid for it), or
they entertained their audience with bawdy songs about crudely

erotic love, or with sentimental songs about sublimated, 'platonic' 'amour courtois'. Allegedly, the Provençal 'troubadours', active prior to the cruel war on the gnostic Albigenses around 1210, excelled in singing ballads of such refined and 'platonic' courtly love. But Briffault has argued quite convincingly that this char- acterization of the troubadours is one-sided, to say the least. They often sang about crudely erotic love in a manner which did not leave much to fantasy.(8)

These entertainers would also perform little plays, sketches rather, in which they would often satirize the worldly and eccles- iastic authorities of the day. But their ilk would also include bear-leaders, rope-walkers, stilt-walkers, acrobats, jugglers, buffoons and pranksters of the Eulenspiegel variety. In short, a multi-coloured, multi-faceted host of individuals - men, women and children - wandered about, calling at fairs and markets in villages and towns, where they would entertain their audiences together with quack physicians who were barbers, surgeons and dentists at once. Many of them, in particular if they were good at singing ballads and telling legends and adventurous stories, would visit castles and palaces. The term 'minstrels' may be reserved for these singers among the entertainers, although it is quite feasible that many of them would also demonstrate considerable skills and talents in the performance of sketches and acrobatic acts. In exchange for food, clothes, shelter and money, these minstrels were eager to perform in villages, towns and castles. It was a hard life, particularly in the recurrent periods of economic malaise, but it had one great advantage: it offered a well-nigh unlimited freedom. We today are rather spoiled with various means of entertainment: books, records, theatres, cinemas, radio and television, musical instruments and technical gadgets such as cameras and do-it-yourself tools. As a result, we can hardly be- gin to understand how tedious life must have been to our medieval ancestors - to the peasants during the long winter months, to the noblemen during the intervals between various war activities, to the noble women during the absence of their spouses in periods of war, to the lower clergy in their rural vicarages. Particularly in the evening, when all outdoor activities had come to a complete standstill (quite inconceivable to modern people), boredom must have plagued these men and women. No wonder that there was this continuous search for diversion. Studying the records care- fully, one begins to realize that there was this well-nigh desperate search for entertainment - a search almost as crucial as the search for food and shelter. These entertainers catered indeed to some kind of primary need! They were in this sense a dire necessity.

Yet, as in ancient Rome, entertainers were considered to be social outsiders. Due to their wandering style of life they did not belong to any specific estate and bore the social and legal stigma of infamy.(9) They were indeed socially free-floating in the sense Karl Mannheim used the expression, and they were at the same time, as I said before, social pariahs, outcasts, in the sense Max Weber used this notion. However, unlike the medieval Jews or

gypsies - typical examples of 'pariah nations' - these entertainers
lacked any trace of social coherence or organization. They were
not in any sense of the word a 'nation'.(10) They did call themselves, as we shall see instantly, 'an order' or 'a family', but this
was meant in a jocular and mocking manner. Individually or in
small bands, they tried to make a living by performing in villages
and cities, castles and palaces, monasteries, inns and farms, ex-
changing their entertainment for a good meal, some clothes, shelter for a few days, and above all material goods and money. They
lived the lives of parasites, attaching themselves to any class or
group of human beings. As a result, their economic dependence
did not at all fall within the confinements of the well-known feudal
bondage. From among these socially free-floating entertainers,
some managed to tie themselves to an estate, like the domestic
bard at a castle, or like the officially appointed jester at a court
or in the household of an influential courtier. But these were
exceptions to the rule that entertainers were generally non-feudal
and socially free-floating. They were appreciated for the entertainment they had to offer, but they were at the same time socially
and legally infamous-marginal people and, in their lower strata,
often the riffraff of medieval society because many criminal elements would join their ranks for the anonymity they would receive
among them. In 'Piers the Ploughman' (c. 1377) William Langland
gave a brief description (11) of

> the professional entertainers, some of whom, I think, are
> harmless minstrels, making an honest living by their music;
> but others, babblers and vulgar jesters, are true Judas'
> children! They invent fantastic tales about themselves, and
> pose as half-wits, yet they show wits enough whenever it
> suits them, and could easily work for a living if they had to!

Naturally, these wandering entertainers did present quite a
nuisance to the powers of the medieval 'establishment' - be they
secular or ecclesiastic. The worldly order had to come to terms
with the criminal elements among them, while the ecclesiastic hierarchy had to worry about their crypto-paganistic secularism and
their anti-clerical sentiments. Who were these strangers?
There was hardly any structural differentiation among these
entertainers, as I said before, but we may single out the socially
critical elements among them who would at times poke fun at the
secular and ecclesiastic authorities of the time under the carefully
maintained disguise of folly. They bore various names, colourful
ones such as 'goliardi', 'scolares vagantes', 'vagi scolares', 'ordo
vagorum', 'familiae goliae', and 'eberhardini'.(12) The precise
meaning of these names is not always clear but 'vagi scolares'
(wandering scholars) and 'goliards' have become most common.
They were monastic monks and secular priests who had fled their
monasteries and parishes, on the one hand, and dropped-out
university teachers and students, on the other.(13)
Wandering clergy roaming through society restlessly existed

already in the very early Middle Ages. During the Council of
Nicea (AD 235), already representatives of the church made a
point of condemning those unstable souls who abused their tonsure
and frock by wandering about restlessly and aimlessly. The council fathers stated solemnly that the clergy should not migrate from
city to city ('ex civitate in civitatem migrare') - a rule which obviously tried to curb the economically conditioned multiplication of
mendicant friars. The Council of Carthage (AD 436) added that
such wandering clerks were not allowed to perform as entertainers
at dinner tables ('clericus inter epulas cantans' - 'clergy singing
at banquets'). Several following councils repeated this prohibition
as in a litany and in some cases the threat was added that such
wandering clerks would lose their clerical status and be defrocked
if they persisted in this infamous style of life. The proposed
measures often came close to excommunication. This long list of
ecclesiastic denunciations of wandering clerks and monks (naturally a very welcome source of historical information)(14) suggests
that many members of the clergy were, from the early Middle Ages
on, plagued by a deeply ingrained wandering itch. Many of them
seemed to have been driven by a yearning desire to fly out into
the world, to leave the strictures of parish and monastery in order
to emancipate themselves from the often rigid hierarchy and discipline of the official church and the society it supervised. One
of them expressed this feeling aptly when he said: 'thuz li munz
est miens envirun' - 'the whole world is my environment.'(15)

Being a 'vagus', or as he was also called more derogatorily, a
'gyrovagus', was indeed an attitude and a mentality in those days -
a kind of state of mind. Waddell relates the illustrative story,
apparently told by the mystic Eckhart, about a young monk of
St Gall who just could not endure the discipline in this famous
monastery any longer. One day he climbed up the campanile and
exclaimed, while looking abroad: 'Oh, that I were where I but
see!' But the poor man missed his step and crashed to the ground.
'Some men no monastery could hold', says Waddell,(16) and she
tells the story of another restless soul who was evicted from one
monastery after another, until he came to Cluny where the wise
abbot William managed to sublimate his endless energy and fantasy
by persuading him to write a historical treatise. The man, who bore
the colourful name of Rodulfus Glaber, must have been quite impossible prior to this scholarly therapy: 'impudent to his superiors, a
nuisance to his equals and a bully to his juniors' - in short the
perfect rebellious material for the making of a 'goliard' or 'vagus'.(17)

Yet, this psychological interpretation of the wandering clerks
and monks should be completed by an economic explanation. The
financial remuneration of secular priests was, during the Middle
Ages, often far from sufficient and in general very irregular
(insecure benefices, unstable sources of income in the rural parishes). They were at the same time prohibited from engaging in
any secular activities and could, therefore, not supplement their
means of existence.(18) As a result, not a few of them were simply

driven to vagabondage by sheer destitution, collecting almonies from charitable believers. It stands to reason that the performance of some songs could yield greater rewards and as they were intellectually more gifted than most of their fellow human beings, these performing clerks were able to engage in satire. That is, if they were quite often entertaining fools, many of them managed to elevate their folly to a certain level of wit, criticizing in particular the church which had left them literally in the cold. We return to this point in a short while but must first analyse in more detail the economic dimensions of the phenomenon of wandering monks and clerks.

Throughout the Middle Ages it was very attractive for peasants to send one or more of their sons to a monastery, because this lightened their economic burden considerably. Moreover, to have one or more children in a monastery or in the secular clergy yielded not only a religious surplus value but also a social benefit in the form of status and prestige. However, most parishes and most (often overcrowded) monasteries had to be self-supporting economically. Even if they possessed large portions of land, a harvest could be unsuccessful due to weather conditions, or a war could destroy it, or invaders could confiscate it.(19) Such events, which were very hard to control in those days, always entailed great economic hardship, to the extent that parish priests or monks in a monastery could no longer be supported. In such circumstances, several of them would be forced to fly out into the world as vagabonds, living from handouts. Their frock and tonsure did, of course, serve them well since their begging could be legitimated as an imitation of the poverty of Jesus Christ - as in the case of the mendicant friars, who begged for alms with official approval. By offering entertainment these clerical vagabonds would collect an additional income. Meanwhile, as there was quite some competition in the field of wandering entertainment, many of these monks and clerks were materially not much better off. Yet, they at least enjoyed the advantage of being feee, and they used this freedom gratefully to satirize the institution that had so badly neglected their material well-being.(20) In particular, those restless souls, mentioned before, who throughout the Middle Ages seemed to carry the very seeds of the Renaissance, must have preferred their wandering style of life above the domestication in monastery or parish.

These 'goliards' should be distinguished from the genuinely religious mendicant monks, which, incidentally, was not always easy, to the detriment of the latter. The Franciscan Minorities present a well-known example. They called themselves the 'fools of Jesus', but it was not always easy to distinguish them from the errant goliards who acted in many cases as popular and thoroughly secularized fools.

One of the few socio-scientific laws that seems to be universally valid states that economic deterioration causes the rise of criminality in a society. This was certainly the case in the Middle Ages when societies were additionally very weakly organized within the

complex feudal system. Banditry was a common phenomenon (21)
and so was vagabondage. Naturally, many criminal elements joined
the ranks of the goliards. The tonsure and the soutane offered
them a special attraction, since they functioned not only as a
cover-up for criminal intentions but also, if the need arose, as a
protection against the long arm of the secular law and its vengeful
courts. As a result, many vagabonds donned the soutane and had
a tonsure shorn on their heads as disguise for their criminal
intentions and practices. The continuous rejections of clerical
vagabondage by the official hierarchy of the Roman Church should
certainly be seen in the light of this fact. But one should also
realize that the same church remained both unable and unwilling
to recognize the economic causes of vagabondage and its inherent
criminality. It did in particular not offer any valid alternative to
the wandering of its lower clergy, continued to voice its often
loud opprobrium of minstrelsy in general and tried to prevent any
ordination on the ground of non-religious motives. As early as
1274, the Council of Salzburg dealt with the issue and stated
tersely: 'Let no prelate give the tonsure to a man or woman, unless they profess a recognized Rule and are going to a definite
place, for otherwise the habit promotes wandering and gives
opportunity to delinquency.'(22) A few decades earlier the Council of Rouen had ruled that clerics who were discovered to be
'vagi' ought to lose their clerical status and be defrocked and
shaven. Waddell summed up what this meant to the goliardic
monk:(23)

> The *vagus* is stripped of his dearest possession, the one
> thing that set him apart from 'the people without the law',
> the other gentlemen of the road, the clowns and the tumblers
> and the performing monkeys and the dancing bears, he who
> had held his head so high, because he knew his Lucian and
> his Ovid, and broke his wildest jests in the ancient tongue.
> To lay him by the heels, the Church will even call in the
> secular arm: repudiation - in the Middle Ages - could no
> further go.

Soon enough, Waddell concludes, 'the word goliard ... becomes
the vilest in the language. By the end of the 14th century the law
courts use it as equivalent to the brothel-keeper'.(23)
   Once more, those occupying the higher and thus economically
safer positions of the church were unable and unwilling to view
the phenomenon in economic terms. They continued to attack it in
terms of theology and ecclesiastic policy. Much theological emphasis was placed on domestication. One medieval abbot formulated it
tersely when he said: 'ubi stabilitas, ibi religio' - 'where there is
stability, there is religion.'(24) The statement is surprisingly
accurate, sociologically, and it meant to say, of course, that
wandering individuals lacked any decent sense of religion and
thus constituted the rabble of society.
   Geographical stability carried a very fundamental religious

significance during the Middle Ages. The most important rule of
the Benedictine vow, for example, was the 'stabilitas loci', the
attachment to one place, i.e. the monastery. The church did send
out its officials to various foreign places - John of Salisbury, for
instance, died as Bishop of Chartres - but it allowed such travels
and migrations exclusively, if they fitted ecclesiastic policies.
They were in actual fact no wandering clerks. Isidor of Seville,
who died AD 636, distinguished between two kinds of clerks:
those obeying their bishop and those not loyal to anyone - a terrible vice in a feudal society - but rather prone to follow their
own free will, wandering about aimlessly - 'solutas et erran-
tes'.(25) One would expect that the bonafide entertainers would
also have second thoughts about this penetration of criminal elements into their rank and file. There is indeed one example of an
attempt to protect the entertaining 'profession' against such degeneration. Reportedly a court of minstrelsy existed in Tutbury
(Staffordshire) which around 1380 issued licences to minstrels
within the area of jurisdiction. From the middle of the fourteenth
century on there have been British attempts at the legislation of
minstrelsy, leading to the decision of Edward IV in 1469 to found
a guild of minstrels, directed by his own household minstrels and
their leader, the marescallus.(26) As Chambers claims, 'the whole
drift of social development was to make things difficult for the
independent minstrels and to restrict the area of their wandering.'(27)

Meanwhile, it was not just impoverished members of the clergy
who went on the road. They were joined by many students and
even some teachers who had not been successful intellectually at
the university, or who were no longer able to support themselves
adequately during their studies and their teaching, or who simply
did not possess the 'Sitzfleisch' needed for scholarly work. Having decided to take off into the wide world, they put their intel-
ligence and wit to practical use in their entertainment, in their
songs and ballads and stories. Sometimes they were students who
travelled from university to university in the serious pursuit of
wisdom and skill, badly in need of food, shelter and money and
therefore moonlighting as entertainers. But most wandering intellectuals joined the band of clerical vagabonds, because they had
failed as students and teachers and yielded to their wandering
itch.

This is not to say, however, that there was no room for folly
within the walls of medieval universities. Several of these stern
institutions, intellectually ruled by the scholars of scholasticism,
knew the yearly 'orationes quodlibetica' in which students and
lower teaching staff ('baccalaurei' and 'magistri') held mock disputations about silly subjects, using all the jargon and debating
manners of the scholars. Sometimes these foolish disputations, in
which the language used apparently had to be foul and barbaric,
would continue for two weeks. The professors usually avoided
these happenings and the humanists of the sixteenth century
characteristically managed to abolish them.(28) Yet, not all the

humanists objected to them. The author of the 'Praise of Folly',
we may assume, must have appreciated these mock disputations,
if he ever attended one. The German humanist Jacob Wimpheling
presided over a session in which Judocus Gallus held such an
'oratio quodlibetica'. This speech was even printed in 1489 at
Strassburg and Wimpheling wrote the introduction to it.(29)

Clerical and intellectual misfits, roaming through the medieval
world, occupied a vantage-point in society which enabled them to
take an independent and critical stance. As coarse and bawdy as
their folly often was, they yet seemed to prelude the secular joy
of life, the delight in material things, and the playful banter
which later became characteristic of the Renaissance.(30) In a
sense they even preluded the modern paganism of the Enlightenment,(31) as non-rational as their folly usually was. That is,
folly's progressive thrust can be found in these entertaining misfits, hidden below much that is rude, primitive, regressive. It is
in particular this tension between the regressive and the progressive that makes it a historical and sociological delight to read
such goliardic songs and ballads as the famous 'Carmina Burana'.(32) A brimful and coarsely joyous reality is created in which
it was apparently fun to dwell because there 'nobody can get at
you' - a world of freedom outside the confinements of church and
society, the world of the freedom of fools, of 'Narrenfreiheit'.

From the vantage-point of this looking-glass reality the goliards
would look back at their society and poke fun at the authorities
of the day, in particular at those in the higher echelons of the
church. Not being plagued themselves by moral norms and values,
solidly entrenched in secular materialism, these goliardic fools
would satirize the corruption, the greed, the simony and the materialism of the leaders of the church, who hid their vices behind
the pomp and circumstance of their authority.(33)

The Cluny Reform Movement of the tenth and eleventh centuries
and the mendicant orders of the thirteenth century had also criticized these symptoms of degeneration, calling for a return to
simplicity, poverty, pure and original Christianity. But they had
remained radically religious, spiritualistic, and loyal to the ecclesiastic hierarchy. Their objective was an inner reform of the
church, and they practised their ascetic ideals in the world as in
a kind of inner-missionary activity. This movement was radicalized
in the sixteenth century by the Reformation, in particular by the
inner-worldly asceticism of Calvinism. The goliards stand in sharp
contrast to this reform movement. They castigated ecclesiastic
degeneration in an utterly unascetic manner, cracked jokes about
the Pope in Rome, ridiculed bishops and cardinals, indulged in
satire and sarcasm - not in the name of Christian faith, but of
secular folly. They would rarely go so far as to touch the essential
doctrines of Christianity (34) but they would the sharper focus
their bough of folly at the bearers of ecclesiastic authority and
religious wisdom.

If the Cluny Reform Movement preluded the Reformation, these
goliards in a way, as I said, preluded the Renaissance and the

Enlightenment. Their secularism and their restlessness should
indeed be interpreted as part of a larger process of unrest in the
Middle Ages which grew into a veritable torrent the closer this
period of European history approached the Reformation and the
Renaissance. It found its adequate outlet eventually in the rise of
the sciences, the emergence of bourgeois capitalism, the discov-
eries of strange continents. That means, as important as the
economic conditions of medieval vagabondage are for a correct
interpretation of the goliards and their folly, one should place
equal emphasis on its spiritual and mental restlessness which was
critical, inquisitive and generally progressive. Prior to the emergence of science, technology and capitalism, much of this unrest
was released in folly.

This unrest, incidentally, did not always lead to vagabondage.
Some of these restless souls were able to make a living as relatively independent intellectuals who were sustained economically
by an ecclesiastic prebend, by a benevolent patron, or by pupils
who were privately taught against remuneration. A combination of
these sources of income was, of course, also possible, as in the
case of Erasmus. He presents, in this respect, an altogether interesting, although, due to his extraordinary capacities, not representative example. He was ordained as an Augustinian priest but
in his mid-twenties left the monastery of Steyn, near Gouda (the
Netherlands), because he could not adjust well to the narrow-
mindedness of the monastic spirit, enhanced as it was at Steyn
by the 'devotio moderna' and its inherent puritanism. While still a
monk, he wrote, together with a very close friend, poems in Latin
in which various secular topics were covered, such as the spring,
love and friendship. Erasmus complained about the barbaric and
stupid reactions of his superiors who apparently found these
activities quite paganistic and unbecoming to a monk. While still
in the monastery, he began a manifesto in defence of profane literature with the significant title of 'Antibarbari'. He was indeed
a restless man who, as he would say himself, read and wrote 'tum-
ultuarie'. Such a spirit no monastery could have confined. Without
breaking with his order, he accepted the appointment of secretary
to the bishop of Cambray around 1493, but not being fit either to
participate actively in politics, which was much part of such a
position in those days, he soon left for the University of Paris for
further studies. This was finally a place to his liking - very lively
and intellectually stimulating, not in the least because of the ongoing debates between the scholastic traditionalists and the modern
humanists.Huizinga wrote about the University of Paris at the time
Erasmus entered it: 'one lived in an almost continuous series of
disputations; there were elections being held constantly, and the
students were disorderly.'(35)

But once more, Erasmus was an exception. It was far from easy
for a restless soul to engage in an independent career successfully.
Most of Erasmus's likeminded contemporaries were forced to end
up among the goliards, certainly if they could not command over
the intellectual capacities which stood at the disposal of the great

humanist. As goliards these restless individuals were constantly
haunted by hunger and cold, marked by social degradation, on
the brink of destitution and thus always close to criminality. Without a wealthy patron among the clergy, the nobility or the higher
bourgeoisie, these clerical and intellectual misfits were generally
dependent on the common people to whom they catered their
brand of entertainment. They could not afford the sharp wit of
Erasmus, even if they possessed but a fragment of his mental
capacities. The medium of their entertainment was and remained
folly.(36)

When we read the songs and ballads of the goliards we are
immediately struck by their earthy quality. This poetry is always
down-to-earth, physical, materialistic and at times simply vulgar
and bawdy. It does not contemplate life after death, or heaven
and hell, or salvation and redemption. Goliards, on the contrary,
boast that they prefer the company in hell above the obviously
tedious company in heaven. This cannot harm them, they claim,
because their souls are lost anyway - a fact, incidentally, that
causes them no distress at all. On the contrary, they are quite
happy about it. Says one of them, bearing the pompous name of
Archipoeta: 'Avid for the world's delight more than for salvation,
dead in soul, I care but for body's exultation.'(37) Naturally, the
tavern not the church is the place they frequent, as it is their
main field of operation. Physical emotions of erotic love and bodily lust, rather than the spiritual exultation of religious-mystical
ecstasy, are the very cornerstones of the goliardic worldview.

A worldview indeed it was: life is like a river without aim and
end, man is like a leaf, floating on this river. Behind the mask of
laughter, under the cover of folly, the goliard hides his nihilism
and immoralism. They are a mirror-image of the norms and values
of Christianity; and what does appear in the mirror? The image
of the higher clergy in its greed, materialism and mendacity! Who
now is the fool? the goliard asks. The difference between the
corrupt clergy and the foolish goliards is not folly/wisdom but
honesty/dishonesty: the goliard does not wrap up his immoralism
in false piety and pompous authority, like the princes of the
church usually do. This point was certainly not missed by the
common people to whom they offered their entertainment. It must
have made these fools very popular.

The goliards tried to be funny all the time. Even such a genuinely lyrical and touching song as Levis Exsurgit Zephirus which
begins with a beautiful description of the emergence of spring,
carries a cynical touch in the appearance of the sighing and love-
sick maiden who sheds some silly tears.(38) Their humour is rarely
witty as in Erasmus. It is sheer folly throughout. But behind this
folly, innocent as it appears, lurks this mocking cynicism, laughing at such values as honour, valour, loyalty and simple decency.
The typically Renaissance opportunist and superbly unreliable
Pietro Aretino (d. 1556), a notorious Italian liar and slanderer,
described by Burckhardt as the first person who used and abused
publicity (the first journalist, Burckhardt added),(39) was indeed

foreshadowed in the songs and poems of the goliards. But one
essential difference remained: Aretino aimed ruthlessly and un-
scrupulously at the promotion of his own personality, whereas
the goliard would always work in anonymity. The target of his
biting folly was never mentioned by name and if his songs circu-
lated, in writing, among a larger audience, this would always
happen under a pseudonym. But it was the systematic permeation
of their folly by cynicism and opportunism, their systematic lack
or moral principles, which brought the goliards close to the first
modern individuals of Western Europe: Aretino and - albeit strip-
ped of all traces of folly - Machiavelli.

The time in which the 'goliardic movement' flourished was a
period in which the power of Rome reached its zenith of imperialist
aspirations (war on the manichee Albigensians of Languedoc, crusades, investiture conflict, etc.). It was also a time in which the
moral decay of the curia and the papacy intensified, paving the
way to the Machiavellian mendacity of an Alexander VI (Borgia)
and the morally vacuous love for pomp and circumstance of a Leo
X. However, this was also a period of reform movements (Cluny,
Franciscan Minorities), mystical reorientation (Eckhart, Tauler,
Ruysbroeck), and sectarian revolt (Joachimism, Albigenses). This
complex, and in many cases contradictory, whole of movements
and counter-movements, of facts and occurrences, was the reality
through which the goliards roamed, singing their ribald, irreverent, foolish songs. They were, of course, not part of any of
these movements. If they satirized the authorities of the official
church, they would also present a kind of mock image of reform
movements. Franciscan Minorites called themselves 'the fools of
Jesus' and they wandered through medieval society while they
ministered their assistance to the needy and helpless, the poor
and the downtrodden, gathering in the community of 'minor brothers', the 'Ordo Fratrum Minorum'. In this order a style of life
was maintained which was opposite to the flauntingly luxurious
life-style of the Roman curia and papacy. The goliards also saw
themselves as fools, but of the people not of Jesus, and they
claimed to belong to an order also, the 'Ordo Vagorum' or 'Familia
Goliae', headed by the 'Grandmaster Golias', an impish monk
image of Bernard of Clairvaux or of Francis of Assisi. They would
not offer Christian charity to the needy, but foolish entertainment to the bored: and they would do so for the sake of remuneration, not of redemption. Moreover, they were not really
shocked by the unascetic life-style of the Roman prelates, and as
immoralists they were not much interested in a spiritual renewal
of Christianity. On the contrary, the morally dismal state of affairs
in the Church of Rome was to their advantage, since it gave them
a butt to point their arrows of folly at. Actually, most of these
goliards probably cherished the secret (yet thoroughly unrealistic)
desire to share even just a fraction of the luxury and comfort of
these popes, cardinals and bishops whom they showered with their
satirical opprobrium. In sum, the goliards were socially critical but
their critique was highly opportunistic as they would not hesitate

to castigate satirically both the Church of Rome and its religious
oppositions, without, of course, offering any valid alternatives.
In other words, their social criticism is non-ideological, and not
founded on any religious, social or political principles. (40)

The goliardic organization 'Ordo Vagorum' did not really exist,
of course. It was the product of foolish make-believe. The pious
monks have their orders, thus the fools among the errant entertainers should have theirs. The valiant knights had their chivalric orders, thus the fools of medieval popular culture should
have theirs. If the 'Grandmaster Golias' had any reality, it was
not much more than the reality of our 'Santa Claus'. Goliards, in
fact, were incorrigible individualists and marginal men who were
hard to organize. Having left the social bonds of monastery, university and social status group, they always took great pains to
avoid new social ties and moral bonds. The notion of a goliardic
organization would make them snicker and that is precisely why
they invented an imaginary one.

An Austrian document, called 'Indulgence given by Surianus,
Arch-Primate of the Wandering Scholars, 1209', demonstrates
handsomely the extent to which this make-believe of a goliardic
organization was driven. (41) It gives a very curious insight into
the folly of goliards and a beautiful characterization of the goliardic mentality:

> swift and unstable as the swallows seeking their food through
> the air, hither, thither, wheresoever the levity of our in-
> constant, fickle and singular mind may drive us, like a leaf
> caught up by the wind or a spark of fire in the brushwood,
> we wander, unweariedly weary, and withal experiencing, in
> accordance with the rigour of our inordinate order, mocks
> and blows....

Surianus, getting apparently caught linguistically in the frisks of
his own mind, is full of metaphors to describe goliardic folly,
likening these restless wanderers to 'bats that can find no place,
either with beast or bird' - silly hybrids in the order of Nature.
His description reminds us of Isidor of Seville's characterization
of a wandering clerk as 'a hybrid, like the hippocentaurs'. (42)

Archipoeta, a goliard from around 1200, whom we met before,
laid also emphasis on the transient nature of these vagabonds. His
description carries definitely a touch of poetry: 'I am of an element volatile in matter, like a frail and withered leaf which the
winds may scatter.' In the next stanza he sighs: 'I a fool, may be
compared to a flowing river, always in the self-same bed, transient yet forever.'(43) In this same song - the famous Vagabond's
Confession - Archipoeta gives air to the goliard's materialism:
'Avid for the world's delight more than for salvation, dead in soul,
I care but for body's exultation.'(44) He ends as a melancholic,
yet mockingly irreverent nihilist: 'In the tavern let me die, that's
my resolution, bring me wine for lips so dry at life's dissolution.
Joyfully the angel's choir then will sing my glory: Sit deus prop-
icius, huic potatori [May God be well-disposed to this toper].'(45)

Once more, one must realize that these goliards were first and foremost out to entertain people. If they were critical, they were so in a non-ideological, highly opportunistic manner, turning on any social group, religious position, or political policy if this would yield the desired result, namely laughter and, in exchange for that, food, shelter, clothes, drinks, and money. The following little verse may demonstrate the fact that the sheer fun of making jokes transcended by far the desire to air criticism of a status quo. It was composed by the goliard Hugh of Orléans and runs as follows: 'Bishop, you're scummy, the dregs of the clergy, your throat has a crop. Winter is here and you gave me a coat without fur on the top.' Taking these lines on their literal meaning, they seem to express feelings of anger and frustration, aired by the use of desperately insulting words: the voice of the downtrodden which expresses powerless opposition against a repressive establishment. However, if one reads loudly the original Latin lines, it becomes quite apparent that they were composed primarily for the linguistic fun of alliterations and of charmingly primitive rhymes and rhythms: 'Pontificum spuma, fex cleri, sordida struma, qui dedit in bruma mihi matellum sine pluma.'(46) Rhymes and rhythms were to these goliardic fools far more exciting than revolt and rebellion. Unlike the latter, the former provided their audiences with simple entertainment and fun. Yet, I venture to say that without their own knowledge these fools criticized their society in a much more fundamental sense than rebels and revolutionaries do, albeit this criticism was less effective politically than a well-organized revolution probably would have been. The goliards, namely, represented a reality which transcended what Schutz would term the 'paramount reality' of their daily life - a looking-glass reality in which, as in a weird dream, parts of a future, as of a yet metaphysical world, seemed to have come into existence. If these fools were not rebels or proto-revolutionaries, they were neither simple functions of a status quo. Their vision of reality was such that they transcended the status quo. To many, goliards must have been the typical representatives of a general, late-medieval degeneracy, components of a larger syndrome which included utterly cruel, legalized tortures, and perverse interests in dwarfs, cripples, idiots and buffoons. Apart from the fact that such a degeneration flourished in all its intensity much later than the Middle Ages (which were indeed far more humane than we commonly believe), one should be very careful with one's evaluation of such phenomena as the goliards. Huizinga's 'The Waning of the Middle Ages' (1919) is a good example in this respect. Apart from a few irrelevant remarks, his otherwise rather detailed study of fools' organizations. He also neglects the goliards. But he went to such issues as court and household fools, festival of fools, and fools' organizations. He also neglects the foliards. But he went to great lengths in giving a picture of the dark shadows hovering over this period of European history, in which people were torn apart by fiery sentiments, dominated by forms and styles, and characterized by pain, cruelty, suffering and death. Although he

did stress the paradoxes of this society, he failed to give fools
and folly their due place in medieval life. He touched this point
briefly in another book in which he discussed man's play instinct
and the cultural expressions thereof - 'Homo Ludens' (1938). Here
he wrote:

> Medieval life was brimful of play: the joyous and unbuttoned
> play of the people, full of pagan elements that had lost their
> sacred significance and been transformed into jesting and
> buffoonery, or the solemn and pompous play of chivalry, the
> sophisticated play of courtly love, etc.(47)

But then he decides to disregard the whole phenomenon altogether
on account of the following argument: 'Few of these forms now had
any real culture-creating function.'(48) Obviously, Huizinga
meant here the creation of 'high culture' which he had analysed
skilfully, when he discussed the life and culture of late-medieval
Burgundian courts. He simply overlooked or disregarded the fact
of a 'popular culture' outside these courts which in many respects
had its own characteristics and which in its own way contributed
to the world yet to come. Medieval fools, including the goliards,
were very much part of this popular culture and in what I have
called the progressive thrust these fools have contributed to the
future world. That definitely is a 'culture-creating function'.(49)

THE FOLLY OF THE LOWER CLERGY

Compared to the inhabitants of traditional societies, we moderns
celebrate only very few festivals in a communal manner. Even the
communal festivals we still do celebrate, of which Christmas is
probably the most universal one, few are sufficiently generalized
in religious meaning as to be useful to a great variety of human
beings. They are quite sober, if not boring, compared to the often
jubilant abundance, and jollity, of most pre-modern festivals. As
Voltaire correctly remarked in his philosophical dictionary: 'nous
sommes un peu secs en tout' - 'in general, we are somewhat
dry.'(50)
    Medieval folly has flourished abundantly in a variety of festivals.
It is quite impossible to give a historically accurate summary of
the many feasts and festivals which contributed to the enchantment
of traditional life and in which fools and folly often received free
rein.(51) Each country had its rather busy festive calendar which -
apart from the Christian festivals like Christmas, Easter, and the
days of the many saints officially acknowledged by Rome - consisted of a broad range of national celebrations. Within these
specific national calendars, various regional differences could
again be distinguished. This is, of course, not the place to discuss all these details.
    Students of folklore have pointed out that many rather ancient
pagan rituals have been preserved in these festivals. The Church

of Rome tried to Christianize them in an attempt to smooth the
transition from heathenism to Christianity. Pope Gregory the
Great, for example, wrote two letters in 601 concerning the missionary policies with regard to paganism. In the first letter he
tells Ethelbert of Kent to see to it that the worship of idols in the
church be curbed and that the temples and idols be destroyed
forthwith. But while his messenger was still on his way to England, the Pope changed his mind and formulated a new policy
which remained typical of the missionary activities of Rome ever
since:

> Do not after all pull down the fanes. Destroy the idols;
> purify the buildings with holy water; set relics there; and
> let them become temples of the true God. So the people will
> have no need to change their places of concourse, and where
> of old they were wont to sacrifice cattle to demons, thither
> let them continue to resort on the day of the saint to whom
> the church is dedicated, and slay their beasts no longer as
> sacrifice but for a social meal in honour of Him whom they
> now worship.(52)

The Christianization of pagan Europe, it stands to reason, was
initially not a very thorough process. In fact, throughout the
Middle Ages men and women wore their Christian skins rather
lightly. Or, to use another metaphor, Christianity remained but
a thin veneer covering a thick layer of paganism. The Reformation
would radically change this, in particular by means of its distinction between natural religion and revelation: the former was
allegedly characteristic of the not yet reborn human being, hope-
lessly caught in the web of original sin, whereas the latter has
come to man from God the Creator through Jesus Christ, as
reported in the Scriptures and preached in the sermon in church.
This was not only a massive intellectualization of religion, as I
indicated before, but also a radical attack on heathenism and its
inherent remnants of magic. As such it contributed strongly to
the disenchantment of the world. But prior to this early modernization, ancient pagan sentiments, couched in magical forms of
thought and experience, would peep through the crevices of the
thin veneer of Christianity. Particularly in their numerous festivities, medieval men and women gave way to pagan impulses and
vented rather ancient, irrational thoughts and sentiments.
   Not amazingly, folly has functioned as the main catalyst of these
ancient, pre-Christian enchantments. When one reads the accounts
of medieval folk festivals, as they have been recorded, for instance, by Chambers in the case of Great Britain, one receives
the distinct impression that these men and women were constantly
driven by frolic and folly, as if these were very basic human impulses which we moderns have managed to bury under layers of
civilization. Civilized people all agree on one point: we should
compose ourselves when we feel the itch of folly because folly is
'primitive', 'childish', 'irrational', 'uncivilized'. In a sense this is

correct. Folly is very much an aboriginal layer of consciousness in the human species, testifying to impulses which lay, as it were, prior to any socializing and civilizing process, piercing through the veneers of culture with an unpredictable, often noisy and irritating force, comparable to the sudden eruption of a volcano which everyone had thought to be 'sleeping'.

In order not to get lost in the overwhelming complexity of medieval festivals and their various degrees and forms of folly, I shall limit myself presently to a short discussion of a most obvious example, the famous and notorious 'Festival of Fools' which was celebrated throughout Western Europe yearly at the end of the old and the beginning of the new calendar year. This period of various foolish festivities, collectively labelled 'Festival of Fools', has been documented best for France during the period from the High Middle Ages up till roughly the sixteenth century. Medieval folly found probably in this festival its most sublime expression and it offers therefore the historical sociologist very valuable information about the nature and the functions of traditional folly.

Here again, however, we are confronted by the undifferentiated complexity of medieval culture and society, because the concept 'Festival of Fools' covers a variety of festivals between Christmas and Epiphany, and there are historians who apply it to the festivities during Lent as well.(53) This is not the place of course to discuss such problems of chronology here. I shall instead focus primarily on the nature of the folly inherent to these festivities. It suffices here to mention the fact that the Festival of Fools consisted originally of a variety of festivities on different days, within and outside the church, during the period at the end of the old and the beginning of the new year. They were organized and performed by different groups of people. Beleth, the rector of the Theological Faculty of Paris in the twelfth century, distinguished four groups, dancing on four different occasions after Christmas: the deacons, the priests, the choir children, and - either on the day of the Circumcision or on Epiphany - the sub-deacons.(54) Apparently, only the latter festivity was initially called 'fête des foux', or 'fête des sous-diacres' which led Chambers to the decision to reserve the name Festival of Fools only for the New Year revels organized and performed by the lower clergy, while he distinguished it from the festival a few days earlier in which a 'boy bishop' was elected from among the members of the children's choir by the deacons and priests.(55) Others, however, call this the 'festival of the innocents' to be held a few days after New Year on Innocents' Day. In short, it is all very complex and confusing, while it is quite possible that many national and regional differences have been existent also. However, it is quite irrelevant to our discussion to acquire definite knowledge about the question of which festival was celebrated on which day. We shall use the concept of 'Festival of Fools' - 'festum stultorum', 'festum follorum', 'festum fatuum', 'festum sub-diaconorum', 'festum baculi', 'asinaria festa', 'fête des foux', 'fête des sous-diacres', 'fête des innocents', 'fête de l'âne'(56) - as an overarching name for various foolish activities in and outside the church in the period between Christmas and Epiphany.

Our main source of historical information about the Festival of Fools consists, ironically, of several theological condemnations and related pastoral admonitions which were issued at regular intervals by official bodies, such as several councils and the Theological Faculty of Paris. Sometimes the descriptions of the denounced festivities were so detailed that the reader begins to suspect that these critics were in fact quite fascinated by the phenomenon. Beleth, the previously mentioned rector of the Theological Faculty of Paris, gave a very fine account of what he called the 'libertas decembris' in his 'Divinorum Officiorum Rationale':

> The freedom lay in an inversion of roles and ranks in the clergy, who played all sorts of pranks inside the churches during the Christmas holidays and at Twelfth-night. Clerks, deacons and subdeacons said mass in place of the priests. The priests danced, shook dice, played at ball, bowls and other games of chance in front of the altar. The choir-boys masqueraded in costume and occupied the stalls of the canons. On Holy Innocents' Eve they elected one of their number bishop, clothed him in episcopal robes, anointed him, and paraded him about town to the ringing of bells and with bands of music. At the Feast of the Circumcision the churchmen appeared at mass, some in female attire, some dressed as clowns or streetperformers, others with their capes and cassocks inside out, and almost all wearing grotesque false faces. They then proceeded to elect a 'Bishop', or 'Archbishop of Fools'. ... At Antibes ... the actors in the festival rushed into the stalls in the choir with their sacerdotal robes inside out or in tatters, and capered about like people who had lost their minds. They held their prayer-books upside down, pretended to read through spectacles with orange-skins in place of lenses, and dusted each other with ashes or flour.(57)

A similar description was given some centuries later in the famous letter of the Theological Faculty of Paris, dated 12 March 1444 (or 1445), which contains also a pastoral admonition and fourteen conclusions. The letter was meant to put an end to these allegedly scandalous practices once and for all - without any success though. 'Priests and clerks', the alarmed theologians write,

> may be seen wearing masks and monstrous visages at the hours of office. They dance in the choir dressed as women, panders or minstrels. They sing wanton songs. They eat black puddings at the horn of the altar, while the celebrant is saying mass. They play at dice there. They cense with stinking smoke from the soles of old shoes. They run and leap through the church, without a blush at their own shame. Finally they drive about the town and its theatres in shabby traps and carts;

and rouse the laughter of their fellows and the bystanders
in infamous performances, with indecent gestures and verses
scurrilous and unchaste.(58)

The paraphernalia and the acts described were those typical of
folly and loaded with magical meanings: faces painted grotesquely
or hidden behind masks, weird costumes, often worn inside out,
transvestism (as well as exhibitionism, as we shall see), playing
at dice and other games of chance in front of the altar, inversion
of hierarchies and mimicking of authorities, books held upside
down, indecent and blasphemous songs and gestures, burning of
incense made of shoe leather, parading through the church and
in town with silly carts (often, in fact, badly smelling dungcarts),
a child as bishop, riding, as we shall see, an ass and waving the
precentor's conducting staff ('baculus') as a mock sceptre, the
gluttonous eating of peculiar food (blood sausages, as we shall
see later, which carried a specific meaning). In short, a scurrilous reality was established - a reality with inversed structures
based on regressive impulses and sentiments, rubbing as it were
against the routines of a taken-for-granted world.

Although a direct historical link cannot be proven due to the
lack of historical records for the period of the Early Middle Ages,
the similarities of this Festival of Fools and the ancient Roman
'Saturnalia' are so striking that one usually assumes the former
to be a continuation of the latter. There are, incidentally, equally
striking similarities between these two foolish festivals, on the
one hand, and the ancient Babylonian 'Saccaea', on the other.
One element, in particular, suggests some sort of trans-historical
continuity, namely the election of a socially inferior person to a
temporary position of high status with much freedom. Faithful to
the leitmotiv of his classic 'The Golden Bough' (1890), Frazer
links this element to the ritual execution of the king by means of
a substitute and finds the ritual back in many different civilizations with only minor variations. The interesting aspect of this
universal ritual is the element of licentious folly prior to the execution of the royal substitute: his freedom as the previously discussed 'Narrenfreiheit'.

As to the folly of the Saturnalia, Frazer gives a brief account
of the remarkable legend of Saint Dasius in which the celebration
of this festival by Roman legionaries at the Danube in Bulgaria
around the year AD 300 is recorded. 'Thirty days before the
festival', Frazer writes,

they chose by lot from amongst themselves and young and handsome man, who was then clothed in royal attire to resemble
Saturn. Thus arrayed, attended by a multitude of soldiers, he
went about in public with full licence to indulge his passions
and to taste of every pleasure, however base and shameful.
But if his reign was merry, it was short and ended tragically;
for when the thrity days were up and the festival of Saturn
had come, he cut his throat on the altar of the god whom he
personated.(59)

The legend continues to tell that in the year AD 303 the lot happened to fall on a young Christian by the name of Dasius who
refused to impersonate a pagan god and to indulge in Saturnalian
lechery and debauchery. When the threats of his commanding
officer were of no avail, he was summarily executed.

About the Babylonian Saccaea, Frazer reports the following:

> It began on the sixteenth day of the month Lous, and lasted
> for five days during which masters and servants changed
> places, the servants giving orders and the masters obeying
> them. A prisoner condemned to death was dressed in the
> king's robes, seated on the king's throne, allowed to issue
> whatever commands he pleased, to eat, drink, and enjoy
> himself, and to lie with the king's concubines. But at the
> end of the five days he was stripped of his royal robes,
> scourged, and hanged or impaled.(60)

A similar story is told about the sacrifice of a young prisoner
impersonating a god by the Aztecs of ancient Mexico:

> Thus, at the festival called Toxcatl, the greatest festival of
> the Mexican year, a young man was annually sacrificed in
> the character of Tezcatlipoca, 'the god of gods', after having
> been maintained and worshipped as the great deity in person
> for a whole year. The young man singled out for this high
> dignity was carefully chosen from among the captives on the
> ground of his personal beauty. He had to be of unblemished
> body, slim as a reed and straight as a pillar, neither too tall
> nor too short. ... He was honourably lodged in the temple,
> where the nobles waited on him and paid him homage, bring-
> ing him meat and serving him as a prince. ... Golden orna-
> ments hung from his nose, golden armlets adorned his arms,
> golden bells jingled on his legs at every step he took. ...
> On the last day the young man, attended by his wives and
> pages, embarked in a canoe covered with a royal canopy
> and was ferried across the lake to a spot where a little hill
> rose from the edge of the water. It was called the Mountain
> of Parting, because there his wives bade him a last farewell.
> Then, accompanied only by his pages, he repaired to a small
> and lonely temple by the wayside. Like the Mexican temples
> in general, it was built in the form of a pyramid. ... On
> reaching the summit he was seized and held down by the
> priests on his back upon a block of stone, while one of them
> cut open his breast, thrust his hand into the wound, and
> wrenching out his heart held it up in sacrifice to the sun.(61)

Whatever faults and shortcomings one can point out in Frazer's
arguments, it still seems that he had put his finger on a myth
which was based on trans-historical and magical connotations and
sentiments. (One could add as another historical example the
crucifixion of Jesus of Nazareth whom the Roman soldiers treated

mockingly, as in a Saturnalian festival, as the King of the Jews and who was later venerated by his followers as the incarnate god who by his death and resurrection had attoned the sins of mankind.) It is the myth of the Scape Goat who in the shape of a god or a king - i.e. the apex of the cosmos and of human society - assumes the sin or ritual pollution of his fellow-human beings, lives as a fool for a while, enjoying the fool's freedom, and then takes this sin or ritual pollution with him into death.

Vilfredo Pareto showed great interest in these festivals, as they seemed to demonstrate a humanly fundamental and meta-historical sentiment - 'the desire to bring contraries, opposites, together'.(62) They are brought together, we may add, in an artificial reality, the reality of the looking-glass. Meanwhile, in accordance with Pareto's remarkably early notion of structuralism, it would not make much sense to retrace the origins of one of these festivals (e.g. the Festival of Fools) to an alleged historical predecessor (e.g. the Saturnalia). They are rather to be viewed as different expressions of the same anthropologically fundamental and meta-historical sentiment. Or, in Pareto's technical terminology, they are different derivations of the very same residue. In any case, in these various festivals folly and foolish liberty are intrinsic components and share a meta-historical nature. Folly might indeed well be an anthropological residue which can only be reconstructed by a careful analysis of its derivations, i.e. its culturally and historically specific expressions. The Festival of Fools was one of them.

Meanwhile, structuralism has too easily and too often lead scholars to 'discover' meta-historical 'structures', because their research was sloppy and their comparisons facile. When one acknowledges the existence of anthropological structures of a mythological and meta-historical nature - anthropological categories with the Kantian status of being a priori - one should be sensitive in particular, I believe, to historical data and sociological facts. One should in particular analyse carefully the historical and sociological differences among the culturally specific expressions of these meta-historical structures or categories. Semantic meanings are derived from a carefully executed comparative analysis of related words, not from the mere discovery of their common linguistic roots and syntactic rules.

This can, of course, not be the place to engage in such a detailed historical and comparative analysis of various festivals having folly as their main component. Let me just give one brief and simple example. The following difference between the Festival of Fools and the festivals which fascinated Frazer so much, is essential: the boy bishop, or the 'abbas stultorum', was sometimes mockingly and ceremonially whipped but he was never executed, not even in a mocking performance. All one could say to satisfy structuralist desires is that such a ritual murder might well have been superfluous, since the crucifixion of Jesus Christ - the mock king of the Jews, murdered by the Romans as in a Saturnalian feast - was already enacted ritually in every celebration of the holy mass.

Fundamental to these festivals, in the anthropologically cate-
gorical sense of the word 'fundamental', has been the magical
notion that these ritual follies somehow would promote fertility.
Whatever else it also might have been, the medieval Festival of
Fools was, like similar festivals in totally different cultures and
historical periods, primarily, yet covertly, a fertility rite. It was
for this very reason that the official hierarchy of the Church of
Rome, with the assistance of learned theologians, would continue
to castigate its practitioners and condemn its practices. In this
festival, the leaders of the church realized, folly was at once the
cover-up, the legitimation and the carrier of ancient magical paganism. That is, in the eyes of the ecclesiastic authorities these
fools were not at all innocent, as they claimed themselves to be
time and again. I shall try to substantiate this point by relating
some facts. In his very curious book 'Scatological Rites of All
Nations' (1891), John Bourke put heavy emphasis on the wearing
of masks and eating of peculiar food by the medieval participants
of the Festival of Fools and he compared it immediately with the
so-called 'urine ritual' of the Zuni Indians which was part of a
whole configuration of ritual follies among the North-American
Indians, since Bourke's days well documented by various anthropologists (cf. chapter 4).(63) He touched upon an important fact
which, for reasons of prudery and ill-conceived decency, had
been hushed up by our theological informants from the Late Middle Ages, as well as by later more scientifically motivated historians. The fact is so important, because it demonstrates, better
than anything else, the intrinsically magical nature of these foolish festivities.

During the Festival of Fools, namely, members of the lower
clergy - marginal men in the ecclesiastic hierarchy anyhow -
danced and hopped through church, gambled in front of the altar,
burned bad-smelling incense, behaved generally demonically, and
ate strange food. The French sources speak of 'boudins', i.e.
blood sausages. Bourke now claims that these sausages were in
actual fact substitutes for excrement and probably phallic symbols
also.(64) (Freudians will find a wealth of symbolic material in this
foolish festival. Jung, as we shall see in chapter 4, envisaged in
it a depth-psychology archetype.) Moreover, those vehicles
which the fools paraded through the streets of the town, were
devilishly smelling dungcarts. Ordure was thrown by them at the
onlookers. Male fools would not only don female clothes but some
of them would throw off all clothes and go about in church stark
naked. Diderot and d'Alembert discussed the 'Fête des Fous' in
their encyclopedia (1779) but when they came to the scatological
practices of the feast they hastened to state that decency forbade
them to enter into a detailed description.

It stands to reason that the inversion of hierarchical positions
and roles will strike our sociological fancy. This was an essential
component of the Roman Saturnalia and we encounter it again in
the Festival of Fools. It certainly deserves careful attention.

The Saturnalia was originally held yearly, 17 December, in

honour of Saturn, god of sowing and husbandry (fertility), but
extended gradually to a festival which would last for seven days.
It commemorated the golden days in which Saturn still ruled peacefully over primitive and rude, yet happy people, taught them
how to plough the earth, how to sow the harvest, how to live
together in harmony according to just laws – a state of human
affairs with little differentiation and complexity, based on moral
purity and legal justice, a bucolic paradise. As Frazer formulated
it in his poetic style: 'The earth brought forth abundantly: no
sound of war or discord troubled the happy world: no baleful
love of lucre worked like poison in the blood of the industrious
and contented peasantry. Slavery and private property were alike
unknown: all men had all things in common.'(65) The festival was
a commemoration of an aboriginal state of communism, based on
freedom, equality and justice, although embedded in yet unciv il-
ized simplicity and crudity. As if to stress the contrast of this
aboriginal communism with the existent status quo, slaves became
masters for the duration of the festival, and masters served their
slaves – a grotesque inversion of the established hierarchy, a
looking-glass image of the status quo. From among the slaves a
mock-king was selected:

So far was this inversion of ranks carried, that each household became for a time a mimic republic in which the high
offices of state were discharged by the slaves, who gave
their orders and laid down the law as if they were indeed
invested with all the dignity of the consulship, the praetor-
ship, and the bench. Like the pale reflection of power thus
accorded to bondsmen at the Saturnalia was the mock kingship
for which freemen cast lots at the same season. The person on
whom the lot fell enjoyed the title of king, and issued commands of a playful and ludicrous nature to his temporary
subjects.(66)

The 'dominus festi' of the Saturnalia, reigning as a Lord of Misrule, emerged also in the Festival of Fools as the 'episcopus
stultus' (the foolish bishop), the 'papam fatuorum' (the pope of
fools), the 'abbas stultorum' (the abbot of idiots), the 'abbé de
la malgouverne' (the abbot of misrule), the 'abbé des foux' (the
abbot of fools), etc. He is chosen from among the 'innocents' of
the ecclesiastic hierarchy, such as the sub-deacons and the choir
boys. Somehow the ass possessed an important symbolic meaning
during the irreverent reign of his misrule: the mock-bishop was
paraded through church and town on the back of an ass with his
face backwards, 'caudam in manis' (with the ass's tail in his
hands), as happened also to the victims of a 'charivari', to be
discussed in the next section. Apparently, the ass symbolized
folly somehow. In fact, this festival was also called the 'asinaria
festa'. C. G. Jung quotes a codex from the eleventh century
which stipulates when the braying of a donkey is to be imitated
during the celebration of a mock-mass. It says, for instance: 'At

the end of the mass, instead of the words "Ita missa est", the
priest shall bray three times [ter hinhamabit], and instead of the
words "Deo Gratias", the congregation shall answer "Ya" [hinham]
three times.'(67)

Two manuscripts of such foolish masses have been saved, one
of which was allegedly composed, or edited rather, by Pierre de
Corbeil, archbishop of Sens from 1194 till 1222. Du Tilliot called
it 'l'Office des Foux' but the recorded title was 'Office de la Cir-
concision à l'Usage de la Ville de Sens' which indicates that the
mass was celebrated at Sens on the Day of the Circumcision.
L'Abbé Villetard incidentally goes to great lengths to deny the
foolish nature of this missal and its alleged link to the Festival of
Fools. To him this 'officum' was a perfectly normal piece of liturgy
which was connected with the Festival of Fools erroneously by
some historians, simply because they misinterpreted the liturgical
annotations in the manuscript. For example, where it says 'euouae'
some have thought this to indicate a kind of bacchantic cry -
'Evohé'. The word, however, was a standard abbreviation of
'seculorum amen', omitting the consonants.(68) Likewise, the
words 'in falso' meant 'with the harmonized accompaniment of the
"faux bourdon" ' (one of the stops of the organ) and is juxtaposed
to 'in voce', meaning 'in unison'.(69) Yet, Chambers who studied
this missal carefully and who avoided the misinterpretations exposed by Villetard, sticks to the opinion that this is indeed a
'Missel des Fous'.(70) Admittedly, the burlesque in this missal is
rather subdued. The archbishop, when still canon at the Notre-
Dame of Paris, in 1198 cosigned a letter proposing to abolish the
Festival of Fools in this church. In this missal which he most
probably did not compose but edited from existing material, he
tried to mould folly in acceptable forms, as Chambers suggested:
'he may well have compiled or revised it for his own cathedral,
with the intention of pruning the abuse of the feast.'(71)

The history of criticism and defence of the Festival of Fools is
long and complicated. Time and again ecclesiastic powers have
tried to abolish or curb it, generally without much success not in
the least because the lower clergy in particular was wholeheartedly
given to this gay inversion of authority. The rather chaotic Council of Basle, held on and off between 1431 and 1449, issued a ban
on this festival in 1435 and historians have often claimed that this
authoritative prohibition did indeed duly impress the clergy involved. This prohibition received in addition considerable support from Charles VII of France when he included a paragraph
against these festivities in his Pragmatic Sanction of 1438. But
characteristically enough, the Duke of Burgundy, Philip the Good,
who unlike Charles VII was very fond of male and female fools,(72)
issued at the same time an official Privilege - in the form of a goliardic poem - in which he allowed his people to continue to celebrate the Festival of Fools.(73) Equally interesting in this respect
is the result of an attempt by the Bishop of Troyes to end the
licentiousness of the Festival of Fools in his city in the year 1444
by hiding safely behind the Pragmatic Sanction. The clergy of

St Peter's cathedral was willing to obey the bishop's orders, but
their colleagues at St Stephen's revolted openly against them and
produced quite some noise. Chambers gives a lively description
of this rebellion in the name of folly:

> They told the bishop that they were exempt from his juris-
> diction and subject only to his metropolitan, the archbishop
> of Sens; and they held an elaborate revel with even more
> than the usual insolence and riot. On the Sunday before
> Christmas they publicly consecrated their 'archbishop' in
> the most public place of town with a 'jeu de personnages'
> called 'le jeu du sacre de leur arcevesque', which was a
> burlesque of the 'saint mistère de consécration pontificale'.
> The feast itself took place in St Stephen's Church. The
> vicar who was chosen 'archbishop' performed the service
> on the eve and day of the Circumcision 'in pontificalibus',
> gave the Benediction to the people, and went in procession
> through the town. Finally, on Sunday, January 3, the
> clergy of all three churches joined in another 'jeu de per-
> sonnages' in which under the names of Hyppocrisie, Faintise
> and Fauxsemblant, the bishop and two deacons who had been
> most active in opposing the feast, were held up to ridicule.(74)

The bishop, however, was determined to win this battle. He mar-
shalled the support of the Archbishop of Sens and wrote a letter
of complaint to the king. In addition, he wrote to the Theological
Faculty which indeed might have contributed to the decision of
these learned men to issue their now famous letter on the alleged
abuses of the Festival of Fools. The result of his activities was
remarkable. The clergy of St Stephen's decided not to react at all.
Nothing was heard from them for some time. Chambers remarks
wryly: 'Probably it was thought best to say nothing, and let it
blow over. At any rate, it is interesting to note that in 1595, a
century and a half later, St Stephen's was still electing its "arce-
vesque des saulx" and that "droits" wer paid on account of the
vicar's feast until all "droits" tumbled in 1789'(75) Incidentally,
after he had conquered Burgundy, Louis XI solemnly authorized
this festival anew as an official institution in 1482.(76) In sum,
the Council of Basle, or the Pragmatic Sanction for that matter,
had earned very little success in their fight against this popular
festival. Folly was obviously too much entrenched in this kind of
society to be curbed successfully.

Meanwhile, protagonists of folly came to its defence with some
impressive arguments. We find some of these in the previously
mentioned letter of the Theological Faculty of Paris, dated March
1444 (or 1445), where they were recorded briefly with the intent
to refute them systematically.(77) The theologians, this much can
be said in their favour, were able to present a fair account of
these arguments, before they produced their counter-arguments –
an interesting debate which it is worthwhile to summarize briefly,
as it indicates clearly the predominant position of folly in traditional Europe.

The defenders of the Festival of Fools argued that these ribald
festivities were very ancient - an argument that should impress
theologians duly, they must have thought. Great ancestors have
participated in them. Moreover, they went on, we are not involved
in these things in any serious manner but frolic just for fun and
entertainment. In fact, we do all this because the folly which
comes naturally to us and seems to be an inborn human quality,
should somehow be discharged and drained at least once a year:
wine barrels would also crack if one would not, once in a while,
open their bungholes or faucets. (It is remarkable to find the
safety-valve argument as early as the fifteenth century!) A con-
stant devotion to the service of God would simply break us up,
they plead convincingly. That is why we give ourselves to folly
for a few days each year, and we fail to see why the church
should object to that. In fact, it enables us to return with even
more pleasure and zeal to the serious study and practice of religion.(78)

The indignant theologians counter that these are obviously arguments of silly old people who persist in their sins and try to
justify their foolish behaviour. What is worse, young people,
always fond of horseplay and novelties, applaud this abominable
festival.(79) This is indeed a very serious business, because
these abusive rituals are caused by original sin and the work of
the devil. The bishops should follow their great ancestors Saint
Paul and Saint Augustine, as well as the good example of their
colleagues, the Bishops Martin, Hilarius, Chrysostom, Nicholas,
and Germanus of Auxerre who have all condemned these sacrilegious practices. We must conclude, the theologians solemnly
declare, that it all depends on you, the prelates of the church,
whether this pestilential ritual will be continued or summarily
abolished: 'Concludimus, quod a vobis praelatis pendet continuatio
vel abolitio huius pestiferi ritus.' And it is simply inconceivable,
they add more threateningly, that these people will be so obstinate
and demented as to face the Inquisition and the secular arm, i.e.
the cruel punishment, 'cum assistentia inquisitorum fidei, et aux-
ilio brachii saecularis.'

Indeed, they run the risk of being incarcerated and losing their
benefices and their good reputation - their 'credit' so to say. Yes,
they would be in danger of being excommunicated.(80) These
threats obviously foreshadowed the cruel persecution of witches
and heretics. The notorious 'Malleus Malleficarum' (1486)(81) was
only published forty years later.

As a matter of fact, medieval fools were in one respect the predecessors of the fiercely persecuted witches of the late-medieval
and early-modern period: like these witches they were the carriers
of ancient, magically oriented paganism. As different as they have
been otherwise, folly and witchcraft were both seen by the official
church as demonic practices in the service of the devil. Yet the
threats levelled against the practitioners of the Festival of Fools
remained generally ineffective. If necessary, these fools would
just keep their faces straight as long as the heat was on. Unlike

the witches, fools were opportunists who would not be willing to
risk their lives or their freedom for the sake of folly. Like the
lower clergy of St Stephen's Church at Paris, they would simply
keep a low profile for a while and the moment their opponents
would be occupied again by other, more sincere and serious
affairs - such as fighting each other over doctrines and church
policies - they would return to their pranks and banter, their
burlesques and satires. It was only when these fools themselves
began to lose all appetite for folly, due to a general change in
culture and mentality under the impact of the Renaissance, the
Reformation and the Enlightenment, and in particular due to the
rise of capitalistic activism, that the Festival of Fools ceased to
be celebrated. Or in other words, during the growing disenchantment of the world in the process of modernization, traditional
European folly gradually faded away. This curious festival vanished with it. The bourgeoisie, initially given to folly as a means
of expression of its newly acquired class consciousness (see the
next section), began later to reject the irrationality of fools, as
it stood squarely opposed to its economic and social aspirations.
This happened precisely when it began to assume a predominant
position in European history (sixteenth and seventeenth centuries).
As early as 1500, rumours began to circulate about the decline of
fools and folly. The early signs of the world to come were indeed
already visible then. Yet, these rumours were still premature, as
a charming poem, composed around 1513, testifies:

> Me di tu que dame Folie
> Est mort? Ma foy, tu as menty;
> Jamais si grande ne la vy,
> Ny si puissante comme elle est.(82)

THE FOLLY OF PEASANTS AND BURGHERS

Since we must make a selection from the wealth of historical data
about rural and urban folly in medieval Europe, I shall focus in
this section primarily on rural youth groups which exerted a
remarkably strong social control over peasant communities by
means of various foolish exploits, and on the carnivalesque activities of the urban 'Fools' Societies' or, as they have also been
called, the 'Joyous Societies'. Like the Festival of Fools, these
rural and urban groups of fools occurred all over Europe, but
have been documented best in the case of France.
    Some historians believe that when the Festival of Fools declined
under the alleged impact of the Council of Basle (1435) and the
Pragmatic Sanction (1438), this foolish celebration was succeeded
by various bourgeois organizations of folly, called 'compagnies
des fous', or 'sociétés joyeuses' in the cities of the sixteenth century.(83) History, however, follows rarely such straight and
smoothly rational paths. In fact, both points of view are historically questionable. As I argued at the end of the former section,

the Festival of Fools did not end abruptly under the impact of
Basle and the Pragmatic Sanction but withered away during the
emergence of modernization. It simply lost its attraction when the
bourgeoisie had become the leading class in European societies -
a class of busy entrepreneurs given to the rationality of capitalism, technology and science, prone to the calculable and predictable rather than the erratic and inscrutable. Initially, when their
class consciousness had still to be forged in competition with the
predominant powers of feudal society, folly served the bourgeoisie
well, as we shall see instantly. But after it had conquered its own
position of power (sixteenth and seventeenth century), it had to
do away with folly gradually. Folly remained too reminiscent of
the society and culture the bourgeoisie had left behind, it also
contrasted too strongly with its own rationalism.

As to the second point, joyous societies did not emerge in the
fifteenth and sixteenth centuries after the Festival of Fools began
to vanish from the scene. On the contrary, as the historian
Nathalie Zemon Davis argued convincingly, such chapters of
foolish misrule did exist in rural France as early as the thirteenth
century, and there is sufficient reason to believe that they were
much older than the records indicate.(84) Most likely, these rural
chapters of folly have spread out to the cities, where they were
often organized in a guild-like fashion around various professions.
These urban joyous societies of the sixteenth century must also
have borrowed quite heavily from the practitioners of the Festival
of Fools, taking over many of its foolish ideas and practices. In
1552, the council of the city of Dijon abolished the Festival of
Fools officially, whereupon the joyous society called 'Compagnie
Mère-Folle' or 'l'Infanterie Dijonnoise' inherited its privileges, its
costumes, and the right to criticize in public.(85) It stands to
reason, by the way, that these urban chapters of misrule also
borrowed freely from the goliards and other minstrels, particularly
in the case of their 'farces' and 'sotties' - i.e. literary product-
ions, satirical sketches which were performed on the corners of
commercially busy streets and on the markets of fifteenth- and
sixteenth-century cities.(86)

Much of the folly of such fools' organizations like the 'Mère-Folle'
of Dijon, the 'Cornards' of Rouen, the 'Enfants-sans-souci' of
Paris, or the guild-like 'Basoche', the fools' club of legal clerks in
Paris with various chapters in other French cities, is similar to
the noisy and at times irritatingly foolish practices of certain
youth groups in rural France. From the thirteenth century on, we
possess records of countless organizations of young, married men
in rural France which were called 'bachelleries' or 'abbayes de la
jeunesse', or otherwise. Their adolescent members would annually
elect a King of Misrule or Abbot of Misrule from among their midst.
This leader directed the members of his chapter in all kinds of
licentious and generally foolish activities in the village.(87)

These rural youth groups had a variety of functions, some of
which were obviously magical by nature, as is indicated by Davis
when she writes:

In the Fête des Brandons at the beginning of Lent it was
they who bore the brands of blazing straw and jumped and
danced to ensure the village's agricultural and sexual fertility for the coming year, and at All Souls' Day it was they
who rang the bells for the dead ancestors of the village.(88)

The most striking function, however, was the exertion of social
control. These youngsters had some sort of jurisdiction over the
premarital and marital behaviour of their fellow-villagers. They
played various, traditionally established practical tricks on mar-
riageable girls of dubious morals, on young lads from other
villages who ventured to court 'their' girls, on husbands who
beat their wives, or on husbands who were henpecked by their
wives, on newlyweds who after a reasonable period of time failed
to produce a child, or on older widowers who wanted to marry
again but chose a girl or woman much younger in age. Depending
on the severity of the moral transgression, their victims were
ducked into water, paraded through the village backward on a
donkey, or treated with a midnight deafening 'charivari'.(89)
The charivari was, according to Davis, originally restricted to the
teasing of people who had married for the second time, especially
when there happened to be a considerable difference of age between the spouses. Sometimes for a week at a time, these youngsters, wearing grotesque masks, would beat on pots, pans, drums,
and go about rattling tambourines, ringing bells, blowing horns,
until a fine was paid. This behaviour was obviously not rebellious.
On the contrary, as Davis suggests, these youngsters came to the
defence of the morals and customs of the community, and even
watched over the demographic continuity of it, as they tried to
control the fecundity of the marriages: once more, couples that
did not produce offspring in time were treated on a 'charivari'.
    Looked at in terms of modern democratic institutions, these
youth groups with their social control activities seemed to carry
elements of vigilantism. The licence allowed to these young lads
did indeed border on criminality. Yet, Davis assures us that violence and aggressive disorder were considered by the practitioners of the 'charivari' as accidents or mistakes. And if there were
violent brawls or even cases of murder, they were not condoned
but immediately referred to the courts for trial. Therefore, in
general the 'terror' brought upon these rural communities by
these foolish gangs remained within the parameters of traditional
folly.
    Davis adjudicates also a pedagogical function to these groups
which she calls 'abbeys of misrule'. Their mocking practices
assisted adolescents to discover their appropriate place in society.
They were like 'rites de passage', helping youngsters in their
transition from childhood to adulthood. In addition, since these
activities took place within organized groups with a distinct leadership, the youthful members learned, in a playful manner, to adjust
to the life of organized and hierarchical society at large. They
resemble in this respect the fraternities of our universities - one

of the last remaining transitional institutions inherited from the traditional society of the past.

During the thirteenth century such chapters of misrule began to emerge also in the cities of France. While they remained largely unaltered in rural France until the nineteenth century, these groups of organized folly changed their character rather drastically in the cities. To begin with, their folly – although never compatible with the wit of Erasmus – was much less boorish and primitive, more civilized, if not yet truly intellectualized. Several of these urban joyous societies produced interesting pieces of literature – 'sotties' and 'farces' which were generally on a higher level of sophistication than the foolish practices of rural adolescents, but are nevertheless still pretty 'primitive' to the taste of the modern reader.

With the growth and expansion of the cities, the number of such fools' organizations increased also. Lyon counted some twenty different societies of fools in the sixteenth century, each having its own abbot, admiral, prince, king, court judge, or patriarch as Lord of Misrule. They were often organized within specific neighbourhoods and in several cases attached to professions which lend them a guild-like character. Paris, for example, had a joyous society for legal clerks, the previously mentioned 'Basoche', with chapters in Lyon, Bordeaux, Dijon and various other cities. The printers of Lyon were organized in a fools' organization, headed by the 'Lord of Misprint', the 'Seigneur de la Coquille', and so were the painters and the silkdyers. Just as the 'Ordo Vagorum' presented a mock-image of a religious or chivalric order, these joyous societies of artisans and professionals were mock-images of the medieval guilds.

Membership of these urban chapters was no longer restricted to unmarried adolescents. Men of all ages joined these voluntary associations, although many of their names harked back to earlier days, when the membership was younger in age: 'Enfants-sans-souci', 'Infanterie Dijonnaise', 'Enfants de la ville', etc. However, this should also be interpreted in terms of folly: the members of these clubs were innocents, fools, blessed with childish ignorance.

These urban chapters were, according to Davis, solidly middle class. Whereas the rural groups would carry 'the sons of the well-off peasants and landless ones', the urban joyous societies were limited to the middle class: 'The urban elite would be missing from the Abbey as would the unskilled "gagnedeniers" [the dayworkers]: certain classes of newcomers and foreign residents would be excluded too.'(90) However, Du Tilliot who had intimate knowledge of the 'Mère-Folle' of Dijon and in 1751 published a valuable book on the Festival of Fools and the joyous societies, informs us that this particular Dijonnaise association was 'composed of 500 persons of all quality, officers of parliament, of the audit-office, lawyers, solicitors, burghers, merchants, etc.'(91) The retinue of Mère Folle herself was made up of fifty of the richest artisans in town. He concludes his book with a few acts of membership, dating from the early seventeenth century. Mentioned with pride are Henri

Bourbon, Prince de Condé, the first 'prince of blood' to join (in 1626), a certain Comte d'Harcourt, and a couple of members of more recent date belonging to the influential bourgeoisie. The famous 'Enfants-sans-souci' harboured exclusively young men of well-to-do families who as students did not as yet command great sums of money, but who could afford to philander and to give vent to their goliardic impulses. Clément Marot (1495-1544), once member of this organization, but in later age obviously given to more serious exploits when he acquired fame as the poet of Protestant hymns, left a marvellous description of these foolish 'children':

> To bear a good heart, a good body and a cheerful face, to drink in the morning and to flee from brawls and wrangling, to sing a little song to one's beloved at the gate in the evening, to cut a figure as a brave bad fellow, to wander all night without harming a soul, to go to bed – there is our whole baffling plan! Next day we begin all over again. In conclusion, what we seek is lightheartedness, and of it we never tire, and we maintain that it is part of true nobility, for the truly noble heart seeks only innocent solace.(92)

With this remark about 'true nobility' which allegedly lay at the foundation of folly, Marot touched a sociologically highly important fact – namely, the use of folly by the bourgeoisie in its rejection of the norms and values of a bygone, feudal age. Before we discuss this point further, however, we should complete our picture of the garrulous activities of these joyous societies. Naturally, it was great fun to visit other chapters of misrule in other cities in the vicinity and to compete with them in foolish exploits. As the monarchs of those days sometimes exchanged their fools in the hope that the guest jester would come up with yet unknown jests and tricks, while one's own jester would acquire some new tricks of the trade, so these joyous societies would engage in exchange programmes, with the additional element of competition. The city of Cambray, for example, which itself housed several fools' organizations, each year invited the joyous companies from the vicinity for a folly's rodeo – a mock-imitation, perhaps, of the knightly tournament.(93) People paraded in weird outfits through the streets, 'farces' and 'sotties' were produced on street-corners and in market-places, goliardic songs performed and many scurrilous jokes were told in taverns and inns (doubtlessly swallowed with large quantities of wine and beer). These chapters of folly, it should be noted, were male associations. Although folly was certainly not thought of as being exclusively a male affair, since there were obviously as many 'folles' as 'fous' in the world, when organized it suddenly happened to be something fit for males only – which is customary when it comes to the point of organization, and not just in traditional societies. In any case, 'Mère Folle', head of the Dijonnaise 'infanterie', was elected annually and was always a man dressed up as woman. If these organized fools,

whose task it was to guard the husband-wife relationships in town
(maybe a remnant of the rural past), would find reasons to castigate a couple, it was always the man who would fall victim to
'charivari'-like punishments. For instance, in the case of a dom-
ineering woman who had beaten her husband, the latter would be
treated with a 'charivari'-like penalty, such as being paraded
through town seated backwards on a donkey, with the animal's
tail in his hands. Davis relates the interesting case of a rich tan-
ner in Lyon whom the joyous society of the Rue Mercière planned
to parade on an ass, because it was found out, after thorough
investigation, that he had recently beaten his wife. However, the
reason given for this penalty is most surprising. It was deemed
necessary 'in order to repress the temerity and audacity of women
who beat their husbands and of those who would like to do so;
for according to the provision of divine and civil law, the wife is
subject to the husband; and if husbands suffer themselves to be
governed by their wives, they might as well be led out to pas-
ture.'(94) Faithful to folly, the order of events is simply reversed,
as if the wife had beaten her husband.

Such joyous societies still exist today wherever carnival is
annually celebrated during the Lent period. In the southern part
of the Netherlands, a Prince Carnival is elected on 11 November
each year - the eleventh day of the eleventh month being naturally the appropriate day to enthrone a fool. During the carnival
festivities the following Lent, he rules over his unruly subjects
together with his council of eleven fools. In some cities, the mayor
will even hand over a large key to this Lord of Misrule at the
start of the carnival period, symbolizing that the city is his for
the duration of his foolish reign.

Incidentally, such foolish organizations have not always existed
in reality - just as the 'Ordo Vagorum' of the goliards never really
existed. The Dutch historian D. Th. Enklaar devoted one chapter
of his book on the 'vagantes' to the fools' society 'Blauwe Scuut'
('Blue Ship') whose origins allegedly go back prior to 1400. Enklaar assumed that this organization did exist and function as a
joyous society.(95) In a recent dissertation, Herman Pleij argues
convincingly that such a fools' organization did not really exist.(96)
All we have in the manner of historical evidence is an old manuscript in the Royal Library of The Hague which is a poem written
in the fashion of a rhymed charter for a guild, called 'Blue Ship'.
Allegedly, these 'statutes' were drafted on Shrove Tuesday 1414.
It invites 'all mates of wild manners' to join the organization, to
board the ship. Differences of class and status are irrelevant;
everybody is cordially invited to join. Yet, a list of most eligible
people follows, mentioning not only men but also women of all
estates, provided they behave out of the ordinary, yet not crim-
inally. Arsonists, thieves, murderers, pirates and genuine thugs
are explicitly excluded from this company of fools. According to
Pleij, this text functioned in the fifteenth and sixteenth centuries
as a poem to be recited during carnival festivities. It probably
belonged to the repertoire of travelling entertainers. He claims in

addition that the content of this poem deserves a detailed analysis, because it contains under the disguise of folly the basic
elements of a new morality - the morality of the bourgeoisie which
is yet to be forged and which has to compete with the old morality
of a bygone age, the age of feudalism. By mocking the still-
dominant values of feudal society, these fools experiment with
and test a new ethos - the ethos of the emerging bourgeoisie.(97)

This is an important conclusion. During the transition from
feudal to bourgeois society, folly functioned as a means of expression: it helped to express criticism of the norms and values of
the feudal past, still dominant in the fifteenth and sixteenth
centuries - but it also assisted in the expression of norms and
values of a new society, still dormant in these centuries, yet
observable as in a dim light. Folly helped to experiment with them
and to test them.

However, as I shall try to demonstrate in the next pages, at
the moment the bourgeoisie consolidated its socio-economic and
political position (roughly during the seventeenth century) and
forged its own norms and values - above all, its work ethic - it
began to reject folly! In 1729 l'Abbé de Bellegarde published the
ninth edition of his book 'Reflexions sur le ridicule et sur les
moyens de l'éviter' ('Reflections on the Ridiculous and on the
Ways to Avoid It') in which he advises the reader how to adjust
to society, how to acquire crucial virtues like 'civilité', 'complais-
ance' and 'politesse' - in short, how to become a social bore who
is the direct opposite of the fool.(98)

Ironically though, when the bourgeoisie began to ban folly,
fools became solely dependent on the powers of the past, the
monarchs in the first place. That is, while the bourgeoisie forged
its work ethic (cf. the impact of Protestantism) and its rationalism
(cf. the impact of the Enlightenment), folly had to withdraw from
the streets of the cities and thus from the centre of social life.
Its last refuge was the remaining powers of a bygone age: the
monarchs of absolutism and the Renaissance popes of Rome and
their prelates. The history of the court fools tells this story (cf.
chapter 3).

During this emergence of the bourgeoisie as the dominant class
of modern society and its increasing persecution of folly, the
latter probably maintained the same position in the peasantry
which it had occupied throughout the ages. This point, I think,
still needs much historical research.

Meanwhile, the intriguing relationship between folly and the
bourgeoisie - the initial mutual attraction, the later definite rejection - becomes sociologically visible in a widely applied metaphor, as well as in a very popular legend - the metaphor of the
'ship of fools' and the legend of the trickster Till Eulenspiegel.

THE SHIP OF FOOLS - A POWERFUL BOURGEOIS METAPHOR

The paraphernalia of medieval fools are familiar - the two-pointed

hood which obviously satirized the monk's hood, albeit adorned
with the ass's ears; the bauble which ended either in a pig's
bladder, filled with rattling beans or pebbles, or in the carved
head of a grinning fool with whom foolish dialogues were held
(the bauble was the fool's sceptre and symbolized his reign of
folly); the narrow suit with stripes of contrasting colours, often
green and yellow, symbolizing the contradictory nature of the
fool's total being. Many of these symbols of medieval folly are
hard to understand, like the previously discussed stone which
somehow symbolized folly. As is well known, the symbolism of
colours played an important role in medieval culture. Various
colours, but in particular yellow and green, were associated with
folly - but it is again hard to receive any specific and reliable
knowledge about this.(99)

Less opaque, however, is the meaning of the most powerful
symbol or metaphor of folly in the Middle Ages - the notion of a
steerless ship, floating around aimlessly, driven by wind and
currents, doomed to perish sooner or later. There is, as I said
in the previous chapter, no historical evidence for Foucault's claim
that real ships of fools, wandering desperately from harbour to
harbour in search for a place to land, have existed. The ship of
fools was a metaphor, which has enchanted generations of med-.
ieval men and women. Both supporters and opponents of folly
have gratefully made use of it. The more influential bourgeois
norms and values grew, the more often this metaphor was applied
in a moralistic manner - the fateful label for any human behaviour
deemed reproachable. Sebastian Brant did not invent the metaphor, but his 'Das Narren Schyff', first published in 1494, functioned as a catalyst. Obviously, his rhymed treatise fell in the
fertile soil of an emerging bourgeoisie which, from the sixteenth
century onwards, would rapidly forge the mentality of modern
Western human beings. As is often the case with phenomena that
seem to strike some very fundamental chords in men and women,
the origin of this metaphor is multi-layered and hard to reconstruct. In fact, several historical crusts have grown around it,
and it is not always easy to peel them off. I mention just a few of
them.(100) In ancient Rome, to begin with, the licentious god of
ecstasy, Dionysus-Bacchus, was carried through the streets on
a float, called the 'carrus navalis' - probably the origin of the
word 'carnival'.(101) Similarly, Mère Folle of Dijon in the sixteenth and seventeenth centuries was paraded through the city
on a float - a cart drawn by horses, surrounded by dancing fools.
If this cart was not precisely a ship (the illustration given by Du
Tilliot certainly does not suggest this), old Germanic mythology
contains the notion of a ship on which a god is paraded around.
The ship, however, was a cart on wheels in the shape of a boat.
Tacitus mentioned this in his book 'Germania'.(102) Naturally, the
ancient Christian tradition about the church as the ship of Saint
Peter has added to the metaphor. Did not Jesus embark on a ship
together with his disciples, and did he not subdue a heavy storm?
(Matt. 8:23-27; Mark 4:36-41). Did the Lord not step on Peter's

boat and preach to the people on shore? (Luke 5:3). The idea of
the Christian community as a ship, safely carried away to heaven
over rough seas, can be found on the murals of the catacombs of
Rome. It returns as a mythological trope in many sermons and
mystical poems. In one such poem, the mystic Tauler (fourteenth
century) speaks of Mary as the one who steers a ship ashore
safely, with the help of an angel. Her ship carries a most precious cargo - her son, the Redeemer.(103) St Dimphna, mentioned
in chapter 1, was sometimes pictured in a boat, obviously on her
flight from Ireland and the indecent desires of her father. In one
case, her boat carries fools.(104) Nicholas V, to give a last example, the first true Renaissance Pope (1447-55), coined a medal
designed by Andrea Guazzalotti, which shows the holy father on
the ship 'Ecclesia' which he steers with a firm hand through a
fierce storm towards heaven.(105) The notion of the 'ship of state',
including the idea of the party leader as helmsman, is of course a
secularized version of the same trope.

Christian theologians, enchanted by the dualism of believers
and sinners, designed the notion of two ships, long before Brant -
one carries the faithful, sailing to heaven, the other carries the
unbelievers and sinful who float off helter-skelter to hell. This
notion can be found, for example, in an old Spanish morality
play,(106) and returns in one of the woodcarvings that illustrated
the first edition of Brant's 'Narrenschiff'. This enchanting little
picture shows a ship which has already capsized. On top of the
demolished hulk sits the Antichrist, 'der Endkrist', a scourge in
his left hand and a money bag in the other. A rather gruesome
devil blows in his right ear with a pair of bellows, obviously
inspiring him with hideous thoughts and ideas. A fool's hood,
blown off, lies next to him. He shows his true face - which, in all
honesty, strikes the modern reader as not at all unpleasant. The
wreck is surrounded by many little boats, all loaded with fools,
i.e. sinners. Some of them fell in the water and are drowning. In
short, it is flotsam and jetsam. In sharp contrast to all this,
stands Saint Peter, a halo around his stern head, his feet firmly
on the ground. With an oversized key, he draws a boat with pious
believers ashore. They are not dressed like fools, but look perfectly normal, i.e. thoroughly bourgeois. This is Saint Peter's
little boat - 'sant peters schifflein' - obviously on its way to
heaven and salvation.(107) The fools of medieval society could
wholeheartedly embrace this metaphor, while they paraded their
foolish floats through the streets or recited the satirical lines of
a poem, like the previously mentioned mock-charter of an imaginary fools' guild, the 'Blue Ship'. But in this case the metaphor
was still part of innocent banter. This changed after Brant's
'Narrenschiff' appeared in print.

Brant, it should be mentioned in all fairness, was not that
original because he borrowed freely, although admittedly with
great virtuosity, from ancient Roman authors and from the Bible,
as was customary in his day. Perhaps the book was even composed
by compiling previously published moralistic pamphlets, putting
them together in an easily digestible, vernacular rhyme.

One predecessor of Brant should be mentioned separately. This was the Austrian Heinrich Teichner who, some time between 1364 and 1368, composed a poem published for the first time in 1413 under the title 'Das Schif der Flust' (The Ship of Loss).(108) People of all estates and classes are invited cordially to embark on a boat which travels over land for a while in order to collect as many passengers as possible, before sailing off out to sea. The poet issues a warning: the devil stands at the helm of this ship, and his aim is hell. His prospective passengers are 'die gut gesellen' (the good mates) - a medieval expression for morally superficial and vacuous people, moral sunshine boys, so to say.(109) When asked whether women can also embark, the answer is a resounding 'nain', because they are too easily plagued by repentance and then seek refuge in church. The devil can apparently use male fools only. But apart from this elegant discrimination, men of all social strata can enter the ship because in hell king and peasant are alike: 'Sam in der hell, dâ ist küng un paur gesell, dâ die edel nich für trait, dâ ist recht ze gleicher hait.' The poem ends solemnly with 'Also sprach der Teichnaer.' Indeed, the author was a Zarathustra of folly.

'Das Schif der Flust' still breathes an air of religiosity, while at the same time folly is not yet rejected or condemned completely. That is, the author moralizes religiously but is able himself to play the fool. By and large, this poem is still innocent. That changes when in 1494 Brant's 'Ship of Fools' appears in print.

It is a long poem that consists of 112 chapters and discusses various human weaknesses as so many follies. Written in medieval German, soon translated by his student and friend Locher into Latin - 'Stultifera Navis' (1497) - and next into many different European languages, this rhymed treatise was meant as a pedagogic book.(110) It was an instant success - some historians call it the first true bestseller - which indicates that it touched some sensitive chords in its contemporary readers.

The book appeared at the birth of the bourgeoisie, when the Reformation was already in the air. The opposition against the Church of Rome, spiritually and morally bankrupt for some time already, was spreading rapidly - especially in Germany. Where several princes, ever since the ill-fated investiture conflict of the eleventh and twelfth centuries, brooded on a political emancipation from Rome. Initially, great hopes were invested by all in the Council of Basle (1431-49) which started as an attempt to reform the Roman Church spiritually as well as organizationally, and thus politically. Yet, due to the shrewd manipulations of Pope Eugene IV the council fell apart, first in 1437 (the 'progressives' stayed in Basle, the 'conservatives' moved to Italy), and later it just withered away slowly, without bringing about any real reforms.

This must have contributed to the general frustration of the time, and meant eventually a severe loss of authority on the part of the papacy as an institution and of the official hierarchy of the church beneath it. In this theologically and politically heated atmosphere, exacerbated still further by various pre-Reformation

reform movements (cf. Wycliffe, Hus, etc.), Brant published his
scathing critique on the moral weakness of his contemporaries; it
was probably his strength that he did not employ any theological
arguments, as such arguments had lost much of their former
authority. He did not, as some have claimed, belong to the pre-
Reformation movement of protest against Rome. He remained a
loyal, rather conservative member of the Roman Church, although
there is not a shred of religious devotion in his book. On the
contrary, the attentive reader discovers between the deceptively
primitive lines of his vernacular German, thoughts and ideas
which are remarkably rationalistic. They are perhaps the result
of the humanistic studies in which he participated, as had so
many intellectuals of his day.(111)

The main objective of this book, or rhymed tract rather, is to
castigate the 'immoral' behaviour of the men and women of all
social strata. Such behaviour is foolish, and such fools are the
victims of the Antichrist. They float off to the doom of 'Narra-
gonia' ('Fools' Land') where they believe they will find the heaven
of material abundance - 'Schlaraffenland' ('Land of Cocaigne').
Inevitably, they will find hell instead.

If Brant does not use any theological or Biblical arguments, how
then does he propose to heal his contemporaries of their immoralism which he views as folly? It is indeed very curious that he
does not present Jesus Christ as the redeemer of these fools! As
a true Renaissance humanist he rather diagnoses this immoralism
and folly as 'ignorance', as a mental and moral deficiency which
must and can be healed by the patients themselves - a curiously
modern notion of self-help. As we are all potential fools, erring
erratically in our thoughts and acts, we must try to learn to know
ourselves, to acquire a rational, Socratic wisdom, to control our
impulses which come all too naturally to us. This is a curious development in the notion of folly; one which would become even more
predominant during the emergence of the bourgeoisie, and reach
its fulfilment in the Enlightenment. Folly is now equated with
human weakness which can be cured by man himself through his
becoming ever more rational. Brant even designs an ideal human
being: the wise man, portrayed in the last chapter, is not easily
carried away by his emotions. As a stoic 'vir bonus', he knows
what he wants (i.e. he is 'inner directed'), he rationally plans to
get what he wants, but he knows his limits also - rational qualities, in short, which the fools of former days lacked completely!
Brant's wise man is ascetic: 'er halt mosz und zyl' ('he keeps himself within bounds and calculates his aim'). Zarncke summed this
up with a sociological insight, which is remarkable for the time in
which he wrote (1854), when he stated that Brant expressed the
bourgeois-urban mentality of his days and was the first to do
so.(112)

But he did something else, too. He provided his contemporaries
and bourgeois successors with a concept which they could apply
polemically in their persecution of opponents. And because he secularized the notion of folly in terms of a rational moralism, it

remained useful for several centuries after him as a means of
moral and political defamation.
This, incidentally, was already observable in Brant's own time.
I found, during my library research in the Nationalbibliothek of
Vienna, a little tract which obviously tried to imitate Brant's
'Narrenschiff' but aimed at a very specific political target.(113)
It is called 'Narrenschiff vom Buntschuh' ('The Fools' Ship of
Laced Shoe'), published in 1514 and attributed to a certain
Johannes Adelphus. 'Buntschuh' - the name of a kind of sandal,
laced around the foot, the poor man's shoe in contrast to the
riding boots of the rich - was a secret organization of German
peasants, founded at the end of the fifteenth century and rev-
ived again by the peasant leader Jos Fritz shortly after 1500.
This organization prepared several peasant revolts which eventually led to the great Farmers' War ('Bauernkrieg') of 1519-24.
The ideology of 'Buntschuh' was similar to that of Tomas Münzer,
i.e. a combination of mystical and apocalyptic Christianity, calling for a spiritual (rather gnostic) revival, as well as for a socio-
economic and political revolt. There was also a strong call for
justice and liberty on behalf of the repressed peasant estate.
'Narrenschiff vom Buntschuh' attacks this farmers' revolt in
its early stage and criticizes as utter folly the violent attacks on
masters, the raids on private property, the refusal to pay interest and the call for some kind of communism. The author also
warns of the threat of a reversal of hierarchies, of the danger of
secularization and - may God help us - of the ensuing threat of
the Turks and the heathen. The author can hardly restrain his
aggressive anger when he mentions the fact that many members
of this secret organization, after having witnessed how captured
companions have been beheaded, quartered and badly injured,
seek refuge in Switzerland, where they can get away with their
criminal folly. He ends his violent diatribe with a call for obedience and order. Brant's rather secularized moralism which
Barbara Könneker interprets as an early form of rationalism, had
a profound influence on both Roman Catholic and Protestant successors in the seventeenth century.(114) At the end of this
century, the author of 'Narrennest' ('Nest of Fools'), the Catholic Abraham a Santa Clara, draws the conclusion that one could
not actually call fools those people who have an empty and silly
mind and whose reason is wormeaten. But one could really decry
people as big fools who act immorally and sin against the divine
Scriptures. The Protestant Moscherosch adds yet another dimension to this moralization of the concept of folly, namely German
patriotism:

> the fools whom he despises most, and upon whom he heaps
> all the ridicule and invective at his command, are the French-
> ified fools, the 'Alamodenarren', the dandies dressed in
> outlandish clothes, the mercenary soldiers who sell them-
> selves to the foreigner, or the students who return from
> abroad with a smattering of foreign tongues and filled with
> contempt for all things German.(115)

In short, Brant's wise man is not just the Socratic ascetic, who keeps his impulses under strict control, but he is also the bourgeois moralist and patriot. As to the latter Moscherosch and others believed that such anti-foolish values as honesty, courage and simplicity were summed up in the concept 'teutsch' - the anti-fool, i.e. the hero, is teutonic!

Meanwhile, as the middle class began to become established in this century it developed standards of social behaviour to which the individual had to adjust lest he make a fool of himself. Brant's moral wisdom thus developed into social sensibility - the Germans call it 'Klugheit' and 'Salonfähigkeit': the wise man knows not only how to suppress his emotions and impulses but also how to discuss the questions of ethics, aesthetics and politics in a rational and analytic manner. It is in general, as K. G. Knight, whom I have followed here closely, summarizes neatly, 'the calculating philosophy of the self-made man'.(116) The same development, incidentally, can be witnessed in France. Although of a later date, the previously cited tract of Abbé de Bellegarde testifies of the same bourgeois norms and values: a fool is someone who does not know how to behave himself correctly, and wise is the person who contains his emotions and adjusts his behaviour to the predominant bourgeois norms and values.

Thomas Lodge (c. 1558-1625), son of the Lord Mayor of London, man of letters and holder of a medical degree from the University of Avignon, does not beat around the bush when it comes to a rejection of fools and folly. In his 'Wits Miserie and the Worlds Madnasse: Discovering the Devils Incarnat of this Age' (1596) he discusses various vices, like greed, avarice, extravagance, ambition, hatred, etc. and 'demonstrates' that they walk around through the streets of the cities as individuals - especially as fools and as foreigners. They are incarnated devils. Immoderate and disorderly joy, for example, are incorporated in the body of a jester who appears as a pleasant, sociable chap. But, Lodge warns, he is in reality nothing but a devil: 'keep not this fellow company, for in jugling with him, your Wardropes shall be wasted, your credits crackt, your crownes consumed, and time (the most precious riches of the world) utterly lost.'(117)

Swain claimed that the fool became exhausted at the end of the sixteenth century. By then the concept of folly had lost its metaphorical strength through over-use. 'The word itself, grown colourless, became a simple term of condemnation.'(118) This inflation of the meaning of folly, I should like to add, was not merely a process of wear and tear. It was, in the very first place, the rise of the bourgeoisie as a class with a specific worldview and ethos which put an end to the reign of folly.

Brant in Germany, Bellegarde in France, and Lodge in England were typical representatives of this bourgeois worldview and ethos, which were forged into a dominant philosophy and mentality in the following ages. From the seventeenth century onwards everything and everyone non-bourgeois was simply labelled pejoratively as fool and foolish. This was a generalization of the concept of folly which robbed it of all its former metaphorical pith and strength.

TILL EULENSPIEGEL - A POWERFUL BOURGEOIS LEGEND

Various fools have featured in our review: the semi-intellectual
who had failed in his scholarly career, not because he was stupid
but because he lacked 'Sitzfleisch' and was infected with 'Wander-
lust' and the itch of folly, above all because he needed money,
clothes, shelter; the clerical deserter who could no longer endure
the monastic and ecclesiastic discipline, whose vitalistic folly
simply burst out of the soutane, and above all whom the monastery
or parish could no longer support economically; the adolescents
in the villages, who guarded, as in an early form of vigilantism,
the norms and morals of the rural community - rude, coarse and
irreverent in their 'charivaris'; the adults and professional fools
in the cities, organized in mock-orders and mock-guilds, playing
the innocents and indulging in satirical farces and foolish parades;
the lower clergy in the churches and cathedrals, annually organizing their blasphemous, paganistic set of rituals, called collectively the Festival of Fools.
In this curious parade two types of fools are still missing: the
folk fool, like Till Eulenspiegel, and the court fool. Their social
station and position was quite different, but their folly, enacted
in practical jokes and pranks played on people, was very similar.
The court fool deserves an extensive sociological analysis and will
thus be discussed in a special chapter. In this section we shall
focus our attention on the folk fool. This discussion will be restricted to the Till Eulenspiegel legend in which we may find a
crystallization of the many features of early-modern folk fools.
It is sociologically senseless - yet historically quite inviting -
to ask whether Till Eulenspiegel ever really existed. Some time in
the fourteenth or fifteenth century an individual by that name
might indeed have lived, acquiring legendary fame for his naughty
pranks and witty rejoinders. Apparently the only historical record
we possess of him is an item in the municipal archives of Braunschweig, dating from the fourteenth century, in which the name
'Ulenspiegel' is mentioned.(119) However, as is usually the case
with legendary figures, Till Eulenspiegel - or, as he was called
in medieval Dutch and German, Tijl Uylenspiegel - since the sixteenth century has remained a kind of peg on which all kinds of
funny stories about pranks, tricks and jests could be conveniently hung. He went thus into history as a legendary folk hero,
very similar to Nazreddin (or the Hodscha) and A'shab in the
Middle East.(120)
Such folk fools and their legends are sociologically of great
importance as they function as a catalyst of sentiments and ideas,
carrying certain elements of the cultural 'conscience collective'
(Durkheim) of a society. The more legendary they become, the
less important the question of their historical existence will be -
they did exist 'once upon a time'. The important thing is rather
that they are present and alive in the legends as long as these
are being told and listened to. Just as the question is irrelevant
whether Buddha or Jesus really lived in history and what precisely

their emotions, thoughts and actions have been, because they are
alive in the preaching and believing of the faithful,(121) so folk
fools like Eulenspiegel or Nazreddin continued to exist in the
legendary stories told and savoured in the centuries after their
hypothetical existence in history. The point is not to reconstruct
the 'historical Eulenspiegel', but to reconstruct the 'Geist' of the
Eulenspiegel legend.(122)

In some respects Eulenspiegel resembled the goliards but he
was never really a semi-intellectual, or a clerk, and his trademark
of folly was his pranks, rather than songs and ballads. He played
at being a professor, or a medical doctor, or a priest, or a monk,
or an artisan - i.e. he played at being a professional of the early-
modern society. And like the shrewd trickster he was, he knew
how to exploit with great skill the simple fact that people are
generally very uncritical and prone to believe in professional
expertise. His easiest prey were the many 'authoritarian personalities' of his day - people who would blindly follow any authority
that crossed their path. So he would dress up as a doctor of
medicine, make liberal use of medical jargon in dog Latin, display
impressive gestures and facial expressions, etc. In particular he
fed on the superstitious beliefs and fears of his 'patients' and
always brought them to a point where they were prepared to deliver their bodies and souls to his 'care'. Not for long, these
people would do the weirdest, the dumbest, the most foolish things.
Eulenspiegel was indeed a trickster and he was a genuine fool in
that he remained eerie and elusive.

The first collection of Eulenspiegel legends appeared at the end
of the fifteenth century in the Braunschweig region. This original
Low German text which was mentioned twice in the accounts of the
Monastery of Hensburg in 1520, has been lost.(123) It reappeared
in High German in Strassburg in 1515 and 1519, and in Low German in Cologne in 1519. In these editions Eulenspiegel plays his
tricks mainly in the Hanse cities of northern Germany. Bostelmann
therefore concludes that these stories were written in the vernacular primarily in order to be read by the up-and-coming bourgeoisie.(124)

Close economic and cultural contacts were in existence between
Braunschweig and the Hanse cities, on the one hand, and Flanders
(especially Bruges and Ghent), on the other. Not amazingly,
therefore, a Dutch edition of this prankster's stories appeared in
Antwerp as early as 1520. In Flanders, which was in that time
still at war with the Spanish Habsburgers, Eulenspiegel, the rebel
against authority, became soon a folk hero with some political
weight - comparable, for instance, to the soldier Schweyk in
Czechoslovakia during the Second World War. The Duke of Alba,
the hated regent of Spain in the Netherlands, issued an index of
forbidden books on 31 July 1571. Together with the other popular
folk book 'Reinke Vos' which contained satirical stories about a
cunning fox, the Dutch edition of Eulenspiegel was mentioned as
forbidden literature.(125)

There were other foolish folk heroes, such as Pfaffe Amis, or

Pfaffe von dem Kalenberg, but Eulenspiegel remained their un-
crowned emperor. To modern readers, unless they are still children, these stories about Eulenspiegel are rather hard to swallow,
as they are boorish and mostly not funny at all. Bostelmann sees
this as a sociologically significant fact; the Eulenspiegel legend
was indeed rude and boorish because it was part of contemporary
anti-intellectualism and crass naturalism, which suggests a shift
from knightly culture, eulogized by the intellectuals of those days,
to bourgeois culture which eulogized nature and naturally healthy
life. It was the same kind of materialism and vitalism which one
finds in Pieter Brueghel's paintings - a reversal of late-medieval,
knightly culture. This supersession of knightly by bourgeois
culture which began in the sixteenth century was very apparent
in Flanders: it was there that the Brueghels, father and son,
worked and lived; it was there that Eulenspiegel and Reinke Vos
(whose legend was a satire of knightly culture also) emerged as
true folk heroes.(126)

This is again the same dynamics which we discussed before;
when the bourgeoisie began to emerge in the sixteenth century,
fighting for the socio-economic and political emancipation from the
dominant feudal forces, folly in all its anti-intellectual rudeness
would be employed as a weapon. But at the same time, the more
self-confident and cocksure this new class became, the more it
would reject folly as a force adverse to its economic and political
aspirations. When the bourgeoisie had to solidify its socio-
economic and political position, the Protestant work ethic served
it much better than the loitering ethos of traditional fools.

Before we take our leave from these folk fools, we must briefly
discuss one other point. Eulenspiegel was a trickster. As we shall
see in more detail later, many non-Western cultures possess
stories about a mythological trickster who is sometimes an animal,
like the spider (Ghana, Surinam, Sioux Indians), sometimes a
human being, like Nazreddin and A'shab (Middle East), sometimes
a theatre role, like the Vidûsaka (India) or Semar (Indonesian
wajang), sometimes alternatively man, animal and monster, like
Wakdjunkaga (Winnebago Indians), sometimes a god, like the
ancient Greek Hermes. Do these mythological tricksters, belonging to different cultural orbits, refer to a meta-historical, collectively psychological, or depth-psychological source, or 'structure'? To C. G. Jung this is, of course, a rhetorical question
and I merely quote his interpretation in conclusion to this section: the trickster is

> obviously a 'psychologem', an archetypal psychic structure
> of extreme antiquity. In his clearest manifestations he is a
> faithful copy of an absolutely undifferentiated human cons-
> ciousness, corresponding to a psyche that has hardly left
> the animal level. That this is how the trickster figure orig-
> inated can hardly be contested if we look at it from the
> causal and historical angle.(127)

FOLLY AND DEATH - THE TWIN LEVELLERS

There is no need to elaborate here on the social and economic
inequalities of the ancien régime. If there was still a personal
bond between lord and serf in the earlier stages of feudalism, the
more this system expanded the more the various estates would be
separated from each other -socially, economically and politically.
Culturally, however, the ancien régime demonstrated some measure of uniformity but it was a complex uniformity indeed. During
the expansion of the feudal system, two kinds of culture emerged,
the 'high' culture of the elites (the nobility and the higher clergy)
and the 'low' culture of the masses (primarily the peasants, but
also the lower clergy and, as of the sixteenth century, also the
up-and-coming bourgeoisie which later moved up to the 'high'
culture). The 'low' culture is also termed 'popular' culture. It
was the domain of most fools, although they would offer their
entertainment also to the members of the leading estates, many of
whom savoured the 'low'-culture diversions of fools despite their
official adherence to 'high' culture. An interesting example was
Pope Leo X who was a typical Renaissance pope with deep interests in the arts and early sciences, but who was also very fond of
fools and folly. Henry VIII of England was a similar case. That is,
the cloak of civilization was rather thin as yet.
  Despite the diversity and the socio-economic and political complexity of the ancien régime, one should keep in mind also its
uniformity. Structurally, to begin with, one can indeed speak of
a specific regime as the principle of inequality and subordination
was endemic to the whole society. Hierarchy was the predominant
feature of this society. But what is perhaps more important, is
the cultural coherence of this regime: it was, so to speak, borne
by a relatively coherent worldview which was internally divided
in its components, yet descended from and remained permeated by
one single source - the Christian tradition. This cultural coherence is, sadly enough, demonstrated most clearly in the universal
rejection and recurrent persecutions of the Jews.(128) Moreover,
peasant, nobleman, parish priest and university intellectual, and,
as of the sixteenth century, Catholic and Protestant, were both
united in their attitude towards the Turks - the 'godless Mussul-
man'.(129)
  Somehow, fools managed to dodge the structural divergences
without surrendering to the Christian worldview and ethos. They
were pariahs, like the gypsies and the Jews, they were people
allegedly infected with a crypto-magical 'infamae macula', a slur
of infamy. Yet, as entertainers and merrymakers they were also
loved and perhaps even secretly admired. Meanwhile, these fools
did not at all hesitate to castigate their fellow-men and women for
their moral and intellectual weaknesses, and they did so without
mercy. This criticism was in principle directed against individuals
and groups of all estates. They were not driven by a social conscience or political conviction. Their motives were materialistic,
their convictions opportunistic. If they often resembled rebels,

they could not in any sensible manner be compared to revolutionaries like John Ball, Wat Tyler, or Jos Fritz. One would also fail
to find among their unruly number a bandit like Robin Hood, who
would rob the rich and powerful and redistribute this wealth
among the poor and destitute. On the contrary, if this would
yield any material profit, they would gladly attach themselves to
the wealthy and powerful as parasites. These fools were immoralists and non-ideological opportunists. Their darts of folly were
always pointed at everyone, indiscriminately and without much
principle. In this respect, medieval folly was very similar to death.
In fact, to medieval people folly and death were twin levellers.

Many illustrations of the so-called death-dance variety show the
man with the scythe as a fool in cap-and-bells.(130) Death was
ubiquitous in medieval and early-modern society. It could put an
end to one's life unexpectedly, at any moment, and it could do so
with inconceivable suffering and degradation. The foolish thing
about death was that one knew for certain it would come once, but
this moment remained yet unknown. Death was as inscrutable as
the fool. One expected the fool to pull someone's leg, making him
the laughing stock of his company, yet one never knew for sure
on whom he would turn next. Likewise, death and folly both
strike indiscriminately, choosing their victims among the members
of all estates.

This intriguing merger of death and folly comes to expression in
the death-dance, a literary form, usually a poem, in which it is
repeated over and over again that everyone will have to depart
from life as he has entered it, namely naked and helpless: the
rich and the poor, the powerful and the downtrodden, the old and
the young, the conceited and the humble, the wise and the dumb,
the beautiful and the ugly - they all will once be called by the
dancemaster general. 'Mort saisit sens excepcion,' said François
Villon.(131) A sixteenth-century poem gives a melancholic expression to this notion. Its simplicity is charming:

> Come, daunce this trace, ye people all,
>   Both prince and beggar, I say;
> Yea, old, young, wyse, and fooles I call,
>   To grave, come, take your way
>   For sickness pipes thereto
>   By griefes and panges of wo.(132)

Most death-dances breathe the spirit of Ecclesiastes - everything
is vanity, as it all ends in death. But next to this element of res-
ignation there is also an element of Nietzschean 'ressentiment' -
the poor and downtrodden may rejoice because the rich and powerful will be their equals in death!(133)

The dominant spirit of the death-dance poetry of the Middle
Ages is 'contemptus mundi', contempt of this world. Jacopone da
Todi (d. 1306) who joined the Franciscan order after his young
wife died in an accident (1268), and as a friar used to call himself
a 'ioculator Matris Domini' ('minstrel of the Mother of the Lord'),

composed a poem in which death is staged as the leveller who
would eventually visit everyone - 'conti, regi, imperatori, cav-
alier, donn e donzelli, sore e fratris, preti, laici e laidi e belli ...
omne gente è convenuta, e mondana e religiosa.'(134) The same
melancholy permeates the 'Dis des trois morts et des trois vifs'
('Legend of Three Dead and Three Living Persons'), dating from
the last quarter of the thirteenth century. Three young noblemen, full of life still, meet three dead men who remind them of
their approaching death and of the end of their splendour and
wealth.(135)

Fools also exhibit 'contemptus mundi' but their contempt is not
religious and spiritual. It is a materialistic and vitalistic contempt.
They laugh the world in its face, not because it is only an episode, moving irresistibly towards death, but because it is but a
stage on which people perform their silly little roles. This is the
worldwide difference between the grin of the skull and the grin
on the face of the innocent fool, between the mask of death,
carved on the face of the deceased, and the mask of folly, worn
by the foolish performers on their very own stage.

CONCLUSION

The fools of the ancien régime were 'contraries', individuals performing an act in which reality was presented counter-clockwise,
topsy-turvy, the other way about - as in a looking-glass. Hierarchies of power and authority were inverted, established social
roles, like those of men and women, liberally exchanged, norms
and values, rooted in a well-nigh sacred tradition, were violated.
In short, during the performances of these fools the world was
turned inside out and upside down, thus reality changed into a
floating mass without any fixed boundaries and beacons. In this
reality everything goes, and nobody from the outside world could
really get at these fools. They enjoyed, in this looking-glass
reality, the freedom of the fool - 'Narrenfreiheit'.

Contemporaries, if they would not join their frolics, but observe
them from the outside, could still recognize their own mundane reality, but it was badly distorted because radically reversed. Likewise, the protagonists of these frolics, the performing fools, were
still recognizable as human beings, yet they were obviously different - somehow socially and psychologically distorted. These
contemporaries, who still lived in an enchanted garden, must have
experienced what our children, also living still in an enchanted
world, feel when they see the antics of the circus clown - the
clown and his world are awe-inspiring, both attractive and repulsive, endearing and yet somewhat frightening. Sociologically,
these traditional fools were marginal people. They lived and performed in the seams of their society, being in the system yet not
really part of it. They were 'infami', outcasts, pariahs, yet popular for the entertainment they had to offer.

To a traditional world imbued with religious corporatism, fools

showed a world of secularized individualism. To a world founded
on religious fanaticism which was legitimated by religious doctrines
and countless metaphysical notions, these fools held up the image
of secularism and materialism. To a world sensitive to tradition
and ritualized forms of behaviour, these fools held up the image
of vulgar animalism and aboriginal vitalism. While their contemporaries took the authority of various hierarchies for granted,
these fools frolicked around in lighthearted anarchy and improvi-
dent licence. Medieval fools embody a utopia in Mannheim's sense
of the word: by creating their looking-glass reality, they transcended the socio-cultural status quo of their day and exhibited
images of a socio-cultural reality to come. Much of their humour
was regressive, but in this respect they were very much part of
a progressive thrust which emerged from the popular culture of
the lower strata of medieval society, and was taken over later
(since the sixteenth century) by the bourgeoisie. As we saw
before, this new class (in fact, the first stratum that was really
a class in the sociological sense of the word) used folly for its
own purpose initially, but became its greatest foe soon, after it
had acquired socio-economic and political power.

   This, it seems to me, is an important conclusion. The mocking
mirror which the fool holds up in front of traditional medieval
society does not only reflect, as in a profound mimesis, the anim-
alistic, pre-civilized, regressive features of mankind, but presents at the very same time a distorted and fragmented picture of
modernity. Like the ceremonial fools (to be discussed in chapter
4), medieval popular fools enacted the anarchy of a mythological,
pre-institutionalized world - the 'tohuwabohu' prior to any kind
of civilization. But occupying a marginal position in society they
demonstrated at the same time a reality of secularized individualism, opportunism, relativism and immoralism - an ethos which was
largely alien to their contemporaries, but which is readily understandable, cognitively and empathetically, for fully modernized
men and women.

   Naturally, it immediately comes to the sociological mind to interpret medieval folly in terms of social and political conflicts. This
dimension, as we have seen in this chapter, can certainly not be
denied. If fools would not dream of attacking the established
power structures, like John Ball, Wat Tyler, or Jos Fritz
attempted, they would yet shower the authorities by which power
was legitimated with their ridicule and satire. Folly was never
designed to attack power straightforwardly, but it did relativize
authority, and that definitely was a critical function. But such an
analysis remains too much on the surface still. Folly, as we have
seen, also functioned as a carrier of ancient paganism. Its brutish
presence testified to an unresolved conflict between Christianity
and aboriginal forms of paganism. In many foolish festivities, the
ancient state of a pre-civilized society, founded on primitive magical rites, was celebrated and commemorated - not Christianized
in substance, like Christmas or Easter, but thoroughly pagan in
both form and content.

We should probe even deeper still. I suggest that in these foolish celebrations and performances, a colourful and illustrative
demonstration was presented of a pre-civilized state of mankind,
reminding people as in a kind of proto-sociological and proto-
psychological mimesis, of the very nature and functions of the
society they live in and they take so much for granted. In the
midst of daily routines, people rarely ponder over the norms,
values and meanings which constitute the parameters of reality.
The fool holds up a mirror in which is shown, as in a badly distorted reflection, where man and society have come from and what
would happen if they rejected the burdens of their civilizing tradition. In this sense, folly was definitely a regressive sustenance
of the status quo.

Likewise, it comes to the psychological mind readily to interpret
medieval folly in terms of a ritualized outlet of repressed sentiments. This dimension too can hardly be denied by anyone who
has studied traditional folly carefully. As a matter of fact, the
practitioners of the Festival of Fools themselves came up with this
explanation when they had to defend their annual debauchery
against stern critics. Being rather serious all year round, they
argued, as we have seen before, it is healthy to take the lid off
once a year, as it makes us fit to return to serious things, like
religious observances. However, this dimension of traditional folly
should not be overemphasized, as psycho-analytically oriented
social scientists in particular tend to do. It is, to begin with,
rather questionable whether such a modern notion as 'repression'
is adequate, analytically, when one deals with thoroughly traditional men and women, living in a web of values and meanings
which was much nearer to their skins than is the case in modern
'abstract' society. There was indeed a widespread restlessness in
medieval society, foreshadowing great changes in mentality, social
structure, culture, politics and economics. Folly was a good medium of expression for this restlessness. Yet it remains doubtful
whether these were feelings of repression, pressing for some kind
of expression and outlet. It was actually not until the bourgeoisie
had acquired wealth and power, while still being kept in political
bondage by politically and morally vacuous (absolutist) monarchies,
that feelings of repression began to emerge and spread massively.
The experience of repression, in other words, is always linked to
clear images of an alternative socio-economic and political structure,
and there must be a real chance for their historical realization, if
they are to be followed massively. Many peasant revolutionaries
had indeed a more or less clear notion of a truly just and equal
society, but they simply lacked the power of an organized class
to realize their dream. The bourgeoisie, on the contrary, was able
to wipe out the powers of feudalism and absolutism (cf. 1789)
under the ideological banner of the Enlightenment, precisely because it could act politically as a class with class consciousness
and an ideology. Long before the French Revolution the absolutist
monarchies of Europe, the one in France in particular, had become
ideologically hollow and morally vacuous. Their power was conse-

quently devoid of legitimacy and thus experienced as being merely repressive. Real political revolution and not folly and Saturnalian revels was the appropriate response.

Nevertheless, this is not to say that folly did not function as a kind of seismograph of dissatisfaction, indicating that some very profound socio-cultural and political changes were on hand. In the seams of society, thoroughly marginal and eccentric, these traditional fools were not inhibited by any of the repressive strictures of the status quo. They could transcend them, reach beyond them. Without any conscious intentions and without any policy planning, they were the harbingers of a world yet to come - as fragmented and at times distorted their representations of this approaching reality might have been. In sum, traditional folly carried a prophetic quality.

What would have happened had these fools received the opportunity radically to realize this progressive thrust, i.e. had they chanced to radicalize their inherent modern potential? The question is, of course, very rhetorical. Folly dies when it moves from the fringe to the centre of society. It is absorbed when it steps out of the reality of the looking-glass into the reality of everyday existence. It loses force and pith when it attaches itself to the powers that be.

This was precisely the fate of the court fools of the fifteenth, sixteenth and seventeenth centuries. It is a long and complex story, which deserves a special chapter.

3 PARASITES OF POWER: court fools during the reign of absolutism

INTRODUCTION (1)

The officially appointed court jester (2) emerged in approximately the thirteenth century from an undifferentiated host of fools, and developed in particular during the fifteenth and sixteenth centuries into a rather specialized institution and profession endowed with a peculiar kind of influence and power. But while he thus institutionalized and professionalized, he began to lose the original features of a fool. That is, in the specialized institution and profession of the court fool, medieval folly generalized to such an extent that it gradually lost its original meanings and counter-reality values. This complex process of modernization took place in the fifteenth, sixteenth and seventeenth centuries.

European court fools were distinguished by their contemporaries in two main categories, namely 'natural' and 'artifical' fools.(3) For instance, Robert Armin, actor in Shakespeare's company and author of 'Nest of Ninnies' (1608), a curious little volume with stories about fools and folly, speaks about 'the difference twixt a flat foole naturall and a flat fool artificiall'.(4) Natural fools were mentally deranged or feeble-minded simpletons, sometimes physically deformed (cripples, humpbacks, dwarfs, etc.). Artificial fools, whom Shakespeare called 'allowed fools', were by contrast in full command of their wits. If they happened to be physically deformed also, this was appreciated as an asset, but in many instances artificial fools were normally shaped.(5) They played at being foolish, often with much wit and ingenuity. The role of fool was played by them in order to make a relatively decent living. And hard work it really was! The officially appointed court jesters were always recruited from among these artificial fools, provided with room in the palace, clothed in a colourful livery (which was not necessarily always the fanciful motley with cap-and-bells), and at regular intervals endowed with sometimes sumptuous gifts.

In the period which interests us most presently - the fifteenth till the end of the seventeenth century - most European courts possessed a small host of fools. Many of these were natural fools and thus the passive targets of the often cruel mirth and banter of courtiers: chased around through court, tossed up in blankets like dogs, often beaten and kicked. They endured this treatment as it would yield food and shelter in exchange.(6) Theirs was not an official appointment, and they scarcely show up in the official account books of the courts, unless on a rare occasion a special

gift was presented to one of them.(7) Usually, the majority of
these passive fools roamed around through court namelessly. They
followed the court as parasites during its journeys along the various residences, always in the hope of receiving some clothes and
the leftovers from the table. A fool belonging to this category was
called in France 'un fou suivant la cour', a fool who follows
court.(8) They were in general a pitiful lot - playthings for bored
courtiers, targets of their aggressive and often cruel impulses.
They lived at the very fringe of courtly abundance, always in
danger of being summarily kicked out.

The passive fools stood in sharp contrast to the artificial fools
who were 'wise enough to play the fool' ('Twelfth Night', III, i)
and had reached the apex of their career, namely an official
appointment as 'domini regis joculator', as 'fou en titre d'office'.
There were usually many fools at court, but only very few of
them held such an officially remunerated, often tenured, and generally very influential position. Some of these top fools were
honoured during their career with large endowments of gold and
even land, and in one notable instance a court fool was even
ennobled - although this did cause some opposition among the
higher courtiers.(9) Since an accomplished court fool was hard to
come by, monarchs were quite reluctant to banish an appointed
jester from court. Moreover, after one had obtained a good one,
he represented quite a substantial investment, since he had to be
dressed up in expensive outfits. Moreover, in most instances he
had to be trained for the job by an attendant who would teach
him the basic rules of courtly etiquette - which he had to know
before he could jocularly violate them - as well as the standard
tricks of the trade. Quite often such an attendant would also act
as the court fool's bodyguard which was certainly not a superfluous function when the fool was still young and new at the job,
or when he happened to be a dwarf.(10) In any case, good court
fools were precious possessions and I know of no instance in
which an officially appointed court jester of the sixteenth and
seventeenth century was incarcerated or received capital punishment. 'It is the court fool, not the foolish courtier, whom the king
can least afford to lose,' Walter Lippman once wrote.(11) Accomplished artifical fools were kept as expensive pets, comparable
to the prestigious and expensive pedigrees of the modern bourgeoisie.(12) In short, the 'domini regis joculator', as he was solemnly called in England, the appointed jester of the lord king,
occupied a rather firm position at court.

Unlike the natural fool, the artificial fool remained usually the
proud master of the situation, always in search for a suitable
victim at whom he could point the arrows of his folly. Constantly
out to please his master and owner - in France he was aptly called
the king's 'plaisant' - he would try to tease and trick the people
around him. Famous jesters of this period - the Gonellas of Italy,
Will Sommer and Archie Armstrong of England, Triboulet and
Brusquet of France - were the true professionals of folly. Each of
them was a virtuoso, feared for his sharp comments and for his

often painful practical jokes. Only Will Sommer (also: Somer, Sommers, Summer), the compassionate fool of England's Henry VIII, seems to have been an exception to this rule. He was generally loved by courtiers and Londoners for his kindness and social awareness, of which Armin gives a few touching examples.(13) It is said in a little song, recorded by Armin, 'hee was a poor mans friend, and helpt the widdow often in the end.'(14) His position at Henry's court must have been very firmly established, the love extended to him by this monarch was solid, otherwise he would certainly have lost control over the situation and degenerated into a passive fool. Because one thing is certain, very few fools could afford to be compassionate and kind. The fool of France's Louis XIV must have been the very opposite of this friendly jester. Despite his name, chosen obviously for contrast's sake, L'Angéli was a rather freocious fellow who managed to terrorize his fellow-courtiers by his sarcastic comments and rude practical jokes. One of his contemporaries admitted once that during a dinner at court he had not dared to speak for fear that this nasty fool would ridicule him publicly.(15) L'Angéli was the favourite pet of the Roi Soleil who used him adroitly in the complex game of courtly intrigues. He was certainly not a little lapdog, this pet. On the contrary, he resembled more a ferocious hunting dog, as he was always on the lookout for an easy victim and cheap prey. It is even recorded that people would buy his silence! Canel claims that this fool was in fact mentally disturbed, but he admits also that he did command a considerable amount of wit.(16)

Maître Guillaume, jester of France's Henri IV and Louis XIII, predecessor of L'Angéli at the Parisian court, was physically deformed but not mentally disturbed. Yet he was often teased by the lackeys and the pages who could beat him easily due to his physical deformity. After some nasty experiences, he decided to carry a club under his blouse which he called lovingly his 'oisel' - his birdie. He could be rather violent with that thing. No wonder that, as a child, Louis XIII was much afraid of this erratic fellow.(17) Later, as a king, he grew very fond of him.

It stands to reason to view the position of the official court jester at medieval and early-modern courts in the light of feudalism. There was indeed a kind of feudal bond between king and fool, but the feudal oath of allegiance - containing the mutual rights and duties of both parties - was, as far as I know, absent. A feudal remnant was the 'my Liege' by which, in England, a court fool would address his master, but other courtiers addressed their monarch likewise. However, in a document which dates from around 1200, the court jester of John Lackland, Will Piccoll (or Piculphus, as he is called solemnly), is mentioned as someone who received from his king an hereditary piece of land in exchange for his service as a court fool. His heirs were allowed to keep the land on the condition that they paid annually two pairs of golden spurs. A French historian has called this fool 'un fou à titre feodal', and Welsford views him as 'a unique instance of

folly being regarded as an acceptable form of feudal service.'(18)
The case is admittedly very curious, but similar instances have
not been recorded. In fact, this particular feudal arrangement, if
it happens to be authentic, might well have been a royal joke,
faithfully recorded in this document for diversion's sake. In any
case, court fools did indeed at times collect valuable gifts from
their masters, including complete estates, as happened to the
notorious Archie Armstrong. Such an action could, of course,
easily be framed in a semi-serious feudal contract. Anyhow, it is
hard to prove that this profession and institution descended from
the feudal contract which constituted the very foundation of the
medieval social system.(19) Not feudalism but absolutism, as it
developed in early-modern Europe, was the socio-cultural and
political environment in which court foolery could develop into a
profession and institution. Meanwhile, not only courts, but also
influential homes and even cities would employ their official fools.
The city of Lille, to give just one example, had its own fool,
appointed as 'fou en titre d'office'. His activities have been described by an eye-witness. During religious processions, for
example, he would throw water at spectators and perform all sorts
of silly antics. The city fool, who was called Corneille and who
died in 1724, was described by another eye-witness as 'the first
"valet" of the city'.(20) Many villages and cities had their un-
crowned fools - usually simpletons who would roam around the
streets, be seen here, there and everywhere, teased by children,
barked at by dogs, living from handouts. Apparently, some of
them acquired an official status by being appointed by city hall as
the town fool.
   Ever since antiquity, influential households had kept dwarfs
and various sorts of fools, male and female, sane and insane,
physically normal and physically deformed. Domestic fools were
the usual appendage of ancient Greek and Roman households. In
exchange for food and shelter, these fools had to entertain the
guests at table and to follow their masters' footsteps wherever
they went. They bore many different names but were usually
called 'parasites'.(21) Somewhat melancholy is the story of Sen-
eca's female fool, Harpaste. He had inherited her from his parents
and kept her in his household for mercy's sake, although he did
not care at all for fools. 'If I want to see a fool,' he is quoted to
have said, 'I can look in a mirror.'(22)
   In the period under discussion in this chapter, domestic fools
were prestigious objects. It was 'bon ton' to have in one's household at least one fool who would follow one's footsteps like a loyal
dog. Cardinal Richelieu had his fool, the remarkable Bois Robert,
whom we shall meet again later. But so did Cardinal Wolsey,
Thomas More, Hernando Cortés and many others. Prescott tells us
how the fool of Cortés observed the jests and antics of the clowns
of Montezuma - with the jealous eye of a competitor, we may safely
assume. In fact, the great conquistador was so much impressed
by their performance that he caught two of them and shipped them
off to Rome as a special gift to his Holiness Pope Clemens VII, who

always appreciated a good fool when he saw one.(23) Even monasteries would employ fools in their household, where they were
ranked together with dogs and falcons. This usage might have
occurred quite early in the Middle Ages, as is indicated by a
Carolingian regulation which stated tersely that monasteries were
not allowed, among other things, to keep hunting dogs, falcons
and jesters.(24)

Meanwhile, queens, princesses and ladies of influential households often kept their own female fools. Like their male colleagues,
many of these 'folles', as they were called in France, were natural
fools, but a few famous ones were obviously of good wit and
rather smart. There is little information about domestic female
fools,(25) but we possess quite substantial material about court
'folles'. Canel, for instance, discusses a few of them who had
very colourful names, such as Madame de Toutes Couleurs, mentioned in 1453 as the 'folle' of the Duchess of Bretagne, La Jardinière, Cathelot and Jacquette, the three of whom were the
property of Catharina de Medici.(26) Maybe some of them came
from the Middle East, as the names La Turque and La More seem
to suggest.(27) Sometimes a queen would keep a male jester, like
queen Marguérite, wife of France's Henri IV whose jester was
called Guérin,(28) while a king would employ a female fool. A famous example of the latter was Mathurine who served at the courts
of Henri III, Henri IV and Louis XIII.(29) She was apparently
quite a character, well known in the streets of Paris because she
used to wander through the city in the company of her friend and
colleague Maître Guillaume,(30) both of them wearing outlandish
outfits and cracking the wildest jokes. Mathurine often wore a
long, wildly coloured, velvet dress, or the outfit of an Amazon,
or of a military officer with a huge sabre - maybe a remnant of the
days she served in the Picardic regiment as a 'goujate'. She was
far from stupid, as is testified by the fact that, after her master
Henri III had been murdered, she had the good sense to join
Henri of Navarre who entered Paris in 1594 and became King
Henri IV. Her loyalty was honoured and she was reinstated as
the official court 'folle'. Her personality was not all that pleasant
and she was described by someone who was in a position to know
that she was as malicious as an old ape. But she was, of course,
very careful not to extend this malice to the king.(31) Her relationship with Henri IV was reportedly quite intimate. She was
allowed to enter his quarters freely at all times, and she used to
eat meals with him frequently.(32) It is reported that she received
a pension in 1622,(33) but she was still seen at the court of
Louis XIII.

Mathurine entertained some outspoken political ideas. Unlike
Maître Guillaume, she was strongly opposed, for instance, to the
League whose endemic fanaticism she particularly disliked - a
political difference, incidentally, which did not throw any shadow
over their friendship. She hated the morally strict and stern
Protestants as much. If they ever got the chance to reform the
world, she once said to Maître Guillaume, they would certainly cut

down on fools and jesters. Referring to the two of them and to a third fool, called Angoulevent, she added: 'Et pauvre Mathurine, pauvre Angoulevent, pauvre Maître Guillaume ... où seraient vos pensions désormais?'(34) As a smart fool, she certainly knew her allies and foes.

Within this host of fools and 'folles', midgets and dwarfs occupied a very special position. Some of them did rise to the rank of 'fou en titre d'office', but in most instances these little people remained passive fools, often subjected to a cruel fate in the hands of fellow-human beings in and outside the court.

Throughout the ages and in various cultures, little people have fascinated their fellow human beings. The curiosity extended towards them was usually linked to a magical awe for the uncommon and acquired easily a rather perverse nature.(35) Cassiodorus related how several influential ladies in ancient Rome would keep dwarfs who ran around their homes stark naked, adorned with a string of pearls.(36) There are numerous stories about queens and princesses of the seventeenth and eighteenth centuries who took great delight in receiving little people in audience. They not only engaged in conversation with them, but would also take them on their lap and fondle them, as if they were outlandish lapdogs. The main attraction might well have been the fact that these individuals were adult males and females, caught, as it were, in the bodies of children - a capricious trick of nature which would allow normal-sized people to push them around as pets or toys. These little people were fondled and touched, but also kicked and tortured. Dwarfs in parrot cages, carried around by giants, dwarfs in the pockets of giants, dwarfs jumping out of huge cakes at the end of dinners, dwarfs fighting each other as mini gladiators, or fighting normal-sized women - history has seen it all. The contrast of a midget and a giant in particular has always attracted man's imagination. During a war raid on Europe, Sultan Soleiman once ordered his soldiers to tie a huge German prisoner to a tree. He then gave order to his dwarf, who hardly reached to his victim's knees, to kill the man with his mini-sword. It took him a long time. The sultan and his soldiers watched the scene with much delight and laughter.(37)

Yet, it should be mentioned in all honesty that the biographies of small people in pre-modern societies were not always as sad as is suggested here. The success story of Antoine Godeau is a clear, although admittedly rather rare, case. The amazing thing is that this man could ever make the brilliant career he made in a society which was fascinated by the appearance of undersized bodies. Born in 1605 at Dreux, France, he developed as a young man some remarkable skills in poetry. After a few ill-fated love affairs, which all ended badly because of his small physical stature, he left for Paris in the hope of building up a literary career. Through his uncle Conrart who, as a man of letters, had access to the higher social circles of Paris, he received an invitation to the renowned hôtel of Madame de Rambouillet who organized her salon in the 'blue room' of her city palace. In fact, he came quite close to

her daughter, Julie d'Angennes, and was often referred to facet-
iously as 'Princess Julie's dwarf'. In her memorable study of the
'précieuses' of Paris, of whom Madame de Rambouillet was the
leading lady, Dorothy Backer writes: 'Throughout the years of its
heyday [i.e. in the seventeenth century] this salon exercised an
unconscious tyranny over the men of letters who went there regularly.'(38) It was 'a cultural landmark in the history of France'(39)
and in this salon 'nobody was allowed to commit bad manners, but
anybody could be crazy.'(40) Godeau was a regular guest and
read his poems to the gathered men and women. Here he met not
only the curious fool and dandy Voiture, whom we shall meet
again at the end of this chapter, but also the great François le
Métel de Bois Robert, usually just called Bois Robert - the domestic fool of Cardinal Richelieu. According to Flögel, this odd
couple organized regular sessions devoted to letters and sciences,
first at the house of Godeau's uncle, later in other bourgeois
homes and salons. The meetings were patronized by Richelieu and
soon received the somewhat pompous name of 'L'Académie Fran-
çaise'.(41) Antoine Godeau was officially appointed by the powerful cardinal as one of the very first members of this august French
institution. However, the cardinal had yet more honours in store
for Godeau. He was appointed Bishop of Grasse, a function which
he carried out allegedly quite conscientiously. Pope Innocent X
granted him the unification of the dioceses of Grasse and Vence
which was, however, fiercely opposed by the clergy of Vence -
not because Godeau was a midget or a bad bishop, but because of
the loss of administrative autonomy. In fact, they asked Godeau
to choose one of the two dioceses, which he did. He moved to
Vence where he died a relatively famous and respected man on 12
April 1672. He is an example of a dwarf or midget who was able
to avoid the process of minstrelization (42) which certainly in his
days was the fate of most little people.

The present chapter focuses mainly on male, artificial fools who,
in the period between the sixteenth and eighteenth centuries,
functioned as officially appointed court jesters. It is these fools
who practised a very curious profession and who were part of a
very specific kind of institution. Through them we can receive
more insight into traditional folly's differentiation and generalization, which were both, as we have seen before, the hallmarks
of modernization. They were surrounded by domestic fools, by
'folles', by many natural fools, inside and outside their courts.
They were surrounded by as many dwarfs and by 'fous suivants
la cour'. But the great, the skilful, the professional jester has
transcended them all, if not in folly and disguised wit, then certainly in influence and power. Sommer, Armstrong, Brusquet and
Triboulet did not merely live and work at courts as the parasites
of wealth and abundance, entertaining bored courtiers by pres-
enting their bodies as the passive targets for their aggression
and cruel impulses. On the contrary, these virtuosos of folly
shared the abundance of their masters, won their confidence, and
even their friendship, and became gradually the parasites of

absolutist power. They managed to remain the supreme masters of
their self-created situations of mirth and banter.

THE COURT FOOL AS INSTITUTION AND PROFESSION

Prior to the fifteenth century when court fools had not yet been
fully professionalized, the position of jesters at European courts
was hazardous and, at times, quite dangerous, as they lacked
the protection offered by an official appointment. In this period,
fools were totally dependent on the whimsical and often cruel
moods of their masters and owners, to whom they had attached
themselves as parasites in order to make a living. If one can
speak of an institution prior to the fifteenth century, the court
fool was exclusively a 'greedy institution'(43) which would not
leave any room for a personal identity. That is, prior to the
fifteenth century, fools were most often passive fools, left to the
cruel mercy of their masters and fellow-courtiers - the lackeys,
the boys in the stables, the kitchen personnel. This fate remained characteristic also after the fifteenth century for natural
fools who just followed the court without holding any official position. It also remained the fate of most dwarfs and midgets. But the
truly gifted jesters from amidst the artificial fools could, after
the fifteenth century, make a career out of their studied and
practised folly, because, as we shall see, the more absolutist the
monarchy grew, the more it needed the fool as an accompanying
institution.
    There was not one single career pattern among these artificial
fools, who managed to rise high above the chaotic host of less
gifted, ordinary fools. But it was not uncommon that foolish
talents were discovered in a young man by a courtier, as happened
with Thoni, whom we will meet again later. After this discovery
he would usually start his career as domestic fool in the house of
an influential courtier. He would then be a servant first, often in
the kitchen, and gradually grow in experience as jester. If he
became a true virtuoso and gained some fame in courtly circles,
he would stand a good chance of being presented to the king as a
precious gift. He had then moved up to the court where he was
usually entrusted to the care of an attendant and guardian who
would train him further in the tricks of the court fool's trade.
Only very few of these gifted fools would reach the top of their
profession - an official appointment as 'domini regis joculator',
which, as I shall show, was a position with great material rewards
and with some measure of influence and power. The officially
appointed court fool - a position and profession which developed
into a true institution during the fifteenth, sixteenth and seventeenth centuries - was not someone to be kicked around anymore.
He had prescribed duties and certain unwritten rights, but,
above all, he had free access to the apex of power, the sovereign
monarch. A good court jester was closer to the king than any
other courtier. This gave him power and influence, and he was

certainly no longer anonymous, as were most of his colleagues in
the world of medieval entertainment.

Roughly after the fifteenth century we find in England, France
and Italy more and more officially appointed fools mentioned in
the financial account books of the courts. They were obviously
fools who had arisen above the common lot of ordinary fools, and
had become talented virtuosos - loved by their masters and
owners, and often feared by their fellow-courtiers. Above all,
these virtuosos were loved by the general public outside the
court. Their practical jokes and witty comments were told and
passed on, first by word of mouth, later by means of printed and
widely distributed jestbooks.(44) Famous court jesters, like the
Gonellas, Sommer and Brusquet, became pegs to hang funny
stories on - a fate which they shared with such popular fools as
Till Eulenspiegel and Nasreddin. Unlike the anonymous host of
natural fools, these topnotch court jesters became unique historical personalities, comparable to famous kings, popes, cardinals
and soldiers. In a sense, they were the first stars in the world
of entertainment. Before we continue our discussion of the court
jester's institutionalization and professionalization after the fifteenth century, I should single out one remarkable, seemingly
paradoxical fact. The rise of the court fool to the summit of parasitical power occurred at the very same time that medieval folly
in general came under the heavy attack of the Reformation, the
Renaissance and the Enlightenment. That is, while his original
soil of nurture - medieval folly as it was discussed in the former
chapter - began to erode and wither away, the court fool reached
the apex of his development.

This is not really a contradiction because, as we shall see in
the remainder of this chapter, the more the court fool moved from
the periphery of courtly society and society in general to its very
centre, namely the throne of the increasingly absolutist monarchs,
the more his folly began to lose its medieval vitality. It grew ever
more artificial and technically routine. In this sense, the court
jester's folly withered away as much as the traditional folly of the
Middle Ages began to disappear from the streets of the cities and,
to a lesser degree, of the villages also.

In fact, the only reason why the court fool could rise in power
and influence, while folly in general began to wither away outside
the king's palace, was the fact that the increasingly absolutist
throne needed him for reasons which were way beyond the need
for entertainment. The fool, to summarize briefly the hypothesis
which will be elaborated further below, was a structurally necessary supplement to Machiavelli's 'Prince'. Although it had already
degenerated before the end of absolutism, one can maintain that
this curious institution and profession came to its definitive conclusion when the absolutist monarchy of Europe collapsed, together
with the total ancien régime, in 1789. Jacob Bibliophile (Paul
Lacroix) tells the melancholy story of his meeting with the last
court fool of Versailles, who was in all probability not a 'fou en
titre d'office'. 'My research', he writes in 1837,

led me to the Château de Versailles where a few years ago
still lived an old man with white hair, surrounded by old
furniture and several souvenirs of the role he had played
during the reign of the ill-fated Louis XVI. He had been
Marie Antoinette's buffoon. With tears in his eyes he showed
me a few grains of coffee which that poor queen had once
given to him. 'For the first time', he had said to her, 'I
regret that such a great lady has such a small hand.'

Lacroix then writes: 'Versailles, empty of its kings, had conser-
ved a court fool as a living ruin of the old monarchy.'(45) It is a
nice and nostalgic story - probably highly apocryphal. Yet Jacob
Bibliophile is able to evoke an image of decline which is very
appropriate. The decline, however, happened long before 1789.

The success of the court jester was a function of the rise of
absolutism - a process which reached its summit during the reign
of the Roi Soleil, but had begun much earlier. In a sense, Machiavelli's treatise on 'The Prince', written in the early sixteenth
century, presented some sort of manifesto of monarchic absolutism.
Even if this author, as some interpreters claim, wrote this little
book as a sarcastic satire with the intention of warning people
about a true prince's rule, he did satirize in a quite illuminating
manner an obviously current conception of absolutist power.(46)
Although he was not an absolutist ruler in the proper sense of
this term, Henry VIII of England definitely had aspirations to
absolutism. His endeavours to build up a Renaissance court, far
outside Italy, in a region still barbaric by the standards of this
cradle of modern civilization,(47) his manoeuvres in the field of
power and his immorality in personal and official matters bore the
main features of absolutism. Although it is far too simplistic to
mould history in this way, one may see the beginnings of absolutism in Henry VIII and its culmination in Louis XIV. After the Roi
Soleil, the decline of absolutism was rapid and radical. It was not
by accident that L'Angéli was the last renowned court fool.

The historical origins of the court fool as an institution and profession are hard to reconstruct. Historians have put forth several hypotheses which are, I believe, not mutually exclusive but
seem to remain rather speculative. Some of them, to begin with,
attribute great significance to the fact that crusaders had allegedly witnessed court jesters at work in Muslim palaces of the Near
East.(48) Upon their return, it is surmised, the crusaders began
to keep court fools of their own. Court jesters did indeed exist in
the Near East, as they did elsewhere - for instance at Montezuma's
court or at the courts of the shoguns of Japan. Yet, one should
not give too much weight to this argument because, first, the
European court fool became a distinct courtly institution much
later than the time of the crusades, and, second, institutions and
professions are rarely transferred from one culture to the other
like pieces of luggage. Third, it remains questionable whether
these crusaders who, in the eyes of the Muslims of Near Eastern

civilization, were incredibly rude barbarians, had free access to the courtly society of the people they attacked and ransacked for centuries. Arabic influences on European culture came rather from Moorish-dominated Spain at a later period. The Provençal troubadours, for example, may well have originated from the Moorish civilization of Spain, as Briffault has argued convincingly.(49) Canel made mention of Moorish buffoons from Tunis who apparently functioned at François I's court next to Triboulet, at the beginning of the sixteenth century. One of them is even known by name: Ortis. The famous Clément Marot wrote his epitaph.(50)

It is more likely that the structural development of the court fool towards a distinct profession and institution has been an inner-European event which ran parallel to the much wider process of modernization. It stands to reason, to begin with, that court poets, who in the early Middle Ages functioned as poets but also as genealogists and astrologers, gradually changed into court jesters. It was part of their function at court to entertain people at dinners and, above all, to boast the great qualities of their masters and patrons. If they did the latter by ridiculing everyone else in and around court, they of course came very close to being court fools.

The ancient Nordic scalds and the Celtic bards present interesting cases in this respect. They were originally (i.e. in the early Middle Ages and probably long before that time) not just poets in the modern sense of the word, but magical seers. Scalds were originally seen as wise persons, sages who could predict the future. They travelled through Scandinavia like minstrels, reciting parts of the 'Edda' and singing their own ballads, in which they would often praise their host and protector. It actually only needs for them to settle down in either a court or a castle in order to change into a court fool. Such domestication had definite advantages, in particular if it would lead to a fixed appointment as the court's official buffoon.(51) Romans such as Appianus mentioned the Celtic bards as parasites who praised their masters and ridiculed the opponents of those who offered them food, shelter and protection. In ancient Ireland, these bards had a low status, far below the 'filid' who served as legal specialists, genealogists and poets of heroic ballads. But the bards were more entertaining than the 'filid', and therefore far more popular. The bards had more prestige in Wales where there were no 'filid'. They were particularly active during the annual poetry festivals - the famous eisteddfods. Again, the Irish 'filid' and the Welsh bards could easily change into court jesters, if settled down at one or other court.(52) But the main origin of the appointed court jester was the vast mass of fools that roamed around through medieval society. 'Normal' people would at times play the fool for the sake of diversion, as in the case of joyous societies, discussed in the former chapter. But if they could afford to do so, they would employ one or more fools in their household - in much the same way as modern bourgeois people keep cats and dogs for pets. They offered badly needed entertainment and heightened one's prestige and status. This vast mass of medieval fools was, so to speak, the field from which the great court jesters of the fifteenth, sixteenth and seventeenth centuries were recruited. And they were in fact recruited from this field because there was a structural demand for them: the increasingly absolutist prince stood in need of a fool.

Natural talent was not sufficient for the making of a successful court fool. Some measure of luck was needed (for instance, one had to be discovered by a courtier), and it took hard work to learn all the tricks of the trade (for instance, one had to have intimate knowledge of the king's ideas and preferences and one had to be able to calculate the consequences of one's jests). Just as there were royal keepers of the hunting dogs and falcons, there were, as we have seen above, royal keepers of fools,(53) who would not only act as guardians and protectors but also as trainers. Some of these guardians and trainers might have been fools themselves in former days. In one of his letters, Henry VIII mentions William Worthy, alias Phip, whom he describes as 'kepar of our foole', referring perhaps to Will Sommer. The name of this man suggests strongly that he himself had formerly been a fool.(54) Thoni's attendant, Brantôme tells us, was called Louis de la Groue (or Proue) but he bore the colourful name 'La Farce' as a kind of stage name. He also instructed Thoni's successor, the strange fool Sibilot.(55)

Although historical evidence is very scanty about this topic, there may have been training schools for jesters. Lacroix, for instance, mentions an 'école de fous' at the time of France's Henri III, but he fails to give any precise and reliable information about the subject.(56) Ever since Flögel, historians mention a letter by King Charles V, called 'le Sage' (1337-80), addressed to the city of Troyes, Champagne. In this letter he publicizes the death of his fool, Thévenin, and requests that a new fool be sent to him, since Troyes had traditionally been the supplier of fools.(57) This suggests that Troyes harboured some kind of training school for jesters, a breeding kennel of fools which de-livered upon request. However, some historians have grave doubts about the letter's authenticity.(58) Even if it is authentic, the content should cause suspicion because it might well have had a facetious intention: maybe the king wanted to be funny by declar-ing Troyes a nest of fools?

The least one can say about the matter is that the more the court fool was institutionalized, the more attempts were made to train jesters in a formal manner. This might even have been done in special schools, but there is no reliable evidence about that. Briffault relates the fact that the city of Ventadorn housed a school for 'jongleurs'.(59) This might have been a training school for all kinds of entertainers, since the concept of 'jongleur' stood for a variety of people in the world of medieval entertainment.

Unlike the infamous professions, like that of the executioner, the position of court jester was not hereditary.(60) Fools would run in families, but an officially appointed court jester was never

succeeded automatically by one of his sons. Or, to use sociological terminology, unlike the profession of executioner which was
necessarily in many instances ascribed, remaining in one family
for sometimes several generations, the profession of the court fool
was acquired. Welsford distinguishes correctly between a Gonella
I and a Gonella II, but they lived far apart in time and did almost
certainly not belong to the same family.(61) As modern people
give the same name to two dogs consecutively, court fools were
often given the name of an accomplished and famous predecessor
who had died and was remembered fondly.(62)

However, this acquired nature of the fool's profession should
not be overemphasized either. Many jesters had not embarked on
their fool's career of their own free will. The fate of the aforementioned Thoni (or Thonin) is indicative of this. Once when the
Duke of Orléans interrupted his journey to Paris in a little village
in Picardy, he chanced to meet a small boy, probably a midget,
who struck him as being exceedingly funny and witty - conceited
and foolish at once. In fact, the lad had all the trimmings of a fine
fool and the courtier was determined to take him with him to Paris.
The boy's mother told this respected courtier that she had two
other sons who were both rather witless. She wanted the boy to
enter the priesthood in order to be able to send up many prayers
to heaven on behalf of his poor brothers. The duke promised to
take Thoni to Paris and to furnish him with a fine theological and
priestly training. However, upon arrival in the capital, he had
him trained as a domestic fool instead - a profession for which
the boy soon demonstrated considerable talents.(63) Brantôme
was full of praise about 'le petit fol Thony', who was loved by
everybody and treated 'comme un petit roi'. This arch-gossiper,
who gave us so much valuable information about the daily lives of
influential men and women in the ancien régime, claimed that
people had never before seen such a funny little fool, who was so
agreeable and so pleasant.(64) When Thoni had become a true
virtuoso and some sort of celebrity, he was presented by his master to the king as a special and much-appreciated gift. Welsford
reports that he functioned ever afterwards as 'the spoiled pet of
three French Kings, Henri II, François II and Charles IX'.(65)

This and similar stories suggest that courtiers were constantly
on the lookout for suitable fools, who were eventually to be presented to their monarch as part of their unending and systematic
flattering. One can indeed speak of some kind of peculiar talent
hunt. Incidentally, this search for entertaining jesters could pose
a real threat to witty individuals who loved to jest but had no
ambitions at all in the direction of a fool's career. Thomas More's
son-in-law, William Roper, tells us in his interesting biography of
the great humanist how much Henry VIII appreciated entertaining
wit and how close More came to becoming this monarch's witty
entertainer.(66) It is worthwhile to quote Roper extensively:

And because he [More] was of a pleasant disposition, it
pleased the King and the Queen, after the Council had

supped, at the time of their supper, for their pleasure,
commonly to call for him to be merry with them. When he
perceived so much in his talk to delight, that he could not
once in a month get leave to go home to his wife and children
(whose company he most desired) and to be absent from the
court two days together, but that he should be thither sent
for again, he - much disliking this restraint of his liberty -
began thereupon somewhat to dissemble his nature; and so
by little and little from his former accustomed mirth to disue
himself, that he was of them from thenceforth at such seasons
no more so ordinarily sent for.(67)

There was obviously in this time a dire need for entertaining
fools, but only a few of them were really talented. As a result,
many fools would try to imitate the great stars and virtuosos of
their profession, by which fact they were automatically doomed
to remain passive fools, pathetic targets for aggression and violence. Unlike their successful colleagues, these second-rate fools
were generally a pitiful lot.(68)

Meanwhile, the very fact that some true virtuosos of folly managed to move up from the anonymous host of ordinary fools to the
much-desired position of 'domini regis joculator' or 'fou en titre
d'office' suggests strongly that absolutist monarchs, from Henry
VIII to the Roi Soleil, stood in need of court fools for reasons
which were not merely those of entertainment. Of course, court
jesters did entertain their masters and owners with their antics
and witty comments, in particular at dinners and on festive
occasions, but then almost any fool could do that. Entertainment
cannot have been the sole and prime reason for the surprising
professionalization and institutionalization of folly into a rather
powerful, official position at the courts of these absolutist rulers.
These very processes rather suggest reasons of a more structural
nature. However, before we discuss this hypothesis in greater
detail, we should first try to gain more insight into the inner
workings of the court fool's trade. It is only after we have glanced
at the court jester's folly that we can begin to understand his
social and political functions.

THE COURT FOOL'S FOLLY

Various painters have counterfeited the fools and midgets who in
late-medieval Europe functioned and performed at courts and in
houses of courtiers, magistrates and members of the higher
clergy.(69) Almost as good a picture can be obtained from various
financial records, the account books of many medieval and early-
modern courts. They give a rare glimpse of the appearance of
these fools. Doran, to give an example, quotes one of these records in which the various parts of Will Sommer's outfit are listed
with apparent care and pleasure. This famous and likeable jester
of Henry VIII must indeed have looked quite pretty:

For making a doublet of worsted, lined with canvass and
cotton, for William Sommers, our fool. Item, for making a
coat and a cap of green cloth, fringed with red crape and
lined with frieze, for our said fool. Item, for making a
doublet of fustian, lined with cotton and canvass, for our
said fool. For making of a coat of green cloth, with hood of
the same, fringed with white and lined with frieze and buck-
ram, for our fool aforesaid.(70)

The British Library (British Museum, London) carries the original manuscript of a psalmbook belonging to this theologically
minded king, who, incidentally, scribbled notes in the margins
for about two-thirds of the volume. The last part has no notes or
comments in the margin. Perhaps his volatile mind got bored with
studying these psalms? In any case, one of the magnificent illum-
inations shows us Will Sommer staring pensively at the reader
while his monarch sits behind his back, playing a small harp. No
scientific research can evoke the experience one has when one
holds this volume which Henry VIII carried around and read, and
stares at this intimate scene of king and jester. For a brief moment, the distant past seems very, very near.
'The impious fool says in his heart "There is no God" ' (Psalm
53). Numerous psalmbooks carry an illumination of a fool next to
this famous line.(71). The serene picture of Sommer and his king
is also an illustration of this psalm verse. It shows the jester not
in motley with cap-and-bells - which might be a sign of his
advanced professionalization. He wore such an outfit probably
only on special occasions, when he had to act and perform professionally as Henry's jester - during dinners or certain festivities. Outside such working-hours he was apparently dressed less
formally. And when not playing the fool in public, he socialized
with his monarch in a confidential manner. Perhaps he was the
only real friend this difficult man had or could afford?(72)
Another account book describes the appearance of Muckle John,
successor to the great and famous Archie Armstrong, alias King
Archie. He must have looked quite handsome in his 'pair of crim-
son silk hose', his 'pair of gaiters and roses' with 'silk and silver
garters, and roses, and gloves suitable for Muckle John'. He wore
'a hat covered with scarlet, and a band suitable', adorned with
'two rich feathers, one red, and the other white'. His gloves were
perfumed and 'lined with sables'.(73) Dressing up these fools was
obviously great fun. 'The apparel oft proclaims the man', Shakespeare said ('Hamlet', I, iii) - certainly, if he happens to be a
court fool, we may add.
As I said before, this profession was not an easy one. A court
fool ought to know intimately the tastes and ideas of his master.
He had to be able to read his mind swiftly, in particular if something out of the ordinary happened. He had to know whom the
king favoured and whom he disliked. Should a change in these
likes occur, the jester had to register them immediately and adjust
his behaviour accordingly. Viola in 'Twelfth Night' (III, iii) sums

up the predicament of the court jester nicely:

> He must observe their mood on whom he jests,
> The quality of persons, and the time;
> And, like the haggard, check at every feather
> That comes before his eye. This is a practice
> As full of labour as a wise man's art;
> For folly that he wisely shows is fit;
> But wise men, folly-fall'n, quite taint their wit.

Most of the pranks and antics of these court fools do not strike
the modern reader as being very funny, let alone witty. I shall
select a few of them, just in order to give an impression of this
type of humour. But before I do so, I should relate a few cases
in which renowned fools fell victim to pranks played on them. A
rather tragic example is the famous fool of Niccolo d'Este, Count
of Ferrara in the fifteenth century, whose name was Gonella.
Welsford correctly calls him Gonella I, as there was a fool later
in time who had the same name. He was already a legend during
his own lifetime but came to his end in a most curious way. One
day, the count pretended to be infuriated by one of his pranks
and gave order summarily to execute the impudent fool. However,
the henchman was secretly told to blindfold the jester and to
throw a bucket full of cold water over his back at the moment
when he would think the sword was going to decapitate him. Gonella believed it was all for real and climbed the scaffold trembling
from fear. The moment the water touched his back, Gonella collapsed and died. The count was reportedly beyond consolation
when he realized this ill-fated result of his obviously very amateurish attempt at folly.(74) One of the many Nazreddin stories
relates how the fool was likewise 'condemned' to death by his
prince. He had to climb a high tree in the middle of an isolated
field, and to sit in its very top. Servants were then ordered to
cut the tree down. But they did not get very far, because the
fool lowered his pants and began to urinate. His aggressors fled
in all directions, much to the amusement of the sultan and his
company. Nazreddin was then allowed to come out of the tree.(75)
Naturally, dwarfs and midgets were the easiest targets of such
nasty pranks. Various horrible stories have been told about the
fate of little people at Russian courts prior to Peter the Great.
Russian princes were, in general, particularly fond of the amusement which little people could offer. Flögel relates the grim fate of
an anonymous dwarf in the possession of Czar Ivan Vasilovitch the
Terrible (1530-84). When in a drunken mood, the cruel monarch
once got fed up with the pranks and jokes of a little fool. He
ordered him to kneel beside his chair, and then poured a bowl full
of boiling-hot soup over the man's bare back. The victim howled
for mercy but was put to death with a knife to his throat.(76) It
seems, incidentally, that the position of court fool never institutionalized and professionalized in Russia to the extent it did in
Western Europe. In fact, Peter the Great (1672-1725) used this

occupation as a special punishment. He would personally examine young men whom he had sent to Western Europe for studies upon their return. If they failed the exam, they were condemned to play the fool at court for a fixed period of time. One day, a conspiracy against the throne was discovered. Two brothers belonging to the nobility had participated in this smothered rebellion. In order to save their necks, they simulated an acute mental disturbance. The czar appointed them immediately as court fools and treated them accordingly from then on. One of them, Flögel adds with some sympathy, became an alcoholic in order to forget his sad fate.(77)

But roughly after the fifteenth century, when the great virtuosos enjoyed the protection of an official appointment, court jesters who had reached the summit of their career were no longer people to be pushed around at random. On the contrary, courtiers grew afraid of them, not in the least because these fools were closer the king than anyone else in court. They were also envious of this influence. The combination of fear and envy created resentment and hatred. But, if necessary, the supervising attendant would protect the court fool and avert possible attacks from courtiers who had recently been victimized by the fool's wit and contemplated revenge.

There is a pattern in most of the jesters' jokes. It is the pattern which is common to all humour throughout the ages: opposites, contraries, which are, logically speaking, mutually exclusive, are peacefully put together, while a certain train of thoughts or events is sent into an unexpected, highly impossible, yet feasible direction.(78) The following prank, attributed to one of the two Gonellas, but also told of Archie Armstrong with a small variation, is a good example. One day, the fool was chased through court by a furious group of ladies, armed with brooms and sticks, determined to give the jester a sound thrashing, because he had gravely insulted one of them. Out of breath but still at a safe distance, he offered the ladies a compromise: he would surrender to their punishment on just a single condition. The ladies decided to comply and asked for the condition. At the top of his voice, he tnen yelled that the lady whom he had kissed last and who was generally considered at court to be the greatest wench, would deal out the first blow. There was much laughter and the fool had won. Flögel, who relates this story, does not mention the source of this prank. It can be found in the Scriptures, because it is, of course, a very witty application of Jesus' words: 'Whoever is without sin, let him throw the first stone.'(79) It is also, of course, a nice illustration of Shakespeare's description of a fool as a 'corrupter of words' ('Twelfth Night', III, i). A universal component of the folly of these court jesters was the ongoing teasing of fellow-courtiers or of visitors at court. Their relationship with holy men and with wise men was in particular strained - to the great delight, of course, of the far less civilized members of court, including most monarchs themselves. Here the leitmotiv of court fools has always been the same: 'What good do holiness and wisdom

do to a man, if he is less popular and less wealthy than a fool?'
A successful jester who had made his fortune by means of his
folly and acquired considerable fame and popularity, never failed
to drive this point home to people who were socially defined as
being 'holy' and/or 'wise', but had to live in poverty. For example,
the longstanding almost ceremonialized feud between Cardinal
Wolsey and Will Sommer acquired near notoriety, and even more
vicious was the hate relationship between Archbishop Laud and
Archie Armstrong. As we shall shortly see, the latter held a fatal
conclusion for the fool as the situation grew ever more political in
nature. The feud between the powerful Archbishop of Canterbury
and the renowned fool Archie had the character of an endless and
rather strenuous mutual bantering and bickering. Often the fool
won on points which was easy because the archbishop could not
allow himself to descend to the mean level of folly on which the
jester operated so skilfully. One day, the king asked Archie to say
grace at table – in itself quite a remarkable fact which illustrates
that this fool was more than an entertainer in the background.
His prayer was short and powerful, and the archbishop could but
grind his teeth in anger. Archie said solemnly and loudly: 'Great
praise be to God, but little laud to the devil.'(80)

The great Dante once experienced what a nuisance these fools
could be when they were out to hurt famous men of letters. Living
in exile in Verona under the protection of Prince Canis (Can-
grande) della Scala (1291-1329), he was constantly abused verb-
ally by his host's (anonymous) fool. Obviously, the jester had
taken an irrational and instant disliking to the poet who at that
time had already acquired great fame. Although but a fool, he
boasted whenever he got a chance, that he had gathered more
wealth than the supposedly wise poet. Dante realized very well
that the jester enjoyed the prince's protection and also that it
would make little sense to stand up to his abuse. But one day he
replied by saying publicly that he would certainly not be as poor
financially as he then was had he found a protector who was as
congenial to his mind as the fool's was to him. The riposte was
clearly directed against the benefactor of the fool and he did not
appreciate it. His revenge followed a few days later. During dinner, the prince and his guests disposed of their gnawed bones by
secretly shoving them under Dante's chair. When the poet rose
after dinner, a coarse laughter arose in the dining hall, whereupon Dante said, in as dignified a fashion as he could: 'There is
nothing surprising about the fact that a dog [i.e. canis] hath
gnawed his bones; but I am no dog and have nothing to do with
these.'(81) The poet had saved his face but he had not beaten the
fool. But then, only very few intellectuals have ever won a victory over a fool. In fact, I know of only two examples. As church
historians know, Luther and Johann Eck crossed their theological
swords in a public debate at the court of Leipzig in July 1519.
Eck won on points, because he made Luther acknowledge that he
accepted the general theological principles of Hus. This admission
marked Luther as an heretic, whereupon the remaining ties

between his Reformation and the mighty Church of Rome, already
worn very thin, were severed radically. Luther was excommunicated soon after the debate. This historically fateful event was
attended by the fool of the Leipzig court. He had been told by
the other courtiers that both famous theologians had been invited
to debate the pros and cons of the fool's marriage, which had
been publicly announced at court the day before. Luther, the
courtiers said, was much in favour of this marriage, but Eck was
strongly opposed to the foolish match. During the ensuing debate,
the fool – who had lost one eye – was seated on the floor in front
of Eck. He constantly stared at the debating theologian with one
very angry eye. Eck tried to ignore him but was yet seriously
distracted by the fool's one-eyed stare. Finally, when he began
to lose his concentration, he put his left hand on his right eye
and stared back at the fool with a mocking gesture. Everybody
present began to laugh, including Luther, I presume, since he
had a good sense of humour. The fool jumped on his feet, began
to shower the noted Catholic theologian with much verbal abuse,
and then left the hall. The intellectual had won but the story suggests that this fool was but a natural one.(82)

The French Cardinal Du Perron related not without pride how
he once successfully put down the aforementioned Maître Guillaume – and that really was an accomplishment, since this fool was
a very skilled and reputed professional. The jester had failed to
counter a biting remark by the cardinal at his expense and he was
teased for this defeat by the king for several weeks in a row.
This was clearly a slur on the professional pride of the court
jester.(83)

People other than theologians, like bishops or cardinals, and
intellectuals, like poets, were probably more qualified to take on
a foolish fight with a court jester – provided, of course, they were
of kindred minds. It took much ingenuity and time successfully
to counter an accomplished court fool – which is demonstrated by
the longstanding, bantering feud between Brusquet and the renowned Marshal Strozzi at the French court in the sixteenth century. The exchange of pranks and tricks which grew increasingly
violent and mean, took in fact a couple of years. Brantôme was
the first to record the whole thing 'in extenso' and several historians have copied him when they wanted to tell the story.(84) I
shall single out one funny incident which suffices to give an impression of the whole drawn-out affair

Strozzi once told the queen how ugly Brusquet's wife was. The
queen's curiosity thus being aroused, she requested the fool to
introduce her to his wife. But he, good professional as he was,
preferred to keep his wife out of his affairs at court. He told her
majesty that there was no point to such an encounter since his
wife was deaf like a stone. There was, in fact, no way to communicate with her sensibly, he lied. But the queen insisted on meeting
her, thus the fool, who was compelled to oblige, told his wife,
before she entered the queen's quarters, that she should speak
loudly, since her majesty was very deaf in both ears. Since he

suspected that the Marshal was behind it all, he told her in
addition that Strozzi too was completely deaf. When introduced to
the queen, the poor woman yelled: 'Madame la reine, Dieu vous
garde de mal!' - 'Majesty, may God protect you from evil!' The
queen, convinced now of Madame Brusquet's impediment, returned
the compliment by yelling out at the top of her voice. Next, a
very weird conversation developed between the two ladies which
could be heard far outside the Louvre. Strozzi, who heard the
noise, rushed in and was loudly yelled at by the fool's spouse.
He understood immediately that the jester was behind this, ran to
the stables, and ordered the keeper of the hunting dogs to follow
him to the queen's quarters with his bugle. He returned to the
shouting ladies and told the queen that he knew an instant cure
for Madame Brusquet's deafness. He held the woman's head between his hands and told the man of the kennel to blow his bugle
full blast in her ears as long as he could. The poor woman was
then sent home, deaf indeed for several weeks.(85)

Such stories give a fascinating insight into the informal parts
of daily life in these courts. They belong to the sociologically
and socio-psychologically relevant 'petite histoire'. Folly was
crucial to it. Flögel, for instance, tells the following anecdote
about Cardinal Richelieu which gives us an unusual glance at (a)
the deference with which a man of his stature was encountered;
(b) the manner in which this great man of history would conduct
his pastime, when he was not engaged in serious endeavours; and
(c) the endearingly small, yet very human frame of this great
man's mind. All this information is easily lost if one treats 'petite
histoire' with disdain.

After sumptuous dinners, Richelieu used to take exercise in
order to stimulate the digestion. But since these exercises were
never very graceful and showed his eminence in a manner not at
all in accordance with his elevated position in society, nobody was
allowed to witness them. However, one day a courtier accidentally
saw Richelieu while he jumped up against a wall with both feet.
The cardinal was much disturbed about this intrusion on his priv-
acy and, in order to save the situation and take away the embar-
rassment, the courtier proposed a jumping match, trying out
which of the two could jump the higher. The cardinal accepted the
challenge and amused himself immensely!(86)

In conclusion of this section I shall briefly summarize the main
features of the court jester's folly, drawing up some sort of court
fool's profile. To begin with, there was this strange combination
of predictability and unpredictability. As the holder of a commonly
known position and the practitioner of an established profession
at court, much of the court fool's behaviour was predictable. His
favourite targets, for example, were well known in advance:
arrogant intellectuals and priests who irritated the king and could
thus be put down freely by means of scathing remarks or practical
jokes; strangers visiting court without having much power and
influence; mental and physical weaklings among the courtiers, who

did not enjoy the protection of the monarch, etc. Moreover, many
of his pranks and jests were predictable because he could not
always and constantly be new and inventive. However, within
this framework of predictability, the fool could suddenly do or
say something which was not expected by anybody – something
exceedingly witty, or stupid, or vicious. A courtier could heartily laugh about a prank played by the fool on someone else, but
within the very next moment he himself could well be the next
victim of his folly. In short, the fool remained eerie and erratic,
awesome and hard to understand. Above all, a fool could never
be trusted, except by his master, the king.

With the exception of Will Sommer and a few others, court jesters were spiteful creatures. They were not really foolish, but
played at being fools in order to make a living. In addition, court
fools were tied parasitically to one person, the monarch. Apart
from him, a court fool was literally nothing. To these monarchs
court jesters were pets – very much loved, but usually not loved
as real human beings so much as dogs, cats or horses. If they
were friends of the king – very often the only friends these kings
could afford to have – their relationship resembled more the bond
between man and dog than between two men, or between a man
and a woman. In such a situation of complete dependence – the
situation of a 'greedy institution' (Coser) – court jesters must
have taken great delight in cornering wise and holy men, or in
putting down powerful courtiers such as cardinals, marshals,
and members of the king's privy chamber. Indeed, many stories
that have been told about them testify to their resentment and
spite, and, as I shall argue later, these qualities were put to use
by the absolutist monarchs of Western Europe after the fifteenth
century.

Finally, these court fools were not bound by any moral re-
straints and ethical standards. Again, apart from such a rare case
as Will Sommer, court fools had no ethics at all. They were amoral
opportunists. The aforementioned court fool Thoni, whom Brantôme described as a pleasant little chap, used to follow an influential courtier like a little dog, but the moment this man fell from
royal grace, the fool would not even look at him anymore. Anne
de Montmorency had protected Thoni and was affectionately called
'Pappa' by the little fool; when this gallant courtier lost his favour
at court, however, the fool ignored him totally.(87)

These fools knew in fact but one loyalty – the one that tied them
to the king. Their only objective in life was to serve their master
and owner by words and deeds which lacked any trace of reason –
logically as well as morally. In sum, the traits most valued in
great court fools were spitefulness, immoralism, opportunism and
total lack of loyalty (except to the king). If looked at with normative moral categories, most of these jesters have indeed been
rather unpleasant individuals. But then, they had to be. These
unpleasant character traits were part of their profession and of
their position at the increasingly absolutist courts of Western Europe after the fifteenth century. Before we pass moral judgments,
we should probe this profession and institution sociologically.

THE COURT FOOL'S MARGINALITY

Domestic fools and court fools have often been called parasites.
On the fringe of society, fools traditionally served entertainment
to the wealthy and prosperous in exchange for food, clothes and
shelter. This structural feature of fools can also be expressed
sociologically by means of the concept of marginality. Fools were
marginal men, living in and from a particular social and economic
system, yet never being fully part of it. They shared this position, as we saw in chapter 2, with Jews and gypsies whom Max
Weber would call 'pariah people'. In traditional society, such
pariah peoples, like Jews and gypsies, and such marginal men,
like fools, shared also the 'infamiae macula', the stain of infamy,
which had social and moral, but also often even legal consequences. It prevented them from being fully human, and deprived them
of very basic rights.(88)

My main argument in this chapter is that due to the rise of
absolutism, court fools institutionalized and professionalized to
such an extent that they moved from the margins of their society
to its very epicentre of power, the absolute monarchy. That is,
they changed from social and economic parasites to parasites of
power. This entailed, of course, a drastic loss of marginality and
since marginality has always been the main structural component
of folly, we may argue that these court jesters lost folly as well.
Their folly grew ever more routine and the entertainment they had
to offer became a sort of secondary asset. Before we discuss this
move of the court fool from the fringe of society to its very epicentre of power where his nature and functioning underwent
drastic changes, we should first analyse his initial and originally
very essential marginality. This is important because even though
he lost this marginality, vestiges of it remained observable until
the moment he had disappeared from history's stage. Initially,
court fools shared the social, moral and legal 'infamia' of the host
of entertainers of medieval society.(89) They were not untouchable, like the executioners, but their fellow-men and women did
not see them as fully human either, be they naturally or artificially
foolish. They were much appreciated for the diversion they had to
offer but one would not like one's daughter to marry one of the
lot. Fools were often mentioned in one breath with falcons and
hunting dogs. Even such an accomplished and successful jester as
Will Sommer who sat next to the king during dinners, would at
night sleep in the kennel among the royal spaniels.(90) He was,
as we saw, Henry's friend - to whom he referred jovially as 'Harry'
- but he was this king's friend in the manner of a favourite dog.

The loss of marginality, as I just indicated, was never total.
Even in his very heyday of influence when he was no longer a
social and economic parasite, the court fool remained a parasite of
power. This is an important structural fact: the court jester had
to operate as an isolated individual, he could never form a party,
thus he could never solidify and fortify the influence bestowed on
him by the fact he had come so very close to the throne. Thus, as

influential as he had become, he could never command over an instrument of power. On the contrary, he was and remained exclusively an instrument of power in the hands of the absolutist monarch, as will be demonstrated in the next section.

It stands to reason that at the summit of influence a court jester would lose sight of the inherently parasitical nature of his position. There are two interesting examples of a court fool who tried to use his influence autonomously - i.e. without the knowledge and consent of his monarch - and in both instances it concerned politically sensitive matters. This was a grave professional error and in both instances it had cost the court fool his job.

Archibald Armstrong, alias King Archie, was not only constantly out to tease Archbishop Laud, but, being of Scottish descent, he also strongly opposed this smart politician's anti-Scottish, high-church policies. Archie began to intrigue against the archbishop outside the field of his competence, namely folly. When he had proof of this behaviour, Laud reported it to the king in terms of treason. The fool was solemnly put to trial by the privy chamber which was probably in itself a mirthful diversion to all involved - except the fool. He was found guilty, to Laud's exultation, and summarily evicted from court - an event which did not pass without ceremony and staged solemnity.(91) But Fortune is a trickster. A few years later, the archbishop fell from power, whereupon the jester published a scathing little pamphlet, called 'Archie's Dreame' (1641). From the handsome estate in the Highlands, once given to him by the king, he wrote triumphantly: 'Changes of Times surely cannot be small, when jesters rise and Archbishops fall.'(92) This was grossly exaggerated because he never returned to his former job.

Brusquet suffered a similar fate. In his function of Postmaster General of Paris - a position he held, strangely enough, conjointly with his office of court fool - this renowned jester once intercepted a few messages which were detrimental to the Huguenot cause. Upon discovery he was accused of Protestant sympathies and treason. He was instantly fired from both lucrative positions, and banished from court. A letter to the son of the previously mentioned Marshal Strozzi in which he speaks of the good relationship he had always entertained with his eminent father (sic!) and in which he requests a good word with the king on his behalf, did, in all probability, lead to nothing. He never returned to Paris as 'fou en titre d'office'. Doran recorded his sad end: 'He lost all heart, patience, and health, sank into a moody despair, and died at the Château Anet, the guest of Madame de Valentinois, in 1563.'(93)

Obviously, these fools had to be reminded of their marginality. I mentioned the fact, related by Robert Armin, that Will Sommer sat next to Henry VIII during dinners but that his bed was made at night among the royal spaniels in the kennel. When in the seventeenth and eighteenth centuries the motley and cap-and-bells, with symbolically coloured contrasting stripes, were no longer in use exclusively, court jesters were often adorned with pompous

outfits made of ridiculously old-fashioned fabrics and patterns.
In addition, they would carry around a little monkey - his next-
of-kin, so to speak. Moreover, throughout the ages the names of
these jesters also emphasized their marginality: Borra, Bolla,
Blue Nash, Clod, Gollet, Hancelin Coq, Joseph Frölich, Jack Pud-
ding, Killian, Master Henry, Nelle, Patch, Pape, Theun, Rees
Pengelding, Robin Rush, Stich, Schwab, Scogan, Sibilot, Wamba,
etc. Not all of these fools were topnotch. In fact, many of them
were natural fools. But each name, often given to several individuals since it is as hard to find an appropriate fool's name as it
is to find one for a dog, intends to underline the marginality of
fools.
  Fools were in the Middle Ages marginal men, but not all medieval marginal men were fools. Physically handicapped people, such
as dwarfs, midgets, hunchbacks, and cripples, are in a sense
still marginal people today - but they were certainly marginal in
the Middle Ages. In fact, they were often marginal to such an
extent that they were forced to sell themselves as fools (usually
passive fools to be kicked and shoved around) in order to prevent
themselves from drifting off to the vast category of 'misérables'.
Ethnic minorities, Jews and gypsies in the first place, have also
been marginal throughout the ages, and certainly during the
Middle Ages. It therefore seems reasonable to assume that fools
were most easily recruited from among them. Yet the historical
data do not support this assumption. Czar Peter did indeed bes-
tow the facetious title of 'King of the Samoieds' on a Pole and a
Jew, who also bore the title 'King of Siberia' and, under heavy
protest from the Orthodox Church, 'Patriarch of Russia'.(94) But
this is really a rather isolated instance. In general, ethnic minorities such as the Jews and the Poles outside Poland were bound
too strongly by the norms and values of their tradition to play
the immoralist and opportunist role of court fool. Appointed court
Jews did exist, particularly in the Germanic world, but they were
economic advisers, not jesters.(95)

THE COURT FOOL'S FUNCTIONS

Under the mounting pressure of absolutism, the profession and
institution of the court fool moved from the societal fringe to the
epicentre of power, losing much of its original medieval spirit and
stamina. In fact, a man like Brusquet who functioned at once as
'fou en titre d'office', as Postmaster General of Paris, and perhaps
at one stage of his career also as magistrate of Antibes, stood so
much in the centre of society that one begins to hesitate to qual-
ify him as a fool. Chicot, who served Henri IV (1589-1610) whom
he addressed with good reason as 'monsieur mon ami',(96) was
even more curious a case: he was a professional soldier and fool
at once - although it is not certain if he held an official appointment. In any case, he was so much appreciated by the king as
friend and courtier that the latter had him ennobled, albeit under

much opposition from the rest of the court. (97) Here again, the
qualities of fool were so secondary that one hesitates to range
Chicot among the great court fools. He was a valiant soldier and
an entertaining wit who came closer to this opportunist king than
anyone else at court. But the loss of folly was clearly observable
in this fascinating man. It had, as it were, evaporated as he
became a parasite of power. (98)

Brusquet and Chicot are but two examples of a general change
that occurred in the institution and profession of the court fool.
This significant process can best be illustrated by a further
analysis of the functions of the court jester, as they gradually
developed during the rise of absolutism in the sixteenth and
seventeenth centuries.

Originally the court fool's main function was that of entertainment. He was expected to please his master and owner, and to
divert his relatives, friends and guests whenever called upon to
do so. As in ancient Greece and Rome, the dinner table formed
the centre of his activities. As some of us today light a cigarette
between the courses of an elaborate dinner, our predecessors
watched the pranks and antics of fools around, under, and sometimes on top of, the table. It was believed that laughter stimulated
the digestion. When Richelieu complained about his health, his
physician Citois would often prescribe 'a quarter of an hour
Boisrobert'. (99)

But after the fifteenth century, the court fool began to attract
other functions which gradually superseded the primary function
of entertainment. The latter never disappeared totally, of course,
but the growing absolutism of the monarchs caused other and
quite different functions to emerge in this institution and profession. They brought the court fool to the centre of society, so
to speak, his institutionalization and professionalization.

After the fifteenth century Western European monarchs, particularly in England and France, began to curb the administrative
and socio-economic anarchy of feudalism. Charles the Great, as
Barraclough argued, (100) left his giant empire in an administrative
chaos which could only be put to order again by cutting it up into
smaller units. These, in their turn, had to have administrative
order restored on a smaller scale. The latter was mainly done by
the feudal contract on a man-to-man basis. But by the fifteenth
century this highly compartmentalized feudal system had again
created an anarchic situation. It was monarchic absolutism, inspired by Renaissance ideas and aspirations, as well as by papal
practices in Rome (cf. Machiavelli and the Borgias respectively),
which tried to solve the great problems of order that formed the
legacy of medieval feudalism. England's Henry VIII stood at the
start of this process, France's Louis XIV was its summit and
imminent end. As the parasites of these absolutist kings of the
sixteenth and seventeenth centuries, the court fools rose to power
and influence, attracting many functions which transcended the
original function of entertainment.

To begin with, one of the unintended consequences of absolutism is necessarily the social isolation of the monarch. When political power is not distributed over various bodies (such as councils and parliaments which exert real influence on matters of policy), but instead concentrated in one single institution - the monarchy - the occupant of the throne is doomed radically to isolate himself from the rest of society, even from its higher echelons that are closest to him.

An absolute prince cannot afford, for instance, to confide in friends, since, as courtiers, they would expect and demand a certain amount of power and influence in exchange for their confidence and friendship. To confide in someone else entails always a certain loss of autonomy and power, not in the least because one is prone to allow glances at one's weaknesses. Naturally, an absolutist prince can least afford such a loss of autonomy and power and this places him in a very isolated and lonely position. In this respect, the court fool presented an ideal solution: being marginal and thus isolated from the rest of court, dependent solely and totally on the monarch, the fool could be allowed to come close to the throne and taken into confidence without any danger. In fact, due to his marginality the fool was the only one in court who was as isolated and lonely as the absolutist monarch!

Meanwhile, his position was such that he could not put to any political use whatever intimate knowledge he might have gathered about the king, because, outside this very greedy dyad which tied him to his master and owner, the fool was an absolute nobody. Even if he developed political aspirations - which would be a very unprofessional thing for him to do - he would not be able to form a party and thus seriously threaten the throne and its absolutist power. Kings have been dethroned by rebellious noblemen, but never by a court jester. The influence and power which a court fool possessed due to this closeness to the throne and its incumbent, remained strictly parasitical and personal. In fact, court fools remained instruments in the hands of absolutist monarchs.

Unless he is an utterly inhuman and rigidly calculating dictator, not in need of any bond of friendship, the absolutist monarch stands in need of a parasite whom he can trust and confide in. Since he must heed his autonomous power, he must see to it that the parasite is kept in total bondage. The court fool was the ideal response to his need and, contrary to the widespread opinion fed by humanism and rationalism, one can indeed view this need for a court jester on the part of these kings as a sign of their humanity. The fool was really the only friend they could afford to have. Nevertheless, it was an attachment - it should be said once more - which resembled more the love for pets than the tie of friendship between two individual human beings.

The elective affinity between the institution of absolutist monarchy and the institution of the court fool is structural by nature. To begin with, both were parasitical. During the reign of the Roi Soleil, for example, the monarchy absorbed vast portions of the national product, not least because of an insanely luxurious pattern of consumption. The monarchy lived off the fat of the nation as a parasite - economically by consuming large amounts of money (partly compensated for by mercantilist policies, for the rest procured by heavy taxation); politically by centralizing all power in the throne; and culturally by dictating tastes and norms from the court in Paris. In this perspective, l'Angéli was indeed a parasite's parasite. Furthermore, the fact that both were without friends for structural reasons, as we have just seen, was another similarity between these two institutions. In a letter dated 16 January 1777 Lady Wortley Montague writes from Vienna to a lady friend about a curiosity which she encountered in all German courts: 'All the princes keep favourite dwarfs. The emperor and empress have two of these little monsters, as ugly as devils, especially the female, but they are all bedaubed with diamonds, and stand at her majesty's elbow in all publick places.' She obviously tries to grasp this strange habit and continues to write:

> I can assign no reason for these pieces of deformity, but the opinion all the absolute princes have, that 'tis below them to converse with the rest of mankind, and, not to be quite alone, they are forced to seek their companions amongst the refuse of human nature, these creatures being the only part of their court privileged to talk freely to them.(101)

The court fool lacked his own identity. But then did the isolated monarch of absolutism possess an identity of his own? Was he not, in a sense, as anonymous as his fool, as much a non-person as his jester? In fact, being both isolated from society, king and fool seemed to be each other's mirror-image, each defining his own identity as being the very opposite of the other. Small wonder that they would at times swap roles in front of the court which had to observe the strange travesty of power from a distance, and, above all, with obliged laughter.

The only formidable competition in this respect was the 'maîtresse' who functioned at the French court also 'en titre d'office', in the shadow, as it were, of the marital bond between king and queen.(102) However, in comparison with the court fool the court mistress had one severe structural drawback: she could, and actually did, entertain social connections with other people - inside the court, and even, when the salon gained momentum, outside the court in the circles of the higher bourgeoisie and nobility. The salon was an attempt by these circles to realize a cultural emancipation from absolutism after the political revolt of the two ill-fated Frondes had failed miserably.(103)

Being radically isolated at the pinnacle of a huge power structure entails an organizational hazard also. The absolute monarch, namely, lacks adequate channels of information. Here again the court fool institution is able to fill a structural void. It has been recorded of numerous court jesters after the fifteenth century that they roamed around through court and through the city in order to gather information for their monarch which they reported back to him upon their return. Much of this information, for sure, was not more than social gossip, but there are instances in which these fools clearly engaged in spying and in intriguing on their masters' behalf. Flögel tells the interesting story of Pastore, the domestic fool of Cardinal Albert, the 'Kurfürst' of Mainz, who participated in a sinister plot on behalf of his master. In 1527 a certain Georg Winkler came to Halle and preached the gospel like a Protestant. He also celebrated communion the Protestant way by distributing both bread and wine. The cardinal summoned him to his palace and reprimanded him severely. He then confiscated his horse and servant as a punishment and told him to leave the city immediately. When he left, Pastore offered him his own worn-out hackney and another servant. But the latter had been instructed by the fool to assassinate the heretic which he did after they had entered a lonely forest. The fool had most certainly been instructed by the cardinal.(104)

A few stories indicate that these fools would also operate as spies. The most reliable proof of this theory is offered by a curious letter which was dictated to a courtier (perhaps the Earl of Buckingham) by Archie Armstrong on 28 April 1623, and sent from the court of Spain to King James I. Archie had obviously joined the notorious journey of Prince Charles to the court of Spain at Madrid where an unsuccessful attempt was made to establish a marital match between this English crownprince and the Spanish 'infanta'.(105) In this letter, the fool boasts that, unlike the other members of the English delegation, he has free access to the Spanish king, due to the fact that his majesty enjoys his pleasant company. Close to the throne, he continues, he is able to hear a lot - but, regretfully, his knowledge of the Spanish tongue is inadequate. He therefore requests his master to provide money for a 'trunchman', an interpreter - 'then you shall know from your fool, with God's help and Christ's help, and the Virgin Mary's, more secret business than from all your wise men here.'(106) The letter is signed with a cross by the obviously illiterate fool. Beneath this signature the following words appear in the same handwriting as the rest of the letter: 'your best foole of state, both here and there'.

Briandas, mentioned as 'bouffon de cour' (probably not 'en titre d'office') after the death of the renowned Triboulet, was once involved in a rather tricky affair. In those days, François I and the Dauphin were seriously at odds. The fool, who had free access to the latter's quarters, one night overheard a conversation between the crownprince and a few friends. He boasted that he would soon usurp the throne and oust his obviously incompetent father. The fool listened silently to this treacherous talk and then reported the whole thing to his king - first in the form of a joke, then, after some mild pressure had been put upon him, in the form of an accurate description. The Dauphin and his cronies were severely punished for their conspiracy. However, one courtier, an older professional soldier, had not participated in the conspiratory discussion. The fool, fairly enough, had mentioned this to the king who consequently exempted him from punishment.(107)

The court fool was not only a channel of information for the absolutist monarch, he also began to function gradually as a kind of passage to this summit of power. Will Sommer, as we saw, would regularly bring the pleas of commoners to his king. L'Angéli, his opposite in character, would arrange an audience with the Roi Soleil against the payment of a handsome sum of money. Fra Mariano, the secretary and jester of Pope Leo X, also arranged audiences with His Holiness in an informal, rather odd manner. This Renaissance pope who competed in absolutism with his secular colleagues, was a notorious lover of fools and folly. Fra Mariano held the 'Offizio dei Piombi' which gave him the right to seal the papal letters and documents. He was, however, very close to this erratic pope because of his enacted folly and wit.(108) If someone urgently requested an audience with His Holiness, the jester was always obliged to arrange one on the condition that the person in question would play the fool in front of the pope. It is not known whether he also demanded some money for such an arrangement.

The more absolutist these monarchs grew, the more their fools would function as buffers between the throne and the rest of society, guarding carefully, so to speak, the integrity of the royal power. In this particular function the fool's freedom of speech, his 'Narrenfreiheit', was used quite deviously. Court jesters have become notorious as people who could at times point their arrows of folly at the king himself, ridicule him, shower him with verbal abuse, and yet get away with it. This curious, often cited, fact has been interpreted time and again in terms of a substitute for the absence of democracy in absolutism: nobody was allowed to speak out openly, to criticize the summit of power, except the fool who, by doing so, exercised some sort of cathartic function. I take strong exception to this interpretation which is, incidentally, quite old and is still repeated over and over again today.(109) I shall argue that even when he showered the throne with his foolish abuse, he still did so as its parasite and as an instrument in the power game of the absolutist monarch. If one carefully reads the stories about the activities of appointed jesters at absolutist courts, one is struck by the simple fact that their jocular remarks and practical jokes at the king's expense were, first of all, not very frequent, and, second, still obviously part and parcel of their parasitical position. The real point was that the monarch, by allowing his fool this kind of impudence, demonstrated in a rather painful manner how utterly powerless the rest of the court actually was. The fool, solidly and solitarily tied to the throne, was allowed to show off his politically innocent, parasitical power in order to demonstrate, as in a reversed, looking-glass manner, how utterly powerless everybody else outside the dyad of king and fool really was. To make things worse, king and jester would at times even swap roles, while everybody present was obliged to laugh heartily about all this folly. They were, of course, obliged to laugh about their own powerlessness!

This is sociologically very ingenious. Precisely because the fool was allowed to ridicule the king and because he was even at times allowed to mount the throne and sway his 'marotte' - that sceptre of parasitical power - the monarch demonstrated to all present the true nature of his sovereignty. The humiliation of everyone with political aspirations must have been complete! This was certainly not a substitute for democracy in a repressive society. It was an ingenious device to heighten absolutist repression.

Indeed, the court fool thus became a dialectical symbol of monarchic power. This can be illustrated by a comparison. If one wants to emphasize the glory and power of God, one can of course surround him with a splendid host of angels and archangels, with saints and all sorts of beatified creatures. But it is, in fact, as impressive and convincing to contrast God with the Devil. Actually, if one wants to describe God's glory and power as something absolute - which in the case of the Supreme Being must, of course, be done - it is rather inadequate to construct a hierarchy of holy beings, starting at the bottom with earthly beings and gradually ascending to the sanctified in heaven - the saints, the angels, the archangels, and finally at the summit: God. Such a hierarchy keeps God's glory and power grounded, and thus relative. It is infinitely more convincing to contrast the glory and power of God with an opposite, the power of Evil, and next to tie the latter to the former parasitically - as, for instance, Luther did when he called the Devil the monkey of God.

Likewise, if one wants to remind one's subjects constantly of the absolute nature of one's power, it will simply be insufficient to construct an impressive hierarchy of power, from the commoners in villages and cities, to the magistrates, the nobility, the clergy, the courtiers, and finally, at the top: the Monarch. Neither is it sufficient to bath in splendour and to surround oneself with flattering lackeys and courtiers. It is necessary to demonstrate one's absolute power by means of a parasitical institution as the pendant of God's Devil. For such a position the court fool was, of course, perfect! By his sheer presence, but in particular by his jests at the king's expense, the court fool demonstrated constantly the absolute nature of the monarch's power - he did so contrariwise, in a mirror fashion. One of Luther's theological dictums was: 'Sub contrario agit Deus' - 'God acts contrariwise.' The kings of absolutism, who thought their power was invested in them by God, acted likewise by employing court fools. But this court fool's praise of absolute power did not remain merely symbolic. The historian J. Mathorez informs us that some French court fools in the sixteenth and seventeenth centuries were actually used for propaganda.(110) He claims, quite remarkably, that there was freedom of the press, even during the reign of Louis XIV and after, journalists could say what they wanted in satires, pamphlets and brochures, as long as this happened anonymously. The dictum was: 'pas vu, pas pris'. Ever since François I, the kings of France employed journalists, called 'libellistes', who would counter criticisms aired in anonymous pamphlets, by defending royal policies in brochures and pamphlets. Two enterprising brothers, called Du Bellay, even opened a press office and employed financially needy men of letters to write pro-monarchy propaganda. This was, in short, a very curious, early form of organized public relations.

Official 'libellistes' who defended royal policies or private authors writing about non-political matters, would publish their pamphlets under their own name. For the rest, all anti-government propaganda got published under feigned names. Even the names of the publishers and of the cities where it was printed, were mostly faked. However, in order to heighten the effect, pro-government propaganda would also quite often use the names of famous contemporaries and here the names of famous court fools served a good purpose. Chicot, Angoulevent, Maître Guillaume, Le Comte de Permission, and Mathurine figured regularly on the first page of these booklets. Maître Guillaume was a favourite. He might even have written a few of the many booklets that were printed and sold under his name. It is established, in any case, that he went through the streets of Paris, accompanied by his colleague Mathurine, selling these pamphlets to the people. He was, one author claims, 'un grand partisan de l'ordre dans l'état, et de l'économie dans les finances et de l'obeissance aux princes' - 'an avid partisan of order in the state, of economy in financial matters and of obedience to Princes'.(111)

We should conclude this section with a few words about domestic fools. In the period under discussion, courtly society functioned as a social, political and cultural model, in particular for the nobility and the higher bourgeoisie.(112) Forms of thought and patterns of behaviour - 'etiquette' - were imitated outside the walls of the royal palace. Thus the domestic fool followed much of the structural developments of the court fool. If we view courtiers and urban influentials of the sixteenth and seventeenth centuries as a 'leisure class' - which they were, in particular since they could not participate in political power and policy (113) - we can define the domestic fools as a piece of conspicuous 'consumption'. It testified of wealth and 'bon ton' to have at least one fool in one's household. He would not do any hard work, like the other servants, but hang around idly, constantly on the watch to flatter, gossip and joke, part of the prestige-promoting appendage of his master's household. His flat fatuity functioned as a mirror-image of the bombastic pomposity of his noble or high-bourgeois master, who remained powerless and endlessly bored as long as the king at court kept all power to his throne.

By the time of the French Revolution all these fools had disappeared. Only a few faint vestiges of this once famous and influential institution remained, like Marie Antoinette's fool visited by Jacob Bibliophile. What had happened? How did it happen?

THE COURT FOOL'S DISAPPEARANCE

One of the sociologically intriguing facts about court fools is their

sudden disappearance. Here we have this widespread institution
and profession, solidly entrenched in the socio-political structure
of absolutism, and suddenly, after roughly 1700, it vanishes from
the stage of history never to return again. When such a prominent institution and profession disappears, something fundamental must happen to its surrounding society and culture.

We should, of course, to begin with, take into account the
general decline of medieval folly under the impact of the Renaissance, the Reformation, and the Enlightenment. In essence, all
three of them were strongly opposed to the uncivilized and irrational nature of folly. Thus, the court fool lost his general soil of
nurture outside the walls of the king's palace. However, as we
have seen before, the general decline of folly in early-modern
society concurred with the rise of the virtuosos of folly to the
summit of their parasitical power at absolutist courts. The great
fools 'en titre d'office' moved from the fringe of society to its
very epicentre, and on the way indeed lost all the original characteristics of medieval folly. In fact, some of the last great court
jesters were hardly genuine fools.

With regard to the disappearance of this institution and profession, one often refers to the collapse of the ancien régime in the
French Revolution, as if the fool tumbled from his elevated position together with his master and owner.(114) The problem with
this explanation, however, is that the officially appointed court
jester had actually already disappeared from these European
courts rather long before 1789. There were still fools at European
courts after 1700, but they were usually of the 'suivant la cour'
variety. Great virtuosos were no longer produced after Muckle
John in England and L'Angéli in France.

The main cause for the disappearance of this institution and
profession must rather be sought in the gradual goal-succession
to which it was subjected under the impact of absolutist demands.
That is, the court jester institutionalized and professionalized to
such an extent that he lost his marginality - which is an essential
ingredient of all folly - and grew into just another courtier, albeit
with a very special position close to the throne. This increase in
functionality which I described in the former section of this chapter, entailed an essential change of this institution's goal: the
court fool of the sixteenth and seventeenth centuries was no
longer primarily an entertainer, but changed gradually into friend,
spy, communication channel, and buffer of the increasingly isolated monarch. The more the king isolated himself from the rest of
court and society, the more his fool changed from a stranger at
the margin to an influential courtier at the epicentre of power.

However, it stands to reason that the fool was not at all sufficiently equipped for such non-foolish functions! He had been
selected for the job of court jester because of natural talents in
matters of folly and a training in foolish exploits and witty remarks; he was not at all a professional in matters of royal friendship and secret information - let alone matters of state and
administration. In these matters most court fools must have been

rather pitiful amateurs. Naturally, these power-hungry monarchs, probably without much genuine taste for folly anyhow, would easily dispose of their court jester, when they discovered from experience that a court fool cuts a strange and pathetic figure when called upon for functions that lie far outside the domain of folly. Structurally the position of court fool seemed to be ideal for the demands of absolutism, but its incumbents were just not able to function satisfactorily simply because they were indeed fools. In fact, this goal-succession manoeuvred most court jesters into an impossible position. To sum it up briefly, the very structural success of the court jester during the reign of absolutism spelled at the same time his fall. After 1700 court fools were predominantly anonymous, passive, and often very pathetic creatures; by the end of the eighteenth century all fools had withered away.

Fools were still at work in German courts during the eighteenth century, but interestingly enough the job was often done by individuals who occupied regular positions in society. They came to court to play the fool in order to augment their insufficient salaries - a moonlighting which stood squarely opposite to Brusquet's holding of positions outside court in bourgeois society.

Flögel tells some remarkable anecdotes about German intellectuals who in this century played the fool at court in an attempt to avert poverty - which might have been an older German tradition as Friedrich Taubmann (1565-1613) was a well-known professor of philosophy at the recently founded University of Wittenberg, a popular poet, and a regular guest at the Kursächsischen Hof, where he played the fool or, as he was called, 'kurzweiliger Rat'.(115) In those days the Germans did not always sharply distinguish between professors and fools. A German prince used to say that he did not need an appointed court fool because he could at all times invite two scholars from the university and have them start a scientific discussion. The more jargon they used, the better, because the members of court enjoyed their scientific exchange anyhow as a big joke. The standard expression was 'learned fool', 'gelehrter Narr', or, as he was also referred to in French, 'morosophe'.

Jacob Freiherr von Gundling (1668-1731) acquired great fame as such a learned fool. He had published some articles which were received by the scientific community with mixed reviews, as some deemed them valuable while others did not hold them in high esteem. In any case, within this community he was not simply perceived as a fool. Yet at court he was primarily seen and treated as jester. He would constantly brag about his wisdom, in particular after he had consumed too much wine. This bragging was seen by the courtiers of Friedrich Wilhelm I of Brandenburg as sheer folly. They would make him drunk and then play various tricks on him. Once, for example, when he was brought home in a palanquin, being quite intoxicated, some courtiers loosened the bottom. After a few steps, this bottom fell out, whereupon the bearers began to run as fast as they could. The Herr Doktor had

to run along and was left on his doorstep totally exasperated.(116)
He was not only elevated to the rank of nobility but received also
many titles which the Germans of those days took apparently with
more sport than in the nineteenth and twentieth centuries. He
was appointed in succession 'Geheimrat', 'Kriegsrat', 'Kammerrat',
'Ober-Appellations- und Kammergerichtsrat', 'Ober-Zeremonien-
Meister' and 'Präsident der königlichen Sozietätat der Wissen-
schaften'. It remains questionable whether the university professors of those days could appreciate the joke when Gundling
was appointed President of the Royal Society of Sciences - even
though the title was obviously fictitious.

Less successful was Doctor Bartholdi, friend of Gundling and
philological specialist in Latin. Convicted for slander, he had
spent some time in a Berlin jail but was released when the warden
discovered that the man was actually mad. Bartholdi then applied
for a professorship at the Royal University of Berlin, and explained the rejection as a revenge on the part of some professors
who could allegedly not forget the hard but very true words he
had once said about them. He began to wander around like a hobo,
and gradually lost all wits. When he became a pyromaniac, he was
incarcerated again and locked to a wooden log by an iron chain.(117)

David Fassmann was more successful as learned fool. He published a scathing booklet about Gundling, his competitior, and
used to quarrel and bicker with him all the time at court. When
both were drunk, they would even attack one another physically,
to the bewildered amusement of the prince and his courtiers.(118)
Friedrich II of Brandenburg discharged by decree the last German court fool, Freiherr von Pöllnitz. It happened, quite appropriately, on 1 April 1744, in Potsdam. The discharge, requested
by the baron himself, is granted to him reluctantly, the decree
says solemnly. We shall abolish the office in order to destroy its
memory among human beings, because after the aforementioned
baron no human being will be worthy to hold this office again.
However, the poor baron had considerable problems in making a
decent living in society. In order to marry a rich Catholic lady,
he converted to the Roman Catholic faith, but when the marriage
did not materialize after all, he remained without job and money.
In a letter to his former master at the Brandenburg court, he
humbly requested to be reappointed in his old court jester's position. If necessary, he added, he would return to the Protestant
faith. Friedrich II answered that he could not care less whether
the baron was Reformed, Catholic or Lutheran, and that he could
resume his former profession at court - if he would have himself
circumcised first.(119)

Obviously, these princes were bored with court fools and had
no real use for them anymore. If they needed amusement they
would surround themselves rather with 'précieuses' and 'dandies',
if they needed informal information and personal attention, they
would call on flatterers and gossipers. Meanwhile, their own absolutism wore away also. The political affairs of state were entrusted
increasingly to the successors of Richelieu and Mazarin, such
truly professional statesmen as Thiers and Metternich.

First absolutist monarchs could do without their parasitical fools,
then the society which they themselves lived off as true parasites
could do without these monarchs. In this sense, the decline of
the court fool was the prologue to the decline of absolutism and
thus the prologue to the Revolution of 1789.

THE BOURGEOISIFICATION OF THE COURT FOOL

Ever since his disappearance people have searched for survivals of
the court fool. They have come up with several fanciful suggest-
ions, most of which remain thoroughly unhistorical. For instance,
in 1789 Nick designated the journalists of his days as the main
successors of the court fools whom he had described in detail and
with much historical skill.(120) Ralf Dahrendorf, to take a more
recent example, once likened modern intellectuals to the court
jesters of the ancien régime. He believed - quite incorrectly, as
we saw - that court fools took a critical stance vis-à-vis their
monarchs and thereby established some kind of correction to the
errors of absolutism. Since modern intellectuals tend to cast doubt
on all taken-for-granted opinions, relativizing in particular all
forms of authority and asking questions nobody would normally
ask, they fulfil a similar corrective function. In this sense, they
may be designated as the court jesters of modern society.(121)
Wolf Lepenies, who is historically better informed, comes to the
opposite conclusion which is, however, as fanciful and unhistorical as Dahrendorf's. The court jester did condone the social and
political system of absolutism, Lepenies argues, and his main
function was to dispel the court's endemic melancholy, caused by
the fact that all power was usurped by the monarch, leaving
everyone else thoroughly powerless. The inability to participate
in political matters - which was fortified after the two ill-fated
Frondes - caused a massive boredom and melancholy, to be dis-
pelled by the court fool. Lepenies then continues to argue that
modern sociology has assumed a similar position with regard to
the present status quo: it has failed to contribute to the emancipation of the downtrodden whose powerlessness is alleviated by
sociology, just as the court jester alleviated the melancholy of the
nobility and higher bourgeoisie under Louis XIV.(122) In an
admittedly inventive, yet thoroughly unhistorical manner, the
modern sociologist is furnished with cap-and-bells, provided gen-
erously by the so-called 'Critical Theory' of the Frankfurther
Schule, and next proclaimed 'court sociologist' of capitalism. Let
us stick to the facts first and be fanciful next. Of crucial importance in this matter is the bourgeoisification of the court fool which
took place in the wake of the bourgeoisification of monarchic power.
Both processes began roughly in the seventeenth century, but
became clearly observable in the eighteenth century in England
and France. For the sake of clarity, I shall restrict my ensuing
discussion to the latter.
Several historians of this period have pointed at the fact that

French absolutist monarchs were, for economic and political reasons, driven into the arms of the higher bourgeoisie. The emergence of a 'nobless de robe' next to and competing with the traditional 'noblesse d'épée' was one of the more obvious indications of this development. The two Frondes of the 1650s - two consecutive amateurish rebellions of higher magistrates and nobility against absolutism in general, and the hideous Mazarin in particular - had given enormous power to the very young Louis XIV. They intensified rather than diminished absolutism. Yet after the Roi Soleil the monarchy began to become more and more bourgeois, not in the least because it needed the bourgeoisie as ally against the nobility and as provider of financial means. This bourgeoisification found perhaps its completion in Louis XVI. In his well-known study on the making of the French Revolution, Georges Lefèbvre gives a vivid picture of this pathetic king's desperate attempt to win the support of the bourgeoisie against the higher clergy and the nobility.(123) The hoped-for ally, however, ousted him and drove him with his family into death. When after the Napoleonic adventure the monarchy was restored, in 1830, its king, Louis Philippe, was indeed a very far cry from the Roi Soleil of the seventeenth century. He was nothing but the silly symbol of a flautingly prosperous higher bourgeoisie. 'Le Poire' was his appropriate nickname.

The fool was subjected to a similar bourgeoisification. When the great appointed court jesters had disappeared, fools continued to frequent Versailles as 'fous suivant la cour'. They may have lived in and around the royal palaces, like the old buffoon of Marie Antoinette, visited by Jacob Bibliophile. However, most of them lived in the city and preferred to frequent the salons of the influential Parisian, bourgeois and noble ladies. In fact, the salon became the powerful, cultural competitor of the court and it provided the fool with an altogether different audience. It was in the salon, which gradually developed into a culturally influential institution of the higher bourgeoisie and the politically powerless nobility, that the bourgeoisification of the court fool found its completion.

Regular and popular guests in the 'blue room' of Madame de Rambouillet's hôtel (city residence), where incidentally two fools, Silésie and Maître Claude, were employed,(124) have been Bois Robert, Richelieu's fool, the midget Godeau and the fool Voiture. Dorothy Backer describes the latter as 'a very superior court fool',(125) although there are no indications that he held an official appointment at the French court. Like Chicot, he was probably court jester 'quand il voulait', whenever he felt like going to court and playing the role of fool. In any case, he felt much more at home in the salon.

Voiture was born a commoner in 1597. As a young man he had decided to make it socially to a higher station in life. One possibility was to enter the military or the clergy, and slowly to rise to higher echelons of the hierarchy. Given his penchant for foolish wit, he could also have tried to make a career as appointed court

jester. Instead, he decided to go to Paris and become a man of
letters, as so many after him would do in the eighteenth and nineteenth centuries.(126) Backer's description of this curious man
is worth quoting:

> He was a little man, agile and talkative. Though not handsome,
> his sharp little face was as volatile as his wit. He spent a lot
> of time on that face before the mirror in the bachelor quarters
> across the street from the marquise [de Rambouillet] where he
> took up residence with a pet crow and two fierce dogs. He
> wore cosmetics and perfumes and curled hair. His clothes
> were as coquettish as a woman's. He was a dandy. And he was
> prepared to devote all his time to the celebration of women.(127)

He might have been a midget, like his friend Antoine Godeau,
and he was a fool who would not at all cut a bad figure as court
jester. Yet he was very different from court fools like Triboulet,
Brusquet and L'Angéli. He composed poems, silly as they usually
were. He engaged in polite and civilized conversations, in flattering, flirting and gossiping. He dressed up like a fat, not in order
to play the entertaining fool, but to impress and to please the
ladies. Indeed, he was a model example of the bourgeoisification
of traditional folly.

But one feature in particular separated Voiture from the traditional court fool of his days. His folly was a technique of self-
expression. The traditional court jester was a parasite, the
monarch's instrument, the king's pet, the willing captive of a
'greedy institution' (Coser). Even if he was a celebrated virtuoso,
he still lacked individualized personality, a unique identity.
Voiture, on the contrary, made folly into a system that had to
give him an identity and that had to make of him a personality.
The opportunism and immoralism of court fools which were always
applied to the service of the throne, became in Voiture part of a
worldview and ethos which served Voiture himself. This worldview and ethos got a name: 'dandyism'.

Dandies of the nineteenth century, like Barbey d'Aurevilly and
Beau Brummell, were fools without a court. They lived like parasites either from the interest of family fortunes or from the handouts of wealthy bourgeois snobs. In the dandy of the nineteenth
century self-expression had become a rigid system which placed
a higher premium on forms of behaviour than on moral and intellectual content. His was a life dictated by style. The dandy was
a rigid aestheticist - 'l'art pour l'art' - who radically rejected any
kind of utilitarianism: 'The dandy was the virtuoso of nonutilitar-
ianism'.(128) He was a romanticist, opposed to any kind of rationalism. He was above all a misanthropist who essentially hated
everybody except himself. He was an opportunist who detested
any kind of principle which would not serve his self-expression.
Dandyism, in short, was a cult of narcissism.(129) Baudelaire,
the ideologue of this cult, described its aim tersely: 'the cult of
oneself as the lover of oneself'.(130) And, intelligent as he was,

he proved to be aware of the fascist potential of dandyism, because he added with apparent fear that it was born of boredom
and that a bored individual would willingly reduce the world to
debris.(131)

Apart from this self-expression the dandy would make a perfect
court or domestic fool. In fact, in his illuminating study of the
dandy Otto Mann relates the story of Robert Peel who, in the
days of his career in Ireland, had a dandy, Lord Allen, as close
friend. The man followed him like a shadow and was nicknamed
'King Allen'.(132) Even the powerful themselves have sometimes
been dandies in their younger years. Disraeli was a prominent
dandy during his adolescence. Apparently, under the impact of
bourgeoisification the distance between power and folly tended
to decrease.

Finally, are there any socio-cultural types in the twentieth century which resemble the traditional court fool? The Dadaists of
the 1920s and the Hippies of the 1960s come to one's mind. However, they were aesthetic and political expressionists to such an
extent that they are in essence even further remote from the court
fool than the dandies of the eighteenth and nineteenth centuries.

It stands to reason to focus on the professional comedian. Someone like Charlie Chaplin belongs to the category of the clown,
which is an altogether different kind of fool, but a comedian like
the American Will Rogers comes closer to the traditional court
jester.(133) In a sense, he was indeed a 'fou quand il voulait' at
the White House, serving a couple of presidents as jester. He
addressed Woodrow Wilson often as 'Pres', and Calvin Coolidge as
'Cal' - just as Will Sommer called his king familiarly 'Harry'. When
invited once to attend and enliven a party for a selected group of
people, he sent word to the White House that he could not possibly come since he had too much work to do. Like several court
fools prior to the eighteenth century, Rogers was politically rather
conservative and populist, and he was quite blunt about his iso-
lationism. Once asked in the presence of the president what he
thought about Coolidge's foreign policy, he answered wryly: 'If
we would stay at home and quit trying to prowl around to various
[international] conferences and conventions, we would be better
off.'(134)

In conclusion, I want to draw the reader's attention to one profession which seems to resemble that of the traditional court
jester almost to the letter. This is, strangely enough, the Hollywood press agent, called in the vernacular of this make-believe
world 'the Hollywood flack'. According to one description, it is
the press agent's job constantly to flatter and entertain his client,
the famous star of the big screen - to cheer him up when he is
depressed, to shield him from prowling visitors, to absorb his
irritations and frustrations, even to function as the passive target
of his aggression. In many respects the Hollywood flack functions
as a pet to be fondled and kicked, and as a lightning rod to divert the surplus energy and frustration of the star. In exchange

for these degrading activities, the press agent can expect to
receive a generous share of his client's wealth and abundance. He
is a true parasite: 'The press agent is as weak and vulnerable
without his client as a hermit crab when it is without its borrowed
shell - an analogy that is almost literal.'(135)

The resemblance between the Hollywood flack and the court
jester of the ancien régime is striking. Yet, just as Hollywood is
but a grotesque image of Versailles, and the Hollywood star an
emulation of the absolutist monarch, so is this flack but a ludicrous reflection of the appointed court fool before the eighteenth
century. Historically, the resemblance is deceptive.

Thus, there remains but one conclusion: the court fool is dead,
and he will never return again. Searching for his descendants in
modernity, we are like Hamlet holding the skull of Yorick, the
king's jester, in his hands - 'a fellow of infinite jest, of most
excellent fancy'. Pensively Hamlet says: 'Here hung those lips
that I have kissed I know not how oft. Where be your gibes now?
your gambols? your songs? your flashes of merriment, that were
wont to set the table on a roar? Not one now, to mock your own
grinning? quite chapfallen?' (Hamlet, V, i).

Maître Guillaume's epitaph has been firmly falsified:

L'on me fait mort
Mais c'est à tort
Car ma folie
Demeure en vie.(136)

4 ENCHANTERS FROM BEYOND:
ceremonial fools in non-Western societies

INTRODUCTION

Our discussion in the previous chapters was restricted to fools
and folly within the context of traditional Western-European civilization. Only rarely have I referred to fools and folly outside the
Western orbit. Yet there is a great wealth of material about traditional folly in non-Western civilizations. The data are scattered
over many monographic articles and still lack any trace of interpretive coherence. These accounts by historians of religion and
by anthropologists seem to suggest, however, that traditional
folly was indeed a universal phenomenon. Its forms and appearances may differ from civilization to civilization, although, as we
shall see presently, these were minor differences. Its meanings
and functions have been conditioned by material and immaterial
circumstances, although, as we shall likewise see presently, this
in no way precludes a coherent theoretical interpretation. Yet it
seems that traditional folly has indeed been a prominent and
influential phenomenon over almost all of the traditional world.
Only in the process of modernization, folly is irrevocably doomed
to wither away.

In this chapter, I shall make an attempt to select and interpret
the relevant data about traditional folly in pre-modern and non-
Western (so-called 'primitive')(1) societies. I fully realize the
hazardous nature of this enterprise. For instance, is there any
guarantee that I shall not inadvertently call phenomena 'fools' and
'folly' due to certain similarities with the fools and the folly we
have discussed in the previous chapters? For example, when in
the eighteenth century European travellers observed the erratic
behaviour of shamans, they were inclined to label it, without any
second thoughts, as folly. Naturally, modern observers, applying
the notions of modern psychiatry, have often labelled it as psychotic behaviour. Scholars like Findeisen and Eliade, however,
can easily demonstrate how fallacious such interpretations of
shamanism are.(2)

Yet a fool-proof guarantee against false interpretations of non-
Western civilizations is, of course, not available. The hermeneutic
fallacy of what the Germans nicely call 'hineininterpretieren' - i.e.
interpreting strange phenomena exclusively in terms of one's own
set of meanings and values - cannot be avoided radically - neither
here nor in any historical and anthropological research. It is from
our own orbit of meanings and values that we observe and try to
understand strange phenomena - that they strike us as 'strange'

to begin with! It is in terms of our own set of meanings and values that we give names to these phenomena, employing the semantics of our own language. And it is in terms of these names and of this language of ours that we try to explain and interpret them, attempting all the time to decrease their strangeness. In fact, all one can do, is to remain conscious of the hermeneutic fallacy, and to minimize its impact.

In the case of the present subject, I shall try to demonstrate by means of empirical examples and theoretical interpretations (a) that certain phenomena in non-Western, traditional societies do indeed strongly resemble the traditional fools and folly of Western European civilization, and (b) that these similarities indeed justify the concept of 'traditional folly' which refers to a widespread and deeply influential character trait of pre-modern civilizations.

In his study on 'Tibet's Terrifying Deities' (1966), the Dutch historian of religion F. Sierksma described the New Year's festivities in traditional Lhasa, the capital of Tibet. It was a period of licence, in particular on the part of the otherwise rather ascetic monks. During the New Year's festivities - a period of transition between the old and the new, and thus a time of 'cultural no-man's-land' - these lamas would turn social life upside down, well-nigh literally. A crucial part was played by one man, chosen to be a one-week ruler from among the lower strata of society. In this week, he was allowed to eat and drink and do whatever he desired. After this week of total freedom and licence had passed, he was sent into the desert as a kind of scape-goat - in very old times, it is said, he was executed. According to Sierksma, this one-week ruler was the symbolic representative of evil, symbolizing in particular the hidden and negative part of Tibetan society. During his reign, he would mock the sacred, Buddhist foundations of his society. He would, for instance, say to the monks: 'What we perceive with the five senses is not an illusion. All that you teach is untrue.' Sierksma quotes Schäfer who described this festival:

> At no time do the rules of Buddhism seem to be more heavily transgressed in the holy city than now. The frivolous debauchery of these days forms an unimaginable contrast to the dogma of the church. Unrestricted fornication is countenanced. There is dissipation everywhere. Daily one sees lamas drinking, smoking, gambling. High dignitaries of the church hold orgies with women of the streets.(3)

Schäfer witnessed these carnivalesque activities as recently as the 1930s.(4)

Is it really too far-fetched and irresponsible to liken this Tibetan New Year's festival with the European medieval Festival of Fools, the ancient Roman Saturnalia, the Babylonian Saccaea, the Aztec scape-goat rituals? Would it be irresponsible to generalize this comparison, in an interpretive manner, and to speak of ritual folly with magical functions? If one were to answer this question

affirmatively, i.e. if one rejected the notion of a universal recur-
rence of ritual and magical folly in pre-modern societies, one
would have to abstain from any cross-cultural comparison and
from any theoretical interpretation. Many modern anthropologists
have indeed taken this 'safe' road, recording as faithfully as possible their observations, jotting them down in monographs. They
have thus provided us with many data of a very valuable nature,
comparable to the disconnected facts gathered by historians on
the court fool. However, these data remain unrelated, isolated,
meaningless. If there is one essential feature of science, it is the
continuous search for relationships, for basic patterns, for fundamental structures. In that respect, many of these monographs
remain rather unscientific.

Prescott, as I mentioned before, described the host of entertainers at Montezuma's court. Apparently, these jesters were
Montezuma's favourites: 'he used to say that more instruction was
to be gathered from them than from wiser men, for they dared to
tell the truth.'(5) These are words expressed about many fools in
traditional Western society. It represents, in fact, one of the
basic clichés about traditional folly. Did Prescott put these words
into Montezuma's mouth in order to enliven his description of
Aztec culture and social life, or are they authentic? In his curious
account of the conquest of Mexico, written some fifty years after
the event, Bernal Diaz also makes mention of these jesters. 'Sometimes', Diaz reports with a remarkable love for details,

> some little humpbacked dwarfs would be present at his meals,
> whose bodies seemed almost to be broken in the middle. These
> were his jesters. There were other Indians who told him
> jokes and must have been his clowns, and others who sang
> and danced, for Montezuma was very fond of music and enter-
> tainment and would reward his entertainers with the leavings
> of the food and chocolate.(6)

There is a remarkable similarity between these Aztec entertainers
and the parasites of ancient Greece and Rome, or for that matter
the host of fools, entertaining medieval and early-modern people
at castles and palaces in Europe. It does not seem irresponsibly
facile to interpret them in terms of the concept of traditional folly.

Around 1800 the young Englishman John R. Jewett who served
as blacksmith on a merchant vessel, was taken prisoner by the
Nootka Indians of America's north-west coast, together with
another sailor. They were made the slaves of Maquina, head of
the tribe. The rest of the crew had been slaughtered by the
natives, whose fury was triggered because the captain had
cheated them in a business transaction. Jewett tried to make the
best of his captivity, made an early attempt to learn the language,
and produced knives and daggers which in particular made him
popular among his captors. He was a perceptive young man who
observed the Indians with curiosity rather than prejudice, unlike
his companion who made no attempt to hide his contempt regarding

these 'savages'. It is even likely that he made notes during his
captivity. In any case, a few decades after his well-planned
escape from Maquina and the Nootka Indians, an account of his
adventure was published in Philadelphia. The noted anthropologist Boas refers to this document as a reliable report of an eye-
witness and quotes from it.(7)

Among the many things that drew Jewett's vivid attention was
Maquina's jester, Kinneclimmets, who also officiated as priest in
ceremonial sacrifices:

> He stood with Maquina in the relation of king's jester, on
> account of his tricks of mimicry and other monkey traits,
> that raised him high in his majesty's estimation. He not only
> performed the part of buffoon, but he had also the office of
> master of ceremonies at all the feasts, and that of public
> orator. He harangued the people, showed all to their places,
> and amused them mightily with his antic gestures, his low
> wit, and savage merriment.(8)

His antics, related in this report, belong indeed to the court
jester's folly variety.

Some Tokugawa shoguns of Japan had a court jester among their
personnel, one of whom bore the name of Sorori.(9) The Muslim
rulers of the medieval Near East employed court fools.(10) Thus,
not only licentious folly in general, but even such an institution
and profession as the court fool did occur far outside the orbit of
traditional, Western European civilization, particularly, of course,
in the cases of 'oriental despotism'. They too testified to the fundamental nature and the coherence of the phenomenon of traditional folly.

Several anthropologists have given lively descriptions of the
so-called 'ceremonial clowns', or 'ceremonial buffoons', or as they
have been called also, yet less adequately, 'delightmakers', prac-
tising all kinds of ritualized follies. They can be found among the
Indians of North America, in Middle America, and in various
African tribes. As we shall see in more detail shortly, these
ceremonial fools mocked the most sacred rituals and traditions of
the tribe. They acted contrary to the established hierarchies of
the social structure. They engaged in contrary behaviour (transvestism being especially popular), in backward speech, and in
revolting acts like drinking urine or throwing manure about. Is it
a matter of fallacious 'hineininterpretieren' to liken this behaviour
to that of the medieval practitioners of the Festival of Fools, who -
as we saw in chapter 2 - devoured 'boudins' (a rather obvious
remnant of very ancient ritual coprophagy)? Is it too far-fetched
to speak of fundamental anthropological links, beyond the historically and culturally specific meanings, values and norms of different civilizations?(11)

The American anthropologist Radin recorded and translated the
Winnebago Trickster Cycle - a set of stories about the antics and
weird transfigurations of an awe-inspiring fool called Wakdjunkaga.

He is half man, half god, half animal, and his main activity is
constantly to trick people. It is hard, if not impossible, to grasp
and grab him, because his behaviour is erratic and his body can
assume many different shapes and appearances. He is like the
Germanic god Loki, or the ancient Greek god Hermes.(12) Is it
irresponsible to compare these tricksters with Till Eulenspiegel
or with Nasreddin, rational and as flatly human as these folk
fools may have been compared to Wakdjunkaga, Loki or Hermes?

Finally, to mention one last example, Huizinga who was a student of Sanskrit and Indian culture and wrote his PhD thesis on
the role of the clown ('vidûsaka') in ancient Indian plays before
he became historian, compared this role with that of the clown in
Shakespeare's plays.(13) Was this merely a facile comparison, or,
on the contrary, a profound one which opens our eyes for the
more universal dimensions of traditional folly?

It is obvious that I have answered this latter question affirmatively. But I go also one step further. In this chapter I venture
to interpret non-Western traditional folly as a 'magical' phenomenon, one that carries out specific functions which are again, as
in the case of the court jester's folly, sociologically of great
interest and significance.

CEREMONIAL FOOLS

Travellers, like the energetic Geoffrey Gorer in our century, or
representatives of colonial regimes, like the inquisitive Captain
John Bourke of the last century, were without exception shocked
and struck by disbelief, when they saw ceremonial clowns or fools
at work in so-called 'primitive' societies. They usually recorded
what they saw, with astonishment and barely-repressed disgust.
It is, for example, curious to read Geoffrey Gorer's report of his
encounter with what was obviously such a ceremonial fool, although
at the time of his encounter he was probably not acquainted with
the phenomenon. I quote him at length, since Gorer gives a good
impression of an African ceremonial fool, while he also vents his
own amazed reaction, albeit in a detached manner:

> Our other appointment was at Lasa, a village a few miles
> away; the entertainment we found there is quite impossible
> to describe, even if it were permissible to do so. The dance
> was a mixture of Brueghel and Bedlam, semi erotic, semi
> ecstatic and quite cuckoo. The dancers, who were old men
> and youths, were nearly all stark naked except for head-
> dresses ornamented with horns and cowries and necklaces
> of black and red seeds; as for the dancers - one old and
> bearded man danced chiefly with his left foot which he waved
> in the air; another did the most surprising things with his
> more private parts, throwing them about rhythmically and
> peculiarly; they were of extraordinay size and plasticity. At
> one moment everyone sat on the ground and did the most

eccentric things, advancing with a sort of wiggle of the haunches. One young man with an extremely elaborate helmet had danced himself into a mediumistic frenzy in which he stuck feathers and thorns into his arms; the other dancers threw him about like a ball. Another young man ate earth and smothered himself in it; he was continually being sick and swallowing his own vomit; he had reached a stage at which only the whites of his eyes showed. He continually fell exhausted to the ground, but the music of the drum and the whistly flutes would bring him to and he would start off again. The native guard who was meant to be keeping order was seized by contagion and did things with his rifle which weren't quite nice. It was the oddest evening I have ever spent.(14)

The ecstasy of these dancers demonstrates a clearly shamanistic trait. Yet one should distinguish between such ceremonial fools and the shamans. The latter, as is very clearly the case in Siberia and among the Eskimos, are individuals with the gift of ecstasy which they have developed to a great skill in a long and usually rather painful training. Ceremonial clowns, on the contrary, belong to traditional groups, to socially established associations, often organized in secret societies. Originally, they may have had functions of a shamanistic nature, such as black magic or the healing of sick people, but these wore away in most instances and have been replaced by other functions.

The American anthropologist Hoebel described a group of young warriors among the Cheyenne Indians, whom their fellow-tribesmen call 'Contraries'. These young men are 'driven' to a well-nigh paranoid fear for their virility. As a consequence, they refuse to marry, because matrimony, it is believed, consumes too much virile power. They engage rather in homosexual relationships.

The aim of their particular style of life is to collect virile power which is to be released in warparties. Indeed, they are very brave in battles, excelling in ruthlessness. They isolate themselves in the Cheyenne camp, where they do everything in a contrary manner. They seem to be in opposition all the time, living against the grain in all things. The Cheyenne realize that these Contraries lead very difficult lives, and they admire them for it, albeit with a measure of pity.

The symbol of the Contraries is the Thunder Bow, which represents the phallus – tied and restrained. It may not touch the earth when it is carried about during a battle, since the earth is the bearer of life, the symbol of femininity. The backward behaviour of these rather asocial Contraries is obviously magical by nature. It is totally geared towards the preservation, the stowage, and the release, in battles, of virile power. Acting, thinking and speaking in a contrary and backward manner is, as we have seen in previous chapters, the hallmark of traditional folly. In this sense, these Cheyenne Contraries were indeed fools. It should be emphasized that this folly was believed to contain power, sexual power, virility.(15)

In her disputed 'Patterns of Culture' (1934), Ruth Benedict characterized the Pueblo Indians as the representatives of an Apollinian culture. In particular the Zuni Indians have allegedly been restrained and ceremonial in their behaviour, avoiding excitement and ecstasy: 'The ideal man in Zuni is a person of dignity and affability who has never tried to lead, and who has never called forth comment from his neighbours. Any conflict, even though all right is on his side, is held against him.'(16) Among these Zuni, Benedict claims, 'There is no courting of excess in any form, no tolerance of violence, no indulgence in the exercise of authority, or delight in any situation that the Dionysian counts most valuable.'(17) Sexuality, according to Benedict, is not one of the major concerns of the Zuni - it rather 'is an incident in the happy life'.(18)

Benedict briefly mentions Zuni clowning ceremonies and links them to the hunting and medicine cults. However, she fails to discuss them in greater detail. Had she done so, she would have discovered Dionysian dimensions in Zuni civilization which stand quite square to the Apollinian ethos which she attributes to it. The Zuni clowns, organized in clubs or societies, could at certain moments of time exceed in crassly erotic behaviour and compete in debauchery. Their behaviour seemed a looking-glass reversal of Zuni's Apollinian ethos.

Two years before Benedict published her book, Ruth Bunzel had reported in great detail about the elaborate ceremonies of the Zuni.(19) In this report she devotes much attention to the ritual fools, the 'koyemci' who arose, according to the legends of the tribe, from the incestuous relationship between a brother and a sister. They demonstrate the stain of their shameful birth by their grotesque appearance and by their revolting behaviour. Although no real shamans, they seem to carry shamanistic features: 'They are the most feared and the most beloved of all Zuni impersonations. They are possessed of black magic; in their drum they have wings of black butterflies that can make girls "crazy".'(20)

These same ceremonial fools drew the attention, only a few years later, of Elsie C. Parsons and Ralph L. Beals.(21) Parsons related her astonishment when she witnessed the actions of these clowns during the Lent ceremony at San Ignacio. The Roman Catholic population of the town walked in procession in a devout manner, but suddenly a small band of men appeared, who began to imitate the ceremony with weird gestures and strange bodily movements:

These masked men teased one another; they fell over dogs and rolled in the dust; they displayed mock fear; they set a doll on the ground to venerate it as a saint; and they simulated eating and drinking the excreta they would pretend to catch in their wooden machete from the body of passing burro, or horse, or woman, even of one kneeling in prayer. The last diversion was a variant on the filth eating and drinking practices of the Pueblo clowns, otherwise every new trick

or bedevilment that was enacted on the outskirts of that
religious procession was one I had seen in our Southwest.(22)

Originally, the eating and drinking of filth was not impersonated
mimicly, but occurred in actual fact! Mathilde Stevenson reported
in 1904 that she saw such Zuni clowns competing with each other
in the devouring of revolting things, such as splinters, strips of
old blankets, heads of living mice, etc. 'The one who swallows the
largest amount of filth with the greatest gusto', she wrote, 'is
most commended by the fraternity and onlookers.'(23) Even the
eating of excrement and the drinking of urine originally took
place in actual fact. In his curious study, 'Scatological Rites of
all Nations' (1891), Captain Bourke filed the following report on
the drinking of urine:

> I refused to believe the evidence of my senses. ... This time
> it was a large tin pailful, not less than two gallons. ... The
> dancers swallowed great draughts, smacked their lips, and,
> amid the roaring merriment of the spectators, remarked that
> it was very, very good. The clowns were now upon their
> mettle, each trying to surpass his neighbor's feat of nasti-
> ness. ... [Some] expressed regret that the dance had not
> been held out of doors, in one of the plazas; there they
> could show what they could do. There they always made it
> a point of honor to eat the excrement of men and dogs.(24)

After she had seen these fools at work, Elsie Parsons must have
felt what Gorer felt in Africa, when he witnessed those foolish
dancers. She sighed: 'I gasped in amazement, inwardly - the dust
was smothering.'(25)
Anthropologists have adjudicated various functions to these
ritual clowns. Healing of sicknesses, black magic, bringing about
rain are a few of them which are mentioned recurrently. Parsons
connects their activities with warfare, which would link them to
the Cheyenne Contraries:

> The obscene behaviour of the clowns may be considered as a
> war trait, particularly their formal obscenity towards women
> and their eating and drinking of filth and stereotype gluttony.
> Also their backward speech, saying the contrary of what they
> mean. Backward speech, eating and drinking in excess or
> things ordinarily repugnant, and playing 'practical jokes' on
> old women, etc. were all items in the foolhardy behaviour of
> certain Plains warrior societies.(26)

This warrior dimension, she continues, disappeared once Indians
began to live in reservations and abstained from warfare. Gradually these warfare functions were superseded by functions of
fertility magic and the control of the weather. These fools also
began to function increasingly as bogeys (katcina's) that intimi-
date and socially regulate the members of the tribe, in particular

the children. However, Parsons emphasizes that entertainment remained an important function throughout, and she added that one should not too hastily interpret the erotic elements in their joking in terms of pahllic magic. Their aim is rather

> to give as outright a representation of sex as possible, for fun. Phallic magic is involved but sex play or pantomime is probably also a stimulation, not to direct licence .... but to sex consciousness of a general sort, in groups where sex expression is very limited and sexual emotion is never openly manifested. (27)

Apparently, the impersonations of foreigners and strangers were particularly held in high esteem. It was received with much laughter and delight when these fools mockingly imitated the Navaho shaman, the Mexican bull fighter, or the American tourist. (28)

Ralph Beals studied the Mayo-Yaqui ritual fools who performed during the yearly Lent ceremonies. They organized a kind of passion play which portrayed the life and death of Jesus, and went on for a whole week. Naturally, the play was a strange mixture of Catholic Christianity and remnants of paganism. In many respects, the whole spectacle looked very much like the medieval Festival of Fools. The Mayo and Yaqui called these fools 'Fariseos' or 'Diablos' - two categories, missionaries must have told them, which were quite similar and symbolized the forces of darkness. Sometimes they bore the colourful name of 'Soldados del Pilate'. Here too the same features: reversed language, contrary behaviour, obscene jokes. Beals too suspects an ancient link with warrior cults. (29)

In a well-written survey of various Indian ritual fools, Julien H. Steward sums up skilfully the activities of different ceremonial clowns:

> A great deal of ruffianism is also exhibited by clowns. Things and persons are not at all respected. The Zuni Newekwe and Koyemshi indulge in all manner of acts of physical violence. The Hopi clowns have tussles, tormenting each other with cactus branches, stripping breech-clouts and such-like. The Papago clowns visit people's houses, upsetting things, and like them, the Miwok clowns run about after dance, prying into houses and wrecking what they can lay hands upon. The Cahuilla 'funny man' of Southern California annoys people by throwing water on them or dropping live coals down their backs. And in like manner the Huichol clowns of Mexico torment people with 'botherations' and prevent their sleeping by shaking rattles near their ears, or by tugging at their clothing. (30)

New material on contemporary ritual fools in Mexico has been gathered by N. Ross Crumrine. In the town of Southern Sonora masked dancers annually add lustre to the Lent ceremonies. They are members of the so-called Parisero Fraternity, and are called 'Capakobam' (singular: 'Capakoba'). They perform a passion play, in which Jesus is taken prisoner and crucified. The occasion is used, however, to impersonate in a mocking manner all kinds of facts and events belonging to the routine of daily social life. Two facts in particular fall victims to their scathing jokes and mockery and these happen to be the facts which are the most couched in taboos – sexuality and sickness. The coitus is enacted in panto- mime; illness and recovery are impersonated; and all this happens in the middle of the church.

Crumrine gives a lively description of the appearance of these ritual clowns: they wear masks, tied to what look like helmets, and they carry about wooden knives and swords. Some carry small drums, painted with red and green figurines (like trees, stars and Western pin-up girls), others walk about with violins, toy guns, balls and small wooden phalli.(31)

One of their tasks during the Lent ceremonies is to watch the believers in the church; they may not walk out of the ceremony. Or, during the night watch on Good Friday, they see to it that nobody falls asleep. An interesting detail is that townspeople have been said to believe firmly that these Capakobam confess guilt on the part of the total community.

Again we can witness the same licentious and foolish behaviour:

One Capakoba played with a small metal bucket in which he had placed dirt. Another had a small rubber doll's foot at the end of a sword. He would tickle the bottom of it and stick it in the other Capakoba's faces and poke it around their anuses. ... Other Capakobam used cans or bottles which they put up to the anuses of their neighbours and then 'drank' the 'contents' of the can or bottle. The 'eating' of feces is a very common Capakoba performance. Another common performance is the 'defecating' upon the crosses of the way of the cross. ... The first Capakoba in a line of runners will squat with his anus to the cross. When he is finished, the second performs, etc., until all the line has defecated upon the cross.(32)

The obscene impersonation of the coitus, incidentally, took place always in the presence of children. Asked about this, the adults of the town admitted that this behaviour was actually too crass for children to observe; but then, they added immediately, these clowns are masked and thus not human! Meanwhile, outside the church, erotic acts were impersonated: 'One will climb on the back of the other, with much bouncing and rattling of coccoon rattles. On another occasion a Capakoba was observed climbing a ladder and pantomiming sexual intercourse with the ladder.'(33)

There is a pattern in all these impersonations and crassly dev- iant acts. Behaviour is excessive, often obscene. It is backward in speech and thought, contrary to traditional norms and values, offensive to established taboos. It presents a counter-worldview and counter-ethos - a mocking mirror-image of the existing culture.

What is the use of these blatant deviations, what are the meanings of these ceremonialized violations of the rules, norms, and values of otherwise very traditional people? Is it possible to explain and interpret these strange phenomena?

CEREMONIAL FOOLS INTERPRETED

The ancient Roman Saturnalia and the medieval European Festival of Fools were celebrated in the period of the winter solstice - a period of transition in nature. The ceremonial fools of the Christianized Indians of North and Middle America would go into action during Lent - a dramatic period of transition in the ritual calendar of Christianity. In other words, these were, in terms of Van Gennep's famous 'scheme of rites of passage', typically transition rites, linking an initial separation (the departure of the norms and values of tradition) to an eventual incorporation (the return to the good, old-time culture).(34) Ceremonial fools did not always and exclusively get into action in marginal situations, such as the winter solstice or Lent or the initiation rites. There is, it seems to me, a variety of occasions in which they were, so to say, ritually called upon to supply their foolhardly behaviour. Regretfully, anthropologists have failed precisely to categorize these occasions. Yet it is safe to state that ceremonial folly is indeed most obvious in marginal situations.

The basic dynamics of ceremonial folly seems to be, in terms of Van Gennep's scheme, a ritual withdrawal from the taboos, the norms and values of established society, resulting in all kinds of foolish, contrary behaviour, with the intention of grounding the observer of these fools more firmly in the tradition of their society. The aim of the foolish separation is renewal and affirmation of incorporation. These abstract formulations, still too much couched in flat functionalism, stand in need, of course, of further elaboration.

Before I do so, however, I must briefly deal with a widespread psychological interpretation of ceremonial folly which can be shortly labelled as the safety-valve hypothesis. According to this interpretation, ceremonial fools vent repressed feelings of frustration and aggression on behalf of the total population. The weird and often awe-inspiring actions of these clowns supposedly generated an emotional discharge and relief on the part of the beholders. Ruth Bunzel uses the hypothesis in her syrvey of Zuni ceremonies with great care. In fact, she only alludes to it in a footnote: 'It is a society of strong repressions. Undoubtedly the great delight in the antics of the clowns springs from the sense of release in vicarious participations in the forbidden.'(35) Elsie Parsons and Ralph Beals are equally careful in the use of this psychological interpretation. Parsons refers only to Bunzel's footnote, while Beals remarks, in a footnote, 'That the obscenity and clownishness are in part a vicarious outlet for a rather emotionally inhibited community is quite possible.'(36) This hesitance on the part of knowledgeable anthropologists changes into great enthusiasm, when psychoanalysts focus their attention on ceremonial fools. Jacob Levine, for example, refers to Steward's comment that these clowns usually ridicule those objects most which the community treats with the greatest deference and awe. He then continues to remark: 'These antic excesses of licence and vice provide a mass return of the repressed, sanctioned by long tradition, and confined to ceremonial occasions which, in these instances, absolve the participants of the fear of castrative retaliation. The close relationship of such behaviour to manic elation is apparent.'(37)

Apart from such a heavily psychoanalytic and rather speculative notion as 'castrative retaliation', Levine's interpretation deserves attention as it stresses the regressive nature of these ceremonial fools. According to Levine, this ritual-clownish behaviour is to be viewed as a regression to a pre-repressive animal stage of humanity. It 'provides a socially acceptable mode of releasing libidinal, aggressive, and infantile impulses which might otherwise be expressed in anti-social behaviour in these societies.'(38)

John Honigmann uses a variation of the safety-valve hypothesis. In so-called 'primitive' societies, individuals observe and experience the ritual activities of priests and shamans as awe-inspiring, strange and astonishing. They feel themselves to be helpless and powerless, and this causes in them emotions of fear. The ceremonial clowns, Honigmann claims, translate the extraordinary terms of this magico-religious world into the ordinary terms of daily social life:

> Clowning and burlesque act as common denominators or
> cultural enzymes whereby the religious material is translated
> into a more familiar form. The sacredness and terror are
> taken out of the priests, rituals, etc. and the crowd laughs
> where otherwise it must act with reverence, fear or wonder.
> What may in other societies be done individually or secretly,
> accompanied by severe manifestations of guilt and anxiety,
> among these Indian groups is handled painlessly and collect-
> ively through the ceremonial clowns with whom the crowd
> identifies.(39)

It is, of course, quite impossible to verify empirically this safety-valve hypothesis. As a result, it has been employed in a contradictory manner. Lucille Charles, for example, used it in a way which is squarely opposite to Honigmann's approach. The ritual clown, she claimed, makes conscious what usually remains unconscious, namely 'the humdrum, humble, everyday, earthy side of life.' Like the contemporary circus clown, the ceremonial fool reminds his fellow-tribesmen of poverty, irresponsibility, licence. These elements ferment in man's unconscious and are elevated into consciousness by these clowns:

> It is the locating, naming, bringing to a head, and expres-
> sing of a psychological element which has been causing
> trouble in the unconscious; a renegade element which for
> the sake of self-integration and further progress in personal
> living should be brought up to consciousness, released, to a
> certain extent experienced and consciously related to, and
> so assimilated into the personality of the beholder.(40)

It is certainly not my intention to deny the heuristic value of such
psychoanalytic interpretations, although I definitely want to take
exception to the ill-advised use of typically Western, psychological categories. For instance, to take just one point, non-Western
pre-modern man is never an individual in the sense of Western
society and Freudian psychoanalysis. It is furthermore assumed
that these ceremonial clowns were surrounded by some kind of
eager audience, enjoying the antics of these fools as if it were a
theatre performance, observed in terms of leisurely entertainment.
The reward of this performance was supposedly some sort of
Aristotelean-Freudian catharsis. We know that this was not so.
Fellow-members of the tribe were quite often offended by the
revolting elements of these foolish performances, but they nevertheless encouraged them because they were deemed necessary. In
other words, these ritual fools engaged in revolting and disgusting acts because they were ritually mandatory! If these clowns
would not perform, the tribe would fall victim to disasters. Max
Gluckman touched on this point with much insight: 'These rites
of reversal obviously include a protest against the established
order: and in many rituals their performance is believed to
achieve success and prosperity for the group which practices
them.'(41) As an example, he referred to the ceremonial revolt of
the Zulu women at the start of the planting period, when they
started their toiling in the fields.(42) Only in this period - again
a period of transition - these women were allowed, or, better,
were expected, to assume the role of the men and to treat them
with disrespect. In the time of Gluckman's field work in Zululand
(1937), these ceremonies were no longer celebrated. An old man
told him that this was, without doubt, the cause of those miserable harvests they had recently collected. Gluckman commented:
'These rituals contain the belief that if people perform certain
actions they will influence the course of events so that their group
may be made richer, more prosperous, more successful, and so
forth.'(43)

I shall further elaborate on this interpretation of Gluckman, since
it strikes me as a valuable starting-point which, in terms of sociological relevance, transcends various psychoanalytic elaborations
of the safety-valve hypothesis. Of crucial importance is the notion
that these foolish rites were ritually mandatory for magico-religious
rather than psychoanalytic reasons. However, before we discuss
the ritually mandatory nature of ceremonial folly, we must briefly
deal with yet another, often proposed interpretation. It stands to
reason that contemporary sociologists will tend to view these

ceremonial fools in terms of conflict. The general line of argument
would thus be that the licence of these fools does not just cause a
psychological release of culturally repressed emotions, as the
psychoanalysts have it, but presents also and primarily an alternative to an oppressive status quo. In the absence of any viable
opposition to the status quo, these fools substituted for a dormant opposition on the part of the larger population. The problem
with this kind of explanation is again that political categories are
used which are adequate only in reference to Western circumstances. They are, by and large, alien to those who happen to
live in a magico-religiously enchanted garden.

In a very perceptive exposition, the Dutch sociologist
W. F. Wertheim once claimed that societies rarely adhere to totally
integrated systems of values. Even if one encounters a society
with a dominant set of values, one will find hidden values which
conflict with and stand in opposition to these dominant values.
These hidden and conflicting values supposedly express dissatisfaction with the status quo. Wertheim mentions religious movements like the Cargo Cults, humorous legends about folk fools
like Till Eulenspiegel and Nasreddin, and the medieval institution
of the court fool, as examples of conflicting institutions which
express a dormant opposition to the dominant system of values.
Wertheim then proposes to call these counter-values the 'counterpoint to the leading melody'. This is indeed illuminating, since it
indicates that these allegedly opposing values do in actual fact
contribute to the total fabric of social life. Before I elaborate this
notion in further detail - and in a direction which is quite contrary to the conclusions drawn by Wertheim - I mention one other,
inventive example which, according to Wertheim, may illustrate
his idea of cultural counterpoint. The Sunday is, he says, a typically Western institution. On this day, the dominant values are
turned upside down, because until modernity the rich and powerful were in the Sunday church service showered from the pulpit
with threats of damnation together with the poor and humble. Both
categories of people were radically treated as equals, despite the
fact, I may add, that the rich and powerful usually occupied the
better and more richly ornamented benches, especially reserved
for them. Wertheim says: 'The poor people rejoiced intensely when
listening to the damnation thrown at those to whom they had to
bow in daily life.' Even today, the Sunday has a similar counterpoint function:

> On that day the prominence of the writing-desk aristocracy,
> who rule on weekdays, is being challenged by the hierarchy
> of physical valour as symbolized by sports. In this sports
> Sunday the protest against the intellectual elite of a manager-
> ial world is embodied in a temporary revaluation of humanity
> according to bodily strength. (44)

Yet, as the metaphor seems to indicate, counterpoint values do
contribute to the total 'music' of social life. They are an integrating

element within the existing system of values and meanings. This
was certainly the case with the court fool during the period of
Western European absolutism, but it also holds true for the ceremonial fools of pre-modern and non-Western civilizations. If these
fools do express any opposition, it is meant to contribute to and
stabilize the existing composition of society! Taken in this sense,
the metaphor of counterpoint is indeed better than the psychologistic metaphor of safety-valve. In any case, the topsy-turvy
world of ceremonial fools with the carnivalesque inversion of hierarchies, is not at all a 'revolutionary' world, as Wertheim seemed
to assume too hastily, but, rather, an intriguingly inventive (and
sociologically fascinating) mechanism to fortify and stabilize the
status quo. However, this should not be taken in terms of a
rather flat functionalism. These fools constructed for the duration
of this ceremonial performance a looking-glass reality which had
to demonstrate in a vivid representation the deeper, magico-
religious and metaphysical foundations of everyday-life reality.
In order to substantiate these statements further, we must first
return to the previously mentioned ritually mandatory nature of
ceremonial folly. Only when we view these fools as the instruments
of magico-religious ideas, embedded solidly in the cultural context
of a pre-modern enchanted garden, shall we be able to understand their nature and their social functions.

Gerard van der Leeuw was one of the first students in the comparative study of religion, who ventured to place religion in the
context of phenomenology. In the phenomenology of religion, he
claimed, one is not primarily interested in the historical origins
and social functions of total religions, like the so-called world
religions, or of isolated religious phenomena, such as prayer,
sacrifice, initiational ritual, sect, church. In this field of study,
one rather focusses on the meanings and functions of religious
phenomena within the total context of their tradition.(45) One will
try to study a phenomenon like shamanism, for instance, within
historically and geographically different contexts of meaning, as
Mircea Eliade did, rather than focusing, in the manner of a monograph, on the phenomenon of shamanism within, say, one single
Siberian tribe at one single moment in history. In such a comparative analysis, it is hoped, one will lay bare and understand the
meta-historical, common and essential features of the magico-
religious phenomenon under study. That is, without sacrificing
its historical and cultural singularities (the phenomenologist is
indeed in danger of generalizing too hastily), one will attempt to
reach the essential common denominators, the basic structures, if
one wishes, of the phenomenon, prior to its many historical and
cultural differentiations. In this sense, phenomenology of religion
is indeed a form of structuralism.

In accordance with many students of religion, Van der Leeuw
believed that the most fundamental and most general aspect of
religion is the phenomenon of power - 'mana', 'orenda', 'dynamis',
or whatever it has been called.(46) In his religion, man venerates
and serves power. He will verbalize it in legends and myths. In

advanced religion he will theorize about power through theological doctrines, and defend it against possible attacks (theodicy, apology). In magic, man tries to manipulate power, in order to cure the sick, or to hurt the enemy, or to promote fertility, or to cause rain. In most 'primitive' religions, mana is viewed as a cosmic vitalistic power, operating in human beings (cf. sexuality), in nature (cf. fertility of the soil), and in cultural institutions (cf. charisma).

It is in the context of this magico-religious notion of power that one should primarily interpret ceremonial folly. To begin with, the foolhardy behaviour of these clowns is not sheer entertainment, like the antics of the modern circus clown. It is first and foremost ritual behaviour, and rituals are essential to the enchanted garden of pre-modern civilizations. They are not functional forms of behaviour, like the role behaviour of modern man in a bureaucratic society. On the contrary, the rituals themselves are sacred and taboo, loaded - so to say - with power. Performing the rituals - e.g. participating in the ritual dances which have been passed on from generation to generation - this power will penetrate into society, getting hold of individuals, bringing them into a state of trance. In other words, when the members of the tribe dance, magico-religious power spreads out over the community, and becomes very concrete and functional. That is, the rituals are necessary, because without them the community would be deprived of its most essential vitalistic force. It would be deprived of its source of energy. However, these rituals incorporate at the very same time a threatening danger: performing them is playing with fire. The ritual performance, therefore, requires knowledge and skill. It cannot take place at any given moment and in any location. Rituals have boundaries which are contained in formulas and calendars, and safeguarded by priests and sorcerers (cf. the ritual taboo).

The rituals provide social life with a distinct rhythm. They are, in fact, the very foundation of the existing social order, and its sense of time. Thus, magico-religious power is not a purely vitalistic, anarchic force. It is, rather, channelled and constrained by the rituals. The latter are, so to speak, the vessels in which mana is stored up and which prevent it from leaking out uncontrollably. Uncontrolled mana is lethal. Thus, each deviance from the ritual taboos, from the traditional boundaries, would present a grave and irresponsible danger to the community, unless, of course, this deviance is again ritualized in its turn.

However, traditionally restrained and ritually contained 'mana' is routinized power, stale power. In various 'primitive' civilizations, the notion can be found that this magico-religious power tends gradually to lose its stamina - just as happens to male potency, which is a manifestation of mana. Atrophied power, however, is believed to be negative power which may work to man's disadvantage. This places 'primitive' man in a curious dilemma: mana stands in need of traditional rituals, as they must restrain and control its vitalistic impact, yet these traditional rituals have the

tendency to routinize mana into a stale but negative kind of force.
The dilemma can be solved only by negating the ritual negation
of mana. How is this task to be performed adequately?

One such technique, by which mana is kept alive and powerful,
without radically abandoning the existing institutional and traditional system, is the giving of gifts. Marcel Mauss and others
have demonstrated that in a 'primitive' society a gift is infinitely
more than just a physical and economic object, while also the act
of gift-giving is more than a mere 'do-ut-des' procedure.(47) The
gift represents the spiritual value of the giver, and symbolizes
his mana. When A presents a gift to B, the latter does not just
receive an object with an economic value, as is predominantly the
case in modern society, but he gets first and foremost a share of
A's mana, of his 'personality', if this modern expression be permitted here. That is why B should return the favour, and present
A with a gift of his.

If he did not make payment in kind, he would deprive A of a
portion of his power. Now, by a continuous process of gift-giving,
structured of course in ritual patterns, power will keep flowing
through the community, as a kind of magico-religious currency,
and it will thus not grow stale. It is certainly in this perspective
that one should view such an astonishing ritual as the 'potlatch'.

Ceremonial folly is, next to gift-giving and various shamanistic
rituals (which cannot be discussed here), another technique by
which magico-religious power is kept alive in a ritualized manner.
Within a highly institutionalized and very traditional cultural context the ceremonial clown seems to play, in an intentionally rough
and blasphemous manner, with the sedimented values and norms
of his society. It stands to reason that sexuality, that prime
example of mana in human beings, occupies a very central position
in the ceremonial fool's licence. One can save sexual power by
abstinence in order to release it full blast in war activities (cf.
sexual asceticism of warriors prior to a battle). The release of
sexual power can be ritualized in order to make it subservient to
the well-being of the total community, as in the case of temple
prostitution. It is also canalized in daily social life (cf. marriage
as a sacrament and traditional institution) in order to prevent it
from running rampant. But these processes of institutionalization
run the risk of routinization by which sexual power may gradually
grow stale and lose its vigour. This is prevented by ritualized debauchery, as can be found in the Saturnalia, the Festival of Fools,
and the activities of 'primitive' ceremonial clowns. Sexual taboos
are violated, the most disgusting erotic acts are performed by the
ceremonial fools. They seem to turn upside down all the values
and norms of their society related to sexuality. They in fact seem
to violate all the rules, norms and taboos. The violations are expected, they have to be done. It is ritual behaviour which re-
enacts the aboriginal power that lays at the very foundations of
all institutionalized, traditional routines. Naturally, such licentious
behaviour is not without danger. These fools play with fire. They
open the box of Pandora, and cause a pandemonium in which

human beings begin to lose their human appearance, changing
into animals or demons. However, the ceremonial clown does all
this anonymously and within ritual boundaries. He wears a mask,
is dressed up for the occasion, he performs a magico-religious
ritual.

It is a widespread belief that laughter in the face of Fate causes
prosperity, and that laughter about erotic things promotes fertility. The ceremonial fool makes hideously obscene gestures and
movements. It causes laughter on the part of the beholders. This
laughter too has a ritual significance: the fool and his 'audience'
perform a magical drama in which cosmic energy is unleashed,
albeit in a controlled, because ritualized, manner.

Mircea Eliade argues in various studies that 'primitive' myths
and rituals ought to be seen as repetitions of the creation of the
cosmos by the gods - an event that occurred in 'illo tempore', in
the mythical time prior to the existence of man and cosmos.(48)
That is, in his myths and rituals 'primitive' man transfers himself
to the primeval time prior to history in which he becomes the contemporary of the gods and shares their work of creation. This
again throws light on the eerie behaviour of the ceremonial fool:
he is the representative of the primeval chaos, the 'tohuwabohu'
which existed prior to the creation of the cosmos. The anarchic
behaviour of these ritual clowns demonstrates in a lively manner
what the raw material has been, out of which the gods once created the cosmos, the present order - nature, society, culture. It
is indeed a regression - a mythic 'mimesis' of 'illud tempus'.

One should realize, above all, that the behaviour of these ceremonial fools presents a demonstration: it demonstrates, without
much abstraction, what happens if the human individual decided
to forsake his responsibility towards tradition, to leave the traditional confinement of his society, expressed in values, norms,
ritual rules. He would deteriorate to a urine- and faeces-devouring
monster - a plastic non-entity, a formless, witless, insane mass of
rude energy. Ceremonial folly is like lava - pure energy prior to
creation.

Crumrine makes mention of a cognitive function on the part of
the Capakobam. They demonstrate to their fellow-human beings,
in particular the young, how the structure of social relationship
is constituted, and they do so by showing this structure in terms
of atypical and deviating combinations.(49) I should like to expand
this interpretation a little further: the Capakobam demonstrate to
young and old what reality has been prior to its creation by the
gods, 'in illo tempore', when the cosmos was yet an undifferentiated mass of energy. They warn, at the very same time, that
human beings are in danger of falling back into this very chaos,
should they forsake the norms and values of tradition. As the
women of these Capakobam said, these fools were not really human.
In sum, the debauchery of these ritual fools pumps the aboriginal
vitalistic energy, out of which the gods created the cosmos, 'in
illo tempore', into the highly traditional and solidly institutionalized community. Ceremonial folly is a cosmogonic force. It presents

a powerful counter force against the eternally impending routinization of society's fundamental energy. It is a dangerous activity,
which can only be executed anonymously and ritually. But is is
also a necessary activity, because without it social life would gradually wither away in the routinization which tradition imposes on
it. At the very same time, the behaviour of these revolting fools
has a cognitive and instructive function. It demonstrates, in a
vivid and very concrete manner, what would happen to the participants in society should they decide to abandon their culture, to
throw off the repressive yoke of tradition: they would change into
cultural protoplasm, into witless and revolting monsters. The main
function of ceremonial folly is, therefore, a mythological 'mimesis'.
Here, the regressive thrust of folly has become predominant and
over-arching.

FOOLS IN LEGENDS AND PLAYS

Legends about mythological fools running about wildly, playing
nasty tricks on human beings, behaving generally in a highly
undifferentiated way, occur all over the world. In his introduction
to the Winnebago Trickster Cycle, Paul Radin refers to such legends in ancient Greece, China, Japan and in the ancient semitic
world.(50) The trickster was a familiar legendary figure in Africa
as well, where he figured, as in Ghana, in the form of a spider,(51)
as is also the case in the trickster legends of the Caribbean
islands and of the Sioux Indians.(52) Without substantiating this
remarkable claim, Radin states that the most archaic form of the
trickster is to be found among the legends of the North American
Indians.(53) He recorded and translated the legend cycle on
'Wakdjunkaga', the mythological trickster of the Winnebago Indians,
who incorporated indeed, as we shall see presently, all the trimmings of a magical fool.
  The pre-human, monstrous character of magical folly is clearly
expressed by Wakdjunkaga. The legend cycle describes him as a
creature whose entrails and oversized penis are wrapped around
his trunk with the scrotum on top of it. He acts impulsively without any control, he does not know good or evil, he is not
acquainted with any norms or values, but is yet believed to be the
very origin of all norms and values. It is obvious Wakdjunkaga
represents the primeval chaos out of which the cosmos was created.
This creature, Radin claims, incorporates the vague remembrance
of an archaic time in which there was no differentiation yet between the divine and the non-divine: 'For this period the Trickster
is the symbol. His hunger, his sex, his wandering, these apper-
tain neither to the gods nor to man.'(54)
  In forty-nine episodes this legendary ballad relates the adventures of Wakdjunkaga, i.e. 'the tricky one', the knave, the rogue.
As in most Indian tribes, the highest honour in Winnebago society
is to become a successful warrior. This crucial value is symbolized
in a special war-ritual. The Trickster Cycle begins right from the

start with a satire of this sacred ritual and continues with the
story of Wakdjunkaga having to prepare for a war-party. As head
of the tribe he violates one of the most sacred taboos of the Winnebago: he has sexual intercourse with a girl immediately prior to
the battle. In the succeeding stories he does engage in various
human activities, but he does it all wrong. These legends, Radin
remarks, want to tell us this: 'Here is Wakdjunkaga pretending
to be thoroughly socialized and about to embark on a war-party.
But let me tell you what he really is: an utter fool, a breaker of
the most holy taboos, a destroyer of the most sacred objects.'(55)
He acts like a child. His right arm fights his left arm which is
seriously injured, and he is pushed around like a passive fool:
'My, my! Correctly indeed am I named Foolish One, Trickster!
By calling me thus, they have at last actually turned me into a
Foolish One, a Trickster.'(56) Gradually, however, the trickster
acquires human features. But then, nothing human appears to be
alien to him: he changes his gender from male to female and back
again to male; while female, he marries and begets a child; when
his son has grown up, he leaves his house in order to wander
through the world in peace; he protests loudly against family life
and against the responsibilities of house and family; at the end of
the cycle he becomes a god. In short, Wakdjunkaga has seen it all.
    In his interpretation of this fascinating cycle of legends, Radin
employs the following cliché explanation: 'We have here, in short,
an outlet for voicing a protest against the many, often onerous
obligations connected with the Winnebago social order and their
religion and ritual. Primitive people have wisely devised many
such outlets.'(57) I would rather opt for a more cognitive and
instructive function as point of departure for the explanation of
this magical fool: he symbolizes the primeval chaos and shows the
members of society, in particular the young, what was the nature
of the cauldron from which they emerged, and into which they
can be plunged again. His foolhardy behaviour must have entertained the listeners, but the laughter he raised was neither
innocent nor relaxed. Radin speaks appropriately of 'laughter
tempered by awe'.(58) The story of Wakdjunkaga provides a
glimpse into the vortex of human existence.
    In their valuable comments on this trickster cycle Kerenyi and
Jung refer to similar figures in antiquity and in the Middle
Ages.(59) Kerenyi compares Wakdjunkaga with Heracles and in
particular with Hermes, whereas Jung, as we saw in chapter 2,
likens his folly to the antics performed during the medieval Festival of Fools. In fact, Jung believes that this legendary trickster
represents an archetypal psychic structure of great antiquity. He
is 'a faithful copy of an absolutely undifferentiated human consciousness, corresponding to a psyche that has hardly left the
animal level.'(60) Wakdjunkaga, in other words, symbolizes in an
exemplary manner the regressive thrust of magical folly. The
magical fool appears also in oriental theatre plays, notably in
ancient Indian plays and in the Indonesian shadow play, called
the 'wagang'. I shall briefly discuss both, without pretending to
be in any way exhaustive.

In various theatre plays, the texts of which have been saved,
we find in India the role of a fool - the 'vidûsaka' - who follows
the king in everything, is tied to him in a peculiar bond of friendship, and acts in general as a silly jester. However, he is not a
parasite and he is not, in terms of social class, marginal. The
vidûsaka belongs to the brahman caste, although he is a ridiculous
brahmin. Often he is referred to as 'brahmabandhu', which means
literally 'lousy brahmin'.(61) He is the laughing-stock of everyone because he is ugly like an ape and very silly - the exact
opposite of the ascetic and spiritually refined, superior brahmin.
His egoism, clumsiness, cowardice, and silly vanity constantly
underline his foolhardy nature.(62) But he is, above all, a colos-
sal glutton. Says Huizinga:

> Naturally, in a world in which philosophy and asceticism on
> the one hand and fine sentimentality on the other had pene-
> trated into the spirit of poetry, the jovial passion for gluttony
> appeared as being very ridiculous. The vidûsaka does not
> know anything that transcends the ordinary, and for his
> sublimest thoughts he draws his images from the area of
> food.(63)

This is why he is not concerned with heaven: 'there one cannot
eat and drink,' he sighs in one of the plays, 'but just stare like
a fish.'(64) Huizinga does not hesitate to call him, anachronistic-
ally, 'a complete bourgeois'.(65) These character traits and his
silly antics on the stage, combined with the fact that he usually
speaks pakrit rather than brahman sanskrit, made him a very popular figure.
   Huizinga emphasizes the looking-glass nature of the vidûsaka -
he is 'a counter-stroke of the spirit of the play itself; the loftiness
of the sentiments comes out the more strikingly by the contrast of
his vulgarity.'(66) In one of the plays he says of himself: 'in me
brahmin everything turns the other way about, like the image in
a looking-glass, left to right and right to left.'(67)
   Kuiper expands this point even further in his analysis of the
vidûsaka role. He does not believe that the vidûsaka was merely a
buffoon whose function it was to enliven the play and to raise
laughter. Kuiper also takes exception to the common interpretation among specialists of the subject that this role was taken
over into sanskrit plays from an ancient, popular, pakrit theatre.
He also rejects the idea that the role was taken from real life,
e.g. from the courts, where allegedly court fools were at work.
He rather interprets the vidûsaka as a very ancient mythological
figure, taken over from the cosmogonic myths of Vedic religion.
In fact, he is the impersonation of Varuna, who in Vedic religion
was the counterpart of Indra, the Creator. Varuna represents
together with the Asuras, the primordial reality of an undifferentiated chaos - the lord of the primeval waters and of the nether-
world. Just as the nayaka is the theatre role which represented
Indra, the vidûsaka, as its mirror-image, impersonates Varuna.

The nayaka is the hero, the vidûsaka the anti-hero - the mythological fool. This fool, in sum, cannot be understood adequately
if one fails to understand the nature of Varuna.
They belong to 'the other side of reality' which can only be
shown and enacted in a reversed manner. Says Kuiper:

> If the theory that at the beginning of every new year Indra had
> to re-enact his cosmogonical flight is correct, it follows that
> not only the powers of Chaos (the *asura adevah*) temporarily
> returned into this world from the place to which they had
> fled after their defeat, but that also Varuna in this critical
> period must have reassumed his Asura-character of the
> primeval world. This means that at that time of the year he
> was not a *Deva asura* but a dangerous Asura *tout court*. He
> must have been dreaded all the more as also his introduction
> into the world of the cosmos apparently did not result in an
> unambiguous position. Even in sources as late as the
> Mahabharata there are indications to show that Varuna,
> although a god of this organized world, continued to maintain
> secret relations with the suppressed demons and the 'night-
> side' of this world. His majestic character too, was based
> upon his partly transcending the boundaries of the organized
> cosmos.(68)

Thus the vidûsaka is more than a laughter-provoking silly buffoon. Like the ceremonial clown, discussed in the previous sect-
ions, he impersonates the aboriginal forces out of which - once
upon a time 'in illo tempore' - the organized world, the cosmos, was
created. The same metaphysical depth and profundity can be
found in Semar, the clown of the Indonesian shadow-puppet
theatre, the 'wajang'.
Geertz, who gives a brief but lively description of the wajang,
relates that its dramatized stories have mostly been taken from the
Indian epic Mahabharata. In these stories, whose performance
lasts usually a whole night, the cosmic struggle between three
major groups of character is shown: (a) the gods and goddesses,
led by Siva and his wife Durga; (b) the kings and nobles, believed to be the ancestors of the Javanese, and a Javanese addition
to the original Hindu cast; (c) the low clowns Semar, Patruk and
Garèng. They are the companions of the Pendawas, who form an
important group within the nobility. Semar is the father of the
other two clowns and the brother of Siva. He is therefore a god,
but carries at the very same time many human features. He is,
according to Geertz, 'a gross and clumsy fool' and probably the
very centre of the whole wajang cast.
Next to talking episodes in which two groups of nobles discuss
their differences, and to the episodes, in which these differences
are fought out in a less diplomatic manner, there are the slapstick
comic scenes. In these scenes the clowns mock not only the dram-
atis personae, the nobles in the first place, but also individuals
in the audience, in particular those holding powerful office. Like

Huizinga, Geertz draws a comparison with Shakespeare:

> The long formal scenes in the courts with the messengers
> coming and going, interspersed with short, breathless
> transitional scenes in the woods or along the road, the
> double plot, the clowns speaking a rough language full of
> worldy-wise ethics, caricaturing the forms of action of the
> great nobles, who speak an elevated language full of
> apostrophes to honor, justice, and duty, the final war,
> which like those at Shrewsbury and Agincourt, leaves the
> vanquished beaten but still noble – all these suggest Shake-
> speare's historical dramas.(69)

He then continues to stress the difference: Elizabethan plays
occur within a distinct historical and sociological setting, whereas
the wajang as a mythological drama focuses primarily on metaphysical and psychological issues. In Semar many opposites meet,
says Geertz. He is the enchanting fool who reminds his audience
of their regressive nature:

> Like Falstaff, Semar is a symbolic father to the play's heroes.
> Like Falstaff, he is fat, funny, and worldly-wise, and like
> Falstaff, he seems to provide in his vigorous amoralism a
> general criticism of the very values the drama affirms. Both
> figures, perhaps, provide a reminder that, despite over-
> proud assertions to the contrary by religious fanatics, and
> moral absolutists, no completely adequate and comprehensive
> human world view is possible, and behind all the pretense to
> absolute and ultimate knowledge, the sense for the irration-
> ality of human life, for the fact that it is unlimitable, remains.
> Semar reminds the noble and refined Pendawas of their own
> humble, animal origins. He resists any attempt to turn human
> beings into gods and to end the world of natural contingency
> by a flight to the divine world of absolute order, a final stil-
> ling of the eternal psychological-metaphysical struggle.(70)

FOLLY IN AN ENCHANTED GARDEN

The world was an enchanted garden to men and women of traditional societies. In and of itself reality presented a borderless
field of contingencies and surprises which traditional people
enveloped carefully with enchanting notions and rituals of a mythological and profoundly metaphysical nature. That is, to these
people reality was not a field of exploration in which chances,
eventualities and possibilities were scientifically calculated and
technologically controlled. This reality was not viewed in terms of
constructibility and calculability, entered into with cocksure confidence and self-reliance, as we moderns do. On the contrary,
reality – i.e. nature, society, culture, history – was rather
experienced as being essentially unpredictable and very hazardous –

a cosmos which once emerged from and remained ever since surrounded by chaos. If traditional men and women would begin to
work on reality - which all human beings have to in order to
survive - they would always do so with great circumspection and
care, i.e. with the help of metaphysical-mythological notions and
of magical-ritual techniques (cf. the taboo). Despite the massive
routinization brought about by the predominance of tradition, the
contingency of reality was never radically removed by traditional
men and women, as has happened in modern science and technology. They wrapped it up in enchanting myths and rituals.

It is a typically modern prejudice to believe that this enchanted
garden was devoid of any trace of rationality. Not only ancient
Greek philosophy but also the great world religions have produced
systems of thought which carried vast amounts of substantial
rationality, while magic in all its appearances and realizations had
always been typical for its functional rationality. However, this
rationality remained at all times grounded in enchantment. Only
after science, technology and bureaucracy began to develop into
the powerful superstructure of modern life, casting away the
enchanting veils of religion and magic, rationality managed to
emancipate itself from this very enchantment, and grow into the
predominant force of modernity.

Traditional folly, as we have described and interpreted it in
this and the previous chapters, is an essential component of the
enchanted garden. In a world without enchantment, i.e. in a
radically rationalized world, folly is doomed to wither away. The
modern child, not yet fully disenchanted, still living in a mysterious world, is able to enjoy the enchanting performance of the
circus clown. He is subjected (eagerly lets himself be subjected)
to the awe-inspiring, eerie, silly, laughable antics of this weirdly
dressed-up and disfigured creature. To the modern child, the
clown is the only adult representative of their enchanted garden,
but rational adults have lost the capacity to experience such
emotions. They watch the performance of a Popov or a Charlie
Rivel - the last representatives of a great tradition of clowning -
and may at the most faintly recognize in their own amusement
some deeply hidden, residual remnants of a metaphysical experience. The clown's antics seem to convey a message which can
no longer be heard and understood in modernity. Fully modernized
individuals live in a radically disenchanted world, an 'abstract
society'. To them reality is not a mysterious garden with hidden
corners and unsuspected creatures, but a field of calculation and
operation - the reality of science, technology, economics and politics. In this world there is no place for traditional fools.

A disquieting thought lingers on. Modern society is in many respects the very opposite of traditional society. If the latter is
reflected contrariwise by its fools, we moderns should be able to
recognize features in these fools that may strike us as peculiarly
'modern' - their materialism, their blatant lack of values and
morals, of metaphysical sense and loyalty. In fact, the only

distinguishing mark seems to be their total immersion in non-rationality. Our rationalism helps us to keep up a front. Those fools were not interested in any make-believe, except the ultimate make-believe of their looking-glass reality.

There is a second disquieting thought which concerns the vast gap between us and these traditional fools. Although themselves devoid of any metaphysical sense, these fools served profound, metaphysical purposes. These were very much in demand, because the society they lived in yearned for such redeeming functions. Our disenchanted 'abstract' society has lost all metaphysical sense and our rationality, put to use in the sciences, technology and bureaucracy, possesses hardly a metaphysically redeeming quality.

In conclusion to his discussion of the wajang clowns Geertz wrote: 'But whether in the form of a trickster, a clown, a belief in witchcraft, or a concept of original sin, the presence of such a symbolic reminder of the hollowness of human pretensions to religious or moral infallibility is perhaps the surest sign of spiritual maturity.'(71) Rational Man, imbued with the arrogance of the Enlightenment, is inclined to label traditional folly as silly, childish, immature behaviour. Our present journey through folly's looking-glass reality has, I believe, firmly falsified this prejudice. It has established the truth of Geertz's perceptive remark.

Meanwhile, the enchanted garden has by now been invaded massively by modernization. The ceremonial fools have largely become figures of history, like the popular fools and the court fools of medieval and early-modern Europe. As early as 1917, Elsie C. Parsons wrote already about the decay of ceremonialism among the Zuni whom she knew so intimately. It became in particular difficult to find qualified impersonators. Modernity had begun to compete with magical beliefs and practices. Medical care, schools, and all kinds of modern technology had made these beliefs and practices more and more obsolete:

> The great dam at Black Rock and the irrigation ditches
> suggest silently but potently that the fall of rain and snow,
> the supreme object of all ceremonies, is not absolutely
> essential to fertility. ... In the annual impersonation of
> sacred personages in general it is becoming more and more
> difficult to secure personators.(72)

5 CONCLUSION:
folly and modernity

In accordance with some main lines of thought in so-called 'classic' social theory, I distinguished in the first chapter two dimensions of modernization: structural differentiation and generalization of values and meanings. In order to conceptualize the dynamics within the phenomenon of folly, I distinguished in the same chapter two thrusts, the 'regressive' and the 'progressive' thrusts. The regressive thrust, I argued, was very obvious in the case of the magical fool (cf. chapter 4) but could also be observed in medieval folly (cf. chapter 2). The progressive thrust which I demonstrated in the case of the court fool in the era of absolutism (cf. chapter 3), coincides with the process of modernization, that is, with structural differentiation and the generalization of meanings and values. Accordingly, regression in folly coincides with structural de-differentiation and with a fundamentalization of values and meanings.

In conclusion to this book, I shall argue that the generalization of folly in modern society has led to a renewed regressive thrust. That is, the values and meanings of traditional folly have gradually spread throughout modern society, taking leave, so to speak, of its structurally differentiated roles, penetrating into socio-cultural life as a blot of oil that spreads out over water and loses its power to burn. Folly has become a general, opaque, vague and free-floating phenomenon. As such it shares the main feature of contemporary 'abstract society', namely a general inflation of meanings and values.(1) As can be seen in such fields as religion and the arts, this generalization may turn about as in a cultural deflation. In that case, meanings, values, and their related experiences grow increasingly fundamentalistic, simplistic, crass, physically concrete. This is a regressive thrust which sets in when values and meanings have become too abstract to relate to, i.e. when generalization has developed beyond the capacity of human beings to adapt to it existentially. In the case of folly, this regression entails a return to traditional folly, although within the framework of modern society it will hardly be able to reassume the functions traditional folly exerted in pre-modern societies. In fact, it can be argued that the functions of this re-emerged folly are rather contrary to those of traditional folly, and generally quite destructive in potentiality.

I shall furthermore argue that a similar regression has set in on the level of structural differentiation, leading up to a structural de-differentiation which will remind us once more of traditional folly.

Before I discuss the dynamics of progression and regression in modern folly, I have to issue a warning. Throughout this book I have tried to use the concepts of folly and fool as technical terms, abstaining from the natural inclination to apply them in the manner of value-judgments. In other words, in this book a fool is primarily a historical phenomenon and not a derogatory label. However, the moment we begin to speak about folly in contemporary society, it becomes harder to maintain this technical and morally neutral use of the concepts. In fact, one is strongly exposed to the seduction to apply the notion of folly in a derogatory manner, labelling negatively those phenomena of modernity with which one is at odds philosophically, religiously, politically, or in any other ideological manner. This problem was the more pressing for myself, since I shall apply the notion of folly to certain dimensions of modernity to which my own norms and values object rather strongly. Yet, throughout the following argument I have made an honest attempt to use the concepts of folly and fool in the historical and technical sense in which I applied them before. Moreover, if I am worried about renewed regressive folly in modern society, it is not folly in itself which worries me, because it could assume existentially redeeming functions, as was demonstrated by traditional fools in pre-modern societies. What worries me is rather the fact that the renewed regressive thrust of modern, generalized folly lacks any clear institutional setting and grounding. It floats freely and quite ambiguously on uncommitted emotions. As such, this 'modern' regressive folly, gyrating in gnostic subjectivism, cannot contribute to man's social and cultural life. On the contrary, I am convinced that in the long run the effects of this regressive and subjectivist folly will be destructive to social and cultural life. Thus, if I am concerned about the existence of folly in modernity, this should not be seen in the facile and rather petty-bourgeois way – e.g. as if I were 'against' folly and fools, like a modern, sociological Sebastian Brant, labelling as foolish those phenomena in modernity which I happen to reject morally. On the contrary, what worries me rather is the fact that contemporary folly tends to grow 'deflationary' and regressive, without any clear ties to tradition and to the institutions. Traditional folly was a looking-glass of social reality not an exercise in emotional expressionism. Traditional fools were immoralists or even amoralists; they were ambiguous and cynical. But they were so in traditionally expected performances, in which reality was reflected contrariwise for very specific, social and existential reasons. Modern regressive folly has the tendency instead to gyrate without institutional control in morally ambiguous subjectivism, catering more to the emotional desires of its individual adherents than to the social and cultural life at large. In Durkheimean terms, such a force is, in the long run, doomed to be anomic.

For the sake of clarity, I shall use the interpretive scheme represented diagrammatically in Figure 5.1 in the further elaboration of this theme. This interpretive scheme is applicable to modernity in general and indicates in an abstract way the dynamics of

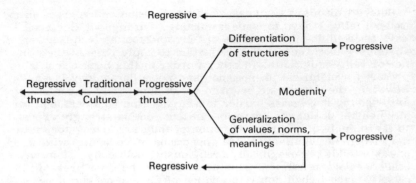

Figure 5.1

'modernization' and 'de-modernization'. The regressive movement
which deviates from the progressive differentiation is an instance
of 'structural de-modernization' which can be observed clearly in
various protests against specialization and professionalization and
in the political call for de-centralization. Regression in generalization is an instance of 'cultural de-modernization' and can be
witnessed clearly in religious fundamentalism or political-ideological
fanaticism. The scheme is applicable to our present discussion on
folly in modernity.
   De-modernization is characterized predominantly by subjectivism and anti-institutionalism - i.e. by attitudes which put a
much higher existential premium on the bodily and psychic experience of emotions than on the social need for institutional order.
The latter is readily identified with 'alienation', without taking
into account that the threat of 'anomie' is inherent in any withdrawal from the reality of traditional institutions to the realm of
emotional experiences and physical impulses. One should realize,
as I have argued elsewhere, that this 'expressionism' is a function
of a fully modernized society, which I called an 'abstract society'.
   As we have seen in chapter 3, traditional folly developed into a
very specific role and position in the case of the court jester. In
fact, due to absolutist demands the court fool became a rather
influential figure at court, holder of an office with its own rights
and duties. This very differentiation reached a level on which the
court fool was actually no longer a fool in the traditional sense of
the word. As a result, he vanished from history even before the
very institution he lived on parasitically, the absolutist monarchy,
declined and finally collapsed. In short, the position of the court
fool had differentiated (modernized) to such an extent that he
changed his foolish nature radically and then became superfluous.
Meanwhile, the role of fool developed further, in particular on the
stage (cf. Shakespeare, commedia dell'arte, the modern comedian,
etc.) and in the circus (cf. the clown). As Welsford has argued,
the fool modernized into a literary figure with some social signif-

icance but without the functions of traditional fools.(2) One
should see the bourgeoisification of the fool, as discussed at the
end of chapter 3, in the same light. Meanwhile, traditional folly
differentiated yet in quite a different direction also. From the
sixteenth century on, fools became people to be cared for in
specialized institutions. This structural development continued up
till our own age. In this line of development, the fool has become
either a simpleton to be cared for by social workers, economically
sustained by the provisions of the welfare state, or a mental
patient to be taken care of by psychiatrists and specialized nurses
in specialized asylums. Due to these structural differentiations,
folly was segregated from daily social life, from the core of social
and cultural affairs - banned, so to say, to the outskirts of the
modern social structure. Structural differentiation, in this case,
became structural segregation.

However, in accordance with a general protest against abstract
society, in which the far-advanced disenchantment and rationalization of modernity is rejected, a regressive movement has set in
within this very differentiation of folly. The most obvious symptom
of this renewed regression within the structural differentiation of
folly is the rather complex phenomenon of so-called 'anti-
psychiatry'. It is an attempt to bring the mental patient back to
the mainstream of social life, and to liberate him from the entangle-
ment in the webs of psychiatric professionalization. Modern pro-
fessionalism with its far-advanced specialization is clearly part of
the progressive structural differentiation. Therefore, any attempt
at de-professionalization in a particular field of action can be
viewed as part of a regressive movement within the structural
component. This is certainly the case with contemporary experiments within the field of psychiatry and psychiatric care which
attempt to curb professionalization. In terms of our discussion,
such experiments try indeed to make fools again out of mental
patients, and to take care of them within, not outside, the structures of daily social life, as was the case in medieval times. Not
amazingly, the Belgian village of Geel, discussed in chapter 2,
draws renewed attention, because there mental patients have been
treated throughout the ages until today, like the traditional fools
with a place in normal social life.

A similar development can be observed in the cultural components of generalization. While traditional folly differentiated in
specific social structures (the theatre, the circus, the asylum), it
began to generalize as to values and meanings, spreading out far
beyond these structural niches, causing the emergence of an
opaque and free-floating kind of folly - hardly discernible, yet
sociologically interpretable. As had happened to the family ('familism'), religion ('civil religion'), education ('permanent education'),
and other socio-cultural phenomena, folly became a general feature
of modernity to the very same extent that it became structurally
differentiated. Wherever structural differentiation occurs as a
rational division of labour, values and meanings will spread out
beyond these structural niches as in an 'inflationary' development.

Values, meanings, norms and motives become hazy, interchangeable, morally unbinding. There are in modern society, as W. I. Thomas once observed, many definitions of the situation but none of them is binding. It led to an 'abstract society' in which well-nigh nothing seems to provide cognitive and emotive security anymore, except the clichés.(3) Apart from the lack of socio-cultural functions, this is indeed a perfect climate for fools. Or in terms of Max Weber's brand of cultural sociology, there is a definite 'elective affinity' between the 'abstract society', on the one hand, and the reign of folly, on the other - except, it must be repeated, for the lack of clearly defined institutional ties and socio-cultural functions on the part of this modern brand of folly.

Traditional fools, as we saw recurrently, are quite erratic in their behaviour. They are not guided by any firm principles, they are not loyal to any particular worldview and ethos, they are not to be held responsible for the things they say, do, think, or feel. If these fools have any worldview and ethos at all they are always tied contrariwise to the worldview and ethos of the people who solicit their foolish performances. Within the boundaries of reality, which they carefully maintain as they are essentially parasites dependent on symbiosis, traditional fools seem to hold up a looking-glass in which this very reality is shown in reverse. At the same time, these fools impersonate the awe-inspiring force of pure energy, the 'tohuwabohu' from which, in a mythological time (Eliade: 'illus tempus'), the organized cosmos arose. In this regressive thrust, traditional fools were neither human nor divine, nor animal. They impersonated undifferentiated monsters which acted impulsively, erratically, demonstrating to the beholders what they themselves once have been 'in illo tempore' prior to the emergence of cultural norms and taboos, of the institutions and their inherent, sacred tradition.

In modernity, emotions, thoughts, and acts have a similar tendency to be erratic, anti-traditional, anti-institutional, lacking loyalty and responsibility. Many a modern individual, protesting in words, thoughts or acts against the strictures of an over-rationalized, 'abstract' society is indeed a foolish contrary. Yet, this moody anti-institutionalism has not been dictated by tradition itself, as in the case of traditional folly.(4) On the contrary, it is anti-traditional, subjectivistic and individualistic - part of the anomic 'cult of the individual' (Durkheim), of the modern 'fall of public man' (Sennett), of a pervasive modern 'culture of narcissism' (Lasch).(5) Not being existentially tied to any traditional and institutional framework, the modern 'homme révolté' rebels rather aimlessly as in a moody and subjectivistic protest. His behaviour does resemble traditional folly in several respects, except for the crucial fact that it is really anomic whereas the anomie of the traditional fool was staged. The latter's behaviour was indeed a cultural imperative. Incidentally, we might have found the source of the very common but false interpretation of traditional folly as a covert rebellion against a repressive status quo: it is a rather simplistic projection of the modern anti-institutional mood on traditional folly.

Yet traditional fools were not merely the ideologues of their
societies either. They cannot be simply viewed as the defenders
of a particular status quo. Theirs was a critical function, but
their criticism was of a metaphysical, rather than socio-political,
nature. These fools, as we have seen, offered a glimpse into the
vortex of human existence by erecting an awe-inspiring, looking-
glass reality which showed to their contemporaries who they could
become, should they abandon the values, norms and meanings of
their tradition. It showed at the same time what they had been
prior to the emergence of the cosmos - undifferentiated protoplasm, pure energy, cultural lava, to be re-enacted by these
fools for the sake of cultural revitalization. These vivid, looking-
glass images withered away when the world-disenchanted and
modern men and women began to lose all sense of and appetite for
metaphysics.

Yet, although for the most part divested of these metaphysical
functions, folly is still present in modernity as an opaque yet
penetrating phenomenon which influences men and women unob-
trusively far outside the structural niches to which it became
restricted in the process of modernization, namely the theatre,
the circus and the asylum. Generalized folly is as such hard to
point at empirically. Modern 'abstract' society has created a cultural climate in which 'everything goes'. It is a climate, as I
argued in chapter 1 (see p. 22), in which not only the values,
norms and meanings of the family, the law, religion and education
have generalized as in an inflationary process, but also those of
folly! However, if we want to indicate this kind of generalized
folly in modernity more concretely, we probably have to look for
it primarily in the areas of humour and laughter. In our humour-
ous exchange of jokes and in the laughter they provoke, we often
play the fool and construct a sort of looking-glass reality which,
however, lasts only for the duration of the laughter. In any case,
in these jokes of ours, traditional folly has been preserved -
albeit in a very generalized manner. In fact, in a very few of
them even the latter's metaphysical dimensions have survived the
onslaught of modernization.(6)

However, as to the cultural component of generalization a renewed regressive thrust might be observed, rendering folly much
less opaque and exclusive. This was clearly the case, for example,
in the 1960s, among the representatives of the so-called youth
culture. The hippies of America, characteristically called (flower)
children - like the 'enfants' of some French Joyous Societies, and
the provos of the Netherlands who like the goliards, or like Till
Eulenspiegel played irreverent pranks on the powers that be -
were fools in well-nigh every respect, except for their blatant
need of self-expression. Much of the behaviour of so-called
'encounter groups', to give another example, reminds the historically aware observer of traditional folly: a premium on impulsive,
non-rational thoughts, acts and feelings, rejection of any kind of
rational control, ongoing search for emotionally gratifying enchantments, etc. But once more, this behaviour too is predominantly

subjectivistic and anti-institutional while it aims primarily at the gratification of individual emotional demands. In sum, this regressive fundamentalization will yield a kind of folly that will resemble its traditional pendant in almost every respect, except one: it is doomed to remain separated from any structural context and thus to float about freely as an uncontrolled and uncontrollable mass of cognitive and emotive energy. Any 'primitive' would warn us against such a situation, because, if not checked ceremonially, he would say, the fool is likely to open a Pandora's box which nobody can keep under control. Durkheim would have argued likewise, although in more 'rational' terms, and spoken of the dangers of anomie. Indeed, folly is an anomic force and if it is not staged ceremonially one may take great risks. But since most regressive folly these days is couched in anti-institutionalism, such a ceremonial staging will remain highly unlikely. It is much more likely that a massive resurgence of folly will eventually be put under control by the use of force.

But there is another possibility still. At this point, someone like Max Weber would probably comment that the magical power of folly, which was formerly legitimated through tradition and/or charisma, can in modern society not be legitimated in the way power is predominantly legitimated in this type of society, namely legally and rationally (bureaucratically). In the second half of the 1960s the city of Vancouver allegedly employed a town fool, financed with the help of a grant from the Canada Council. He was doomed to wander around through this metropolis like a living fossil, looked at with amusement or anger, but devoid of any socio-cultural and metaphysical function. Arguing in the Weberean vein, one must draw the conclusion that in modernity regressive folly is unlikely to grow into a sizeable anomic force. It is much more likely that it will remain marginal – a curious phenomenon without any observable, real effect.

POSTSCRIPT:

Peppi revisited

Our journey through folly's reversed world began with the
encounter I had in Vienna with Peppi. As I reported in the Preface, I felt ill-at-ease with the man. Now that our journey is
completed, I begin to feel more comfortable, because I think that
I have begun to grasp this fool's essence. One thing is definitely
clear, psychiatry would not have been of much help. A historical-
sociological analysis was needed to unveil the mystery that surrounded this fool. But at the very same time, the analysis was
also very revealing with regard to my own supposed rationality.

At the end of this journey through the looking-glass, we should
once more return to Peppi and complete the picture that I started
to paint in the Preface. To this end, I asked my wife, Angelika
E. Dissmann, to return to Vienna in order to collect as much bio-
graphical data on Peppi as she could. She went to the scene of
her childhood and interviewed informally and semi-casually a few
people who had known this fool during various stages of his life.
They would not have talked freely about him to me, certainly not
if they knew that I was preparing a book on 'Narren'. They would
have coloured their stories and distorted their memories. My wife
pretended nostalgia, the desire to collect childhood memories after
having been 'away from home' for so many years. Although she
does in no way suffer from such a romantic yearning for the past,
she pretented nostalgia in order to lead her informants unob-
trusively from general childhood memories to Peppi in particular.

Next to the valuable data she thus collected, which will be
reported briefly in the remainder of this Postscript, she discovered a most peculiar thing which can be understood better now
that the book is completed: her informants began to recollect facts
about Peppi but moved unconsciously from his life to their own
lives, telling sometimes the most intimate stories about themselves,
while referring all the time to the fool. It was as if these fool's
stories offered them a welcome opportunity, yes, a language, to
speak about themselves - indeed, this is the process referred to
in the subtitle of this book, but then on the level of common sense.

From a handful of informants two ladies in particular were very
resourceful: Mrs K., the former janitor of the apartment building
in which Peppi spent his life, who assumed the role of guardian
after his mother had died, and the owner of the dogs' trimming shop
in the court of the apartment building of my parents-in-law in
the centre of Vienna. Peppi used to frequent this shop, and
'Tante Anna', as the lady was referred to by the children in the
neighbourhood, knew very well how to handle the fool.

My wife's relatives were of little help, as they simply took
Peppi for granted, like they had taken Pit, the family spaniel,
for granted. They failed to understand my and my wife's interest
in 'diesen Narr'. Peppi's own relatives also could not be of any
help. His father died during Peppi's early childhood when 53
years old. His mother passed away a few years before his own
death in 1978. His only brother, who had kept an eye on him from
a distance, was married and had a job as an engineer. He saw
Peppi as a stain on the petit-bourgeois reputation of the family,
in which he was strongly influenced by his sister and his wife.
The two ladies preferred to deny Peppi's existence - he was such
a shame to them. Shortly after Peppi's death, his brother, at 53
years of age, drove to his country house outside Vienna and com-
mitted suicide. His widow refused to talk to my wife, and his
sister was likewise not available for an interview. There simply
was no need, they both stated tersely, to recollect memories about
this stupid fool. After his death, they went to his apartment and
destroyed all the photographs taken of him. The lady janitor kept
one in a drawer secretly and showed it to my wife.

Peppi was born on 18 August 1925. In those years this date was
still commemorated as the birthday of the last Austrian emperor.
Maybe it testified to the high expectations his parents had of
their newly born son that they gave him this emperor's first names
at his baptism: Franz Joseph.
Both Peppi's parents at that time worked at 'Steinhof', the
asylum for the mentally ill outside Vienna. They were not regis-
tered nurses though, but assistants in the lower echelons of the
staff. Peppi's father died in the early 1930s. His brother and sister both moved up socially from their parents' solidly lower-middle-
class station in society. The brother became an engineer in the
Austrian railroad system, and his sister married an engineer.
Very little is known about Peppi's youth and adolescence. He
grew up in a peaceful, petit-bourgeois family, and attended primary school. The latter fact came out quite unexpectedly after the
death of his mother, in 1973, when he had to live on his own in
his parents' small apartment. Since he was a fool, everyone had
assumed him to be rather witless and illiterate. Now Mrs K. discovered, much to her surprise, that he not only kept the apartment tidy and clean - which was to her bourgeois liking - but also
that he carefully kept a financial record of his modest earnings
and equally modest expenses. He could obviously read and write,
and was able to add, deduct and multiply on a modest scale.
As to Peppi's folly, there are in general two theories. The sophisticated explanation is medical. Supposedly he caught meningitis
in his early childhood and suffered some minor brain damage
therefrom. It was, however, not possible to corroborate this
modern rational diagnosis, as medical records were not available.
Much more colourful and enchanting, however, is the explanation
given by common people. Mrs K. conveyed this theory: when preg-
nant with him, Peppi's mother was once attacked by an 'Irre', a

patient, at 'Steinhof', and thus gave birth to a fool some months later. Sociologically far more relevant, however, is the following chain of events which throws an interesting light on the nature of Peppi's folly. This nature, it will become clear, was not so much congenital as sociological!

Peppi was, this much can be stated with certainty, somewhat strange. He did attend at least some grades of primary school and was certainly not a clearcut psychiatric case. Thus, he was in a way mentally somewhat disabled, but had it not been for the events I shall relate now, he would probably have been trained in some simple skill and become a reliable part of the lower levels of the production process, either as a blue- or white-collar worker.

As in the case of millions of individuals, the Nazi holocaust interfered in Peppi's biography in a rather dramatic way. Shortly before the outbreak of the Second World War, the Nazis put him to work as a labourer in a quarry outside Vienna. He was of an exceedingly strong and bulky physique and thus obviously deemed to be perfect for this hard and degrading slave-labour. Each morning his mother would deliver him at the stone pit, but Peppi simply refused to toil as a convict. Quite regularly, when his mother left him at his work and came back home, she would find her son in front of the apartment door again. She never found out how he managed to escape the quarry and be back home before her. Meanwhile, she fully realized the danger of the situation, because she knew from her experience at 'Steinhof' that the Nazis had already begun with the liquidation of the mentally ill. In order to save the endangered life of her son, she did something extraordinary. She took on for herself the role of a poor, lower-class widow, and, for her son, the role of innocent fool. When she realized that she could not force Peppi to work at the quarry, she went to the Nazi district officer in her neighbourhood and told him that she needed her physically very strong son in order to help her out at home and in her job. She had one crippled arm due to a birth defect and, for the first time in her life, she played out this fact. At the same time she began to dress shabbily, and took up a job in the inner city as a cleaning woman for the janitors of large, upper-middle-class apartment buildings. Her main and rather wearisome task was to clean the large, stone staircases of these buildings. She took Peppi with her on the job and put him in a shapeless cover-all, held together with a large cord around his big belly. She enacted the part of an old, needy widow who gratefully accepted the handouts given to her by the people who pitied her - old clothes and pieces of furniture which, incidentally, were all found unused in her basement after she died in 1973. In private, mother and son behaved and were dressed like 'normal' bourgeois people, but in public they were the lower-class, shabby, somewhat pathetic odd couple - a hard-working, poor widow with her innocent son, the fool. It carried Peppi through the Nazi nightmare.

After the war, Vienna was divided into various quarters, ruled

respectively by the British, the French, the Americans and the
Russians, except for the inner city, the 'erste Bezirk', where
the four occupation forces changed command every three months.
This situation lasted till 1955 when Austria acquired its present
(neutral) autonomy.

In 1946 Peppi was involved in a nasty little incident which went
into the police records as the provocation of a police officer. The
precise nature of the incident is not known and it is also not
known under which occupying force this event took place. It
might have been the Russians, because Peppi always liked the
British and Americans very much (he even knew some English),
stood indifferent towards the French, but simply dreaded the
Russians. In any case, his mother received a stern warning to
take better care of her son and this must have inspired her to
maintain the roles she had devised for herself and her son during
the war.

Then, in September 1947, Peppi was arrested for unruly behaviour and sent to 'Steinhof', probably for observation. Apparently some people in the city had made fun of him, taken him to a
bar and offered him liquor to drink which he had never touched
before. He reacted badly to alcohol and he must have caused quite
some commotion before the police got hold of him. To both the
mother and the son this event was extremely traumatic. The hospitalization in 'Steinhof' in particular came as a severe shock,
because now the fool Peppi was defined as 'mad', as a 'mental
patient'. Ever after, his mother kept him under very strict and
stern control. In fact, she was until her death very tough with
him and kept him in the role of fool by the use of all sorts of
threats.

Peppi was released again in October 1948 and never again came
in touch with the law. Shortly after, his mother requested my
parents-in-law and another upper-middle-class family in the same
apartment building to take up Peppi as a domestic helpout for the
heavy chores, such as cleaning the many flights of staircases,
carrying up heavy coal bins from the cellar of the building to the
apartment, dusting the furniture, running errands, etc. He used
to come in early in the morning and leave in the late afternoon for
almost thirty years.

Initially, he spoke in a very high, childish tone which my wife's
mother found too strenuous to put up with. After a few months of
training, he spoke in a 'normal' voice, at least when he worked in
my in-laws' apartment. He did his very best to behave 'correctly'
towards the 'Herrschaften', as his mother had obviously implored
him to do. But he did so as a fool. For instance, until the very
end of his life he would intersperse his sentences and gestures
with a repetitive 'bitte-danke, danke-bitte' ('please-thanks,
thanks-please'). If a question was addressed to him to which he
did not want to respond, he simply rattled 'bitte-danke, danke-
bitte, bitte-danke, danke-bitte'. It was, as I have observed myself, a very successful 'instant shut-up'.

It was also curious - certainly if seen in the light of the history of traditional folly - that he ate with a spoon only, or preferably with his hands. But Mrs K. discovered after his mother's death that he could eat perfectly 'normally' with knife and fork. More than once he asked my mother-in-law to take him in the house for days and nights, perhaps because he found his mother too stern. He would be very happy, he said, to sleep together with Pit, the family spaniel, under the table.

He would never touch alcoholic beverages, but he did smoke a cigarette once in a while. He always savoured his cigarettes in front of a mirror, staring at the smoke around his silly face with obvious fascination. Asked why he did this, he answered: 'I want to see where precisely the smoke is going.'

Peppi was eager to meet other people, just because he was a very curious fellow, and also because he simply liked to draw attention. When there was a social call on the family, he would always find an excuse to knock at the door and interrupt the conversation with many 'bitte-danke, danke-bittes'. Usually, he asked a silly question or made a silly, superfluous remark. In such cases, one did wisely not to talk down to him or ridicule him in front of the visitors, because that always inspired him to take revenge. My mother-in-law was very good at handling him. If he intruded on the company she entertained, she would tell her amazed, amused or sometimes shocked visitors that this was 'our dear, loyal Peppi', or 'our good old Pepperl', and next, turning to him, she would order him sternly to leave instantly. He simply adored her, like a dog one caresses and disciplines at the very same time.

People in the streets of Vienna, especially the children, often did tease him. But as long as this was done in a good-natured and harmless manner, he would put up with the treatment. But if someone dared to insult him, he would take revenge, always taking care not to be caught by the police again for unruly behaviour. (Indeed, it must have been a narrow path this fool had to tread!) Once, he felt insulted by a shopkeeper in the inner city. There were rumours that the man had made sexual advances to the sexually rather innocent fool. In any case, Peppi went to the market, collected some thoroughly rotten tomatoes and returned to the man's shop. When some customers were present to witness his foe's degradation, he threw the smelly stuff right in the shopkeeper's face. It caused quite some commotion, but the victim decided not to press charges on the condition that the fool never set one foot in his shop again. Peppi kept his promise, but glowed with pride over his victory. For many weeks he boasted to everyone who would listen to him: 'A hab'm b'züt' ('I aimed at him', i.e. I got him right on target).

In 1973 Peppi's mother died at the respectable age of 93. He had nursed her with care for a year. Mrs K. took upon herself the informal task of looking after Peppi, while his brother also regularly checked on his well-being. Looked at from the outside, he did remarkably well. He went out for his work in the apartment building of my parents-in-law each day, kept up his apartment

quite well, saved some money. His hot dinners came from a welfare organization, called meals-on-wheels. Mrs K. collected them
for Peppi and warmed them up at the end of the day. He prepared
his own breakfast in the morning and ate luncheon in the kitchen
of the families where he worked. Mrs K. assisted him with his
laundry. Next to his own earnings, he received a monthly welfare
cheque.

Yet, at the very same time, a curious change occurred in Peppi's life and it was a change for the worse. The good Mrs K.,
namely, was of the sincere conviction that something 'decent'
could still be made of Peppi, whom she loved as her own son.
She began to do the exact opposite of what Peppi's mother had
done ever since the Nazi nightmare. She disposed of Peppi's
sloppy cover-all and bought him decent working-clothes. In the
evenings and during weekends she made him wear straight suits,
with clean shirts and neck-ties. She put him on a diet and made
him lose several pounds of excess weight. She told him always to
eat with knife and fork. She took him on small bus tours outside
the city, through the beautiful hills of the Wienerwald. And she
told him straightforwardly that if he did not behave 'normally',
she would bring him to 'Steinhof', where the real fools were.
(She probably had no knowledge of the traumatic experience of
1947-8.) The threat must have scared Peppi stiff. He began to
change obediently. His whole appearance and demeanour altered
dramatically. In sum, the role of fool which he had played safely
and quite happily for so many years, was suddenly destroyed by
the demands of the petite bourgeoisie, and the threat of 'Steinhof'
always lurked in the background. As a result, Peppi began to
wither away. He became not only slim, but also very silent, pen-
sive and timid.

In May 1978, Mrs K. was hospitalized briefly for a minor operation. Peppi was very shocked and depressed. Upon saying
farewell to the lady, he stammered in his colourful Viennese
dialect that this was the end for him, that he would never see
her again. A few weeks prior to this event, Peppi had complained
about his health, Mrs K. recalled in the interview with my wife.
He had perspiration spells at night and felt generally not well.
But when Mrs K. implored him to see a doctor, he refused and
soon declared himself better again. Mrs K. assumed at the
time that he had suffered an acute attack of the flu. She never
thought about it again. But then, the day after her hospitalization
Peppi came to the apartment of my parents-in-law to start just
another working day. My mother-in-law, whom he had always
trusted as much as his own mother, was in the United States at
that time and an old aunt who took care of the household saw that
Peppi was not well, and sent him back home. He stayed in bed for
two days, checked upon regularly by his brother. On the third
day, the brother took him to the hospital in his car. Upon arrival
in the hospital, while being rolled on a stretcher to a doctor's
office, Peppi suddenly died - like his father and brother, he was
53 years old. There was, apparently, no acute medical reason for

his death. As is appropriate for a fool, Peppi did not die, he just faded away.

NOTES

INTRODUCTION: INNOCENTS IN AN ENCHANTED GARDEN

1   Cf. Max Weber on ancient China in 'Gesammelte Aufsätze zur Religionssoziologie', vol. 1 (Tübingen Mohr-Siebeck, 1963), pp. 512-36, in particular p. 513; also on ancient India in ibid., vol. 3, p. 237. See also Johannes Winckelmann, Die Herkunft von Max Weber's 'Entzauberungs'-Konzeption, 'Kölner Zeitschrift für Soziologie und Sozialpsychologie' (1980:1), pp. 12-53.

2   I borrowed this concept from the phenomenology of religion where it is usually applied to the Sacred. Cf. G. van der Leeuw, 'Religion in Essence and Manifestation', vol. 2, trans. J. E. Turner (New York: Harper & Row, 1963), p. 463. See also Rudolf Otto, 'The Idea of the Holy', trans. J. W. Harvey (Oxford University Press, 1969), pp. 31-41. In the original German edition Otto distinguished within the concept of 'das Heilige' (the Sacred) an attractive and a repulsive dimension which he called respectively 'fascinosum' and 'tremendum'. This ambiguity of attraction and repulsion is also very characteristic of traditional folly.

3   Cf. Arnold Gehlen, 'Die Seele im technischen Zeitalter', 1949 (Hamburg: Rowohlt Taschenbuch, 1957), pp. 87f, and his 'Urmensch und Spätkultur' (Bonn: Athenäum Verlag, 1956), pp. 20, 61, 103, 110, 294.

4   Max Weber, Soziologische Grundbegriffe, in 'Gesammelte Aufsätze zur Wissenschaftslehre' (Tübingen: Mohr-Siebeck, 1968, 3rd edn), p. 543.

5   Cf. my 'On Clichés. The Supersedure of Meaning by Function in Modernity' (London: Routledge & Kegan Paul, 1979).

6   See in particular Utopia, Ideology and the Problem of Reality, in Karl Mannheim, 'Ideology and Utopia', trans. L. Wirth and E. Shils (New York: Harcourt, Brace & World, n.d.), pp. 192-204.

7   For the concept of reality-maintenance see Peter L. Berger and Thomas Luckmann, 'The Social Construction of Reality' (New York: Doubleday, 1967).

8   Anomie is viewed rather simply here as the lack of institutional order and control, whereas alienation may be seen as the result of too much social control. Both seemingly opposite concepts characterize adequately the state of affairs in a fully modernized society. See my 'The Abstract Society', 1970 (London: Penguin Books, 1974).

9   This point will be further elaborated in the conclusion of this book.

10   Cf. Theodor Reich, 'The Greening of America' (New York: Random House, 1971).

1 INTO THE LOOKING-GLASS

1   Cf. Friedrich Schleiermacher, 'On Religion, Speeches to its Cultured Despisers', 1806; trans. J. Oman (New York: Harper Torchbooks, 1958).

2   Cf. the brief methodological note on cultural sociology in my 'On Clichés. The Supersedure of Meaning by Function in Modernity' (London: Routledge & Kegan Paul, 1979), pp. 106-11.

3   Cf. Heinrich Rickert, 'Die Grenzen der naturwissenschaftlichen Begriffsbildung', 1902 (Tübingen: J. C. B. Mohr - Paul Siebeck, 1929, 5th edn); Heinrich Rickert, 'Kulturwissenschaft und Naturwissenschaft', 1898 (Tübingen: J. C. B. Mohr - Paul Siebeck, 1915, 3rd edn); Heinrich Rickert, 'Die Probleme der Geschichtsphilosophie', 1904 (Heidelberg: Carl Winters Universitätsbuchandlung, 1924, 3rd edn). Max Weber applied Rickert's neo-Kantian methodology to the social sciences, in particular to what he called 'verstehende Soziologie' in 'Gesammelte Aufsätze zur Wissenschaftslehre' (Tübingen: J. C. B. Mohr - Paul Siebeck, 1968, 3rd edn). Georg Simmel's methodology in which he tried to combine the rationalism of

neo-Kantianism with the irrationalism of vitalism (in particular of Henri Bergson) can be found in his 'Die Probleme der Geschichtsphilosophie', 1892 (München-Leipzig: Duncker & Humblot, 1923, 5th edn). For Karl Mannheim's position, cf. On the Interpretation of Weltanschauung, trans. P. Keckskemeti in 'Essays on the Sociology of Knowledge' (London: Routledge & Kegan Paul, 1952) pp. 33-83. For Georg Lukács's critique of the previous cf. his monumental 'Die Zerstörung der Vernunft', 1952 (Berlin-Neuwied: Luchterhand, n.d., 9th edn).

4 Cf. Weber's opening statement in the fifth chapter of the second part of 'Wirtschaft und Gesellschaft' (Cologne-Berlin: Kiepenheuer & Witsch, 1964), dealing with the sociology of religion.

5 Historical facts will be provided in the next chapter.

6 Clifford Geertz, 'The Interpretation of Cultures' (New York: Basic Books, 1973), p. 129.

7 Ibid., cf. pp. 126f, 140f.

8 For a thorough analysis of the notion of creation in the Old Testament, cf. Gerhard von Rad, 'Theologie des Alten Testaments', vol. 1 (München: Chr. Kaiser Verlag, 1957, 3rd edn), pp. 140-57.

9 Cf. von Rad, op. cit., pp. 157-64.

10 Cf. Max Weber's analysis of theodicy in section 8, chapter 5, Part II (Sociology of Religion) of 'Wirtschaft und Gesellschaft', op. cit., pp. 405-10.

11 Cf. Max Weber, Die protestantische Ethik und der Geist des Kapitalismus, in 'Gesammelte Aufsätze sur Religionssoziologie', vol. 1, 1920 (Tübingen: Mohr-Siebeck, 1963), pp. 17-206.

12 The literature on gnosticism or Manicheism is by now very extensive. Sociologically relevant is e.g. Gilles Quispel, 'Gnosis als Weltreligion' (Zürich: Origo Verlag, 1952). For a more recent analysis, cf. Elaine Pagel's 'The Gnostic Gospels' (London: Weidenfeld & Nicolson, 1979). Cf. also a volume of essays edited by Kurt Rudolph, 'Gnosis und Gnostizismus' (Darmstadt: Wissenschaft-liche Buchgesellschaft, 1975). My own analysis of modern gnosticism can be found in 'The Abstract Society', 1970 (London: Penguin Books, 1974), pp. 95-102.

13 Cf. Ernst Bloch, 'Thomas Münzer als Theologe der Revolution', 1960 (Frankfurt am: Suhrkamp Verlag, 1967), Cf. also Walter Wakefield, 'Heresy, Crusade and Inquisition in Southern France, 1100-1250' (London: George Allen & Unwin, 1974).

14 Although gnosticism is not discussed specifically in them, the following studies are relevant here: Cesar Grana, 'Modernity and its Discontents', 1964 (New York: Harper Torchbooks, 1967); Richard Sennet, 'The Fall of Public Man' (Cambridge University Press, 1976); Christopher Lasch, 'The Culture of Narcissism' (London: Abacus, 1980).

15 On Marxism and gnosticism see Ernst Topitsch, Marxismus und Gnosis, in Ernst Topitsch, 'Sozialphilosophie zwischen Ideologie und Wissenschaft', (Berlin-Neuwied: Luchterhand Verlag, 1962), pp. 235-71.

16 In a Dutch publication I analysed the 'elective affinity' (Weber) between an 'immoralist ethos' and the modern welfare state, claiming that the one did not cause the other (they both have their own historical origins), but rather that both stimulated each other since the turn of the century, making for a typically modern society and culture. Cf. Anton C. Zijderveld, Het Ethos van de Verzorgingsstaat, 'Sociale Wetenschappen' (1979: 22,3), pp. 179-203.

17 Nietzsche's typology of 'Herrenmoral' and 'Sklavenmoral' ought to be understood in terms of the theodicy problem.

18 Du Tilliot, 'Mémoires pour servir à l'histoire de la Fête des Foux' (Lausanne-Geneva: 1751), p. 89.

19 Enid Welsford, 'The Fool. Its Social and Literary History' (Gloucester, Mass.: Faber & Faber, 1968), p. 78.

20 Friedrich Nietzsche, 'Die frölische Wissenschaft', section 125, in 'Gesammelte Werke', vol. 2 (Munich: Carl Hanser Verlag, 1955), pp. 126-8.

21 Lewis Carroll, 'Through the Looking-Glass', 1871 (London: J. M. Dent, 1970), p. 122.

22 Max Scheler, 'Die Stellung des Menschen im Kosmos', 1928 (Bern-München: Francke Verlag, 1962, 6th edn), p. 38.
23 Cf. Arnold Gehlen, 'Anthropologische Forschung' (Hamburg: Rowohlt, 1961), pp. 18, 48.
24 What follows is largely taken from Arnold Gehlen's writings. Cf. in particular his monumental 'Der Mensch. Seine Natur und seine Stellung in der Welt', 1940 (Frankfurt am-Bonn: Athenäum Verlag, 1962, 7th edn), and 'Urmensch und Spätkultur' (Bonn: Athenäum Verlag, 1956). Vittorio Klostermann Verlag is presently publishing Gehlen's collected works in ten volumes.
25 The biological relevance of symbolic culture in terms of evolution was also emphasized by Clifford Geertz in his essay The Growth of Culture and the Evolution of Mind, in 'The Interpretation of Cultures' (cf. note 6), pp. 55-87. Many of Geertz's ideas concur with those of Gehlen.
26 In what follows I extrapolate some ideas of Gehlen to the phenomenon of folly. More historical and anthropological facts will be given, however, in chapters 2 and 4 of the present study.
27 Cf. Wolfgang M. Zucker, The Clown as the Lord of Disorder, in 'Theology Today' (October, 1967), pp. 306-17. Cf. also William Willeford, 'The Fool and his Scepter' (Chicago: Northwestern University Press, 1969), pp. 73-150.
28 Once more, I have to abstain from methodological discussions of the nature and functions of 'ideal types'. Cf. the literature mentioned in note 3, as they indicate the frame of reference of my approach.
29 I refer once more to Gehlen's theory of 'cultural threshold'. Cf. Introduction, note 3.
30 Bronislaw Malinowski, 'Magic, Science and Religion' (New York: Doubleday Anchor, 1954), pp. 29f, 139f. Malinowski emphasizes the absence of magic in certain 'technological' activities stronger here than in his famous 'Argonauts of the Western Pacific', 1922 (New York: E. P. Dutton & Co., 1961), in particular pp. 105-45.
31 The sociologist Andrew Greeley always emphasizes this point. Cf. for example his 'Religion in the Year 2000' (New York: Sheed & Ward, 1969).
32 This is an elaboration of theoretical notions formulated by respectively Durkheim and Weber. Cf. Talcott Parsons, 'Sociological Theory and Modern Society' (New York: Free Press, 1967) and 'The System of Modern Societies' (Englewood Cliffs, N.J.: Prentice-Hall, 1971). H. P. M. Adriaansens of Tilburg University made me aware of the heuristic usefulness of Parsons's theory of modernization.
33 Cf. Georg Simmel, The Web of Group-Affiliations, trans. R. Bendix, in Georg Simmel, 'Conflict and the Web of Group Affiliations' (London: Collier-Macmillan; New York: Free Press, 1964).
34 This is a crucial element in the previously mentioned 'immoralist ethos' of the welfare state (cf. note 16). In such a society, not only goods and services but also social relationships like friendship and marriage are consumed and disposed of when they no longer satisfy the consumers. Not loyalty and commitment but consumerist satisfaction tends to become the supreme value of such relationships. See also my book on clichés, op. cit., pp. 42-7.
35 Numa D. Fustel de Coulanges, 'The Ancient City', 1864, trans. W. Small (Garden City, N.Y.: Doubleday Anchor Books, n.d.), chapter 13, pp. 198-201. 'It is not surprising that the ancient republics almost all permitted a convict to escape death by flight. Exile did not seem to be a milder punishment than death. The Roman jurists called it capital punishment' (p. 201).
36 On the generalization of Christianity in modern society, cf. Talcott Parsons, Christianity in Modern Industrial Society, in E. A. Tiryakian (ed.), 'Sociological Theories, Values and Socio-Cultural Change' (New York: Free Press, 1963). Cf. also Andrew Greeley, op. cit., pp. 75-103.
37 I have called this cultural climate of modernity 'clichégenic'. Cf. my book on clichés (note 2). See in addition to the well-known books of I. Illich, the interesting study by P. Nonet and P. Selznick, 'Law and Society in Transition Toward Responsive Law' (New York: Harper Colophon Books, 1978).

38 Cf. chapter 4 of this book.
39 Cf. Enid Welsford, op. cit.
40 This concept is meant in the sense given to it by Norbert Elias in his study 'Ueber den Prozess der Zivilization', 2 vols, 1936 (Bern-München: Francke Verlag, 1969, 2nd edn).
41 Cf. Anton C. Zijderveld, 'Humor und Gesellschaft' (Graz-Wien-Köln Styria Verlag, 1976). In this book which is a translated and extended version of an earlier Dutch edition, I failed to distinguish sharply enough between folly and humour. The book intended to present 'a sociology of humour and laughter'.
42 This point was brought to my attention by the Dutch dissertation of André Drooglever, 'De Gevaarlijke Reis' ('The Dangerous Journey') (Amsterdam: Free University, 1974). It is an anthropological study of the initiation rites for boys among the Wagenia of Kisangani at Zaire. On pp. 264ff. he discusses the relationship between folly and transitional situations, ceremonialized in particular in the initiation rituals. He criticizes my chapter on humour in non-Western cultures in 'Humor und Gesellschaft' (pp. 143-72) for missing this important point. I agree with him. The ensuing elaboration in the present chapter is, of course, my own.
43 A delightful description of Charles Darwin's initiation during his first crossing of the equator on the HMS *Beagle* was given by a young crew member, the midshipman P. G. King, aged 14 at the time of the event, but written down later in retrospect. See David Stanbury (ed.), 'A Narrative of the Voyage of H.M.S. Beagle' (London: The Folio Society, 1977), pp. 51f. Darwin noted down in his diary, 17 February 1832: 'I have undergone the disagreeable operation of being shaved.' He was yet treated with some respect, unlike the others: 'dirty mixtures being put in their mouths and rubbed on their faces' (p. 52).
44 Arnold van Gennep, 'The Rites of Passage', trans. M. B. Vizedom, G. L. Caffee (University of Chicago Press, 1960).
45 Jean Froissart, 'Chronicles', 1390, selected, translated and edited by G. Brereton (London: Penguin Books, 1979), p. 212. Froissart who does not at all sympathize with Ball's communist ideas, notes worriedly: 'Some, who were up to no good, said: "He's right!" and out in the fields, or walking together from one village to another, or in their homes, they whispered and repeated among themselves: "That's what John Ball says, and he's right." ' Ibid., p. 213. Together with Jack Straw, this John Ball served as companion of the well-known peasant leader Wat Tyler, of whom Froissart remarks: 'He was a tiler of roofs, and a wicked and nasty fellow he was.' Ibid. On Froissart's very lively description of the peasant revolt of 1381, see pp. 211-30.
46 Orrin E. Klapp, The Fool as a Social Type, 'American Journal of Sociology', 55 (1950), pp. 157-62.
47 Simon Murray, 'Legionnaire. An Englishman in the French Foreign Legion' (London: Sidgwick & Jackson, 1980), p. 40.
48 Ibid., pp. 184f.
49 Peter Gay, 'The Enlightenment: An Interpretation. The Rise of Modern Paganism', 1966 (New York: Random House Vintage Books, 1968).
50 This point made by Max Weber regularly was missed by Peter Gay (ibid.).
51 The idea of the 'dark Middle Ages' stems not from the Enlightenment which used it abundantly but from the Middle Ages! Cf. Lucie Varga, 'Das Schlagwort vom "finsteren Mittelalter" ' (Baden-Wien: Verlag Rudolf M. Rohrer, 1932).
52 Cf. Ernst Troeltsch, Die Bedeutung des Protestantismus für die Entstehung der modernen Welt, in 'Historische Bibliothek', vol. 24, 1906 (München-Berlin, 1909, 2nd edn). Also, 'Historischer Zeitschrift', 97 (1906), pp. 1-66.
53 On the follow-up of various 'ultimate authorities', see Jan Romein, Het Algemeen Menselijk Patroon, in Jan Romein, 'Eender en Anders' (Amsterdam: Querido, 1964), pp. 63-84.
54 Hans Freyer, 'Theorie des gegenwärtigen Zeitalters' (Stuttgart: Deutsche Verlagsanstalt, 1955), in particular chapter 1 which deals with the 'Mach-

barkeit' of things and objects, of human labour, of human beings and of history, pp. 15-78.

55   Cf. Karl Marx's Theses on Feuerbach, in particular the first one. Thesen Über Feuerbach, in 'Karl Marx Frühe Schriften', vol. 2, H. J. Lieber and P. Furth (eds) (Darmstadt: Wissenschaftliche Buchgellschaft, 1971), pp. 1-4.

56   On the fallacy of this one-sided praxis-orientation see Hannah Arendt, 'The Human Condition', 1958 (Garden City, NY: Doubleday Anchor Books, 1959), particularly, pp. 9-22.

57   Cf. chapter 3 of my 'The Abstract Society' (cf. note 12).

58   This point was stressed by Mircea Eliade in his book on shamanism: Mircea Eliade, 'Schamanismus und Archaische Ekstasetechnik', trans. from the French by I. Köck (Zürich-Stuttgart: Rascher Verlag, 1957).

59   Cf. Michel Foucault, 'Histoire de la Folie à l'âge classique' (Paris: Gallimard, 1972). Also H. H. Beek, 'Waanzin in de Middeleeuwen' (Hoofddorp: Uitgeverij De Toorts, 1969). Unlike Foucault, Beek used an admirable wealth of historical material and did himself additional archive research. I used his book in this section gratefully.

60   Thomas S. Szasz, 'Ideology and Insanity' (Garden City, NY: Anchor Books, 1970), in particular chapter 2: The Myth of Mental Illness, pp. 12-24.

61   A. Canel, 'Recherches historiques sur les Fous des Rois de France' (Paris: Alphonse Lemerre, 1873), pp. 249-55.

62   On the mental illness of Charles VI and other European monarchs, see Beek, op. cit., pp. 41-53.

63   On the 'lettres de rémission', cf. Beek, op. cit., 162f.

64   Barbara Swain, 'Fools and Folly during the Middle Ages and the Renaissance' (New York: Columbia University Press, 1932), p. 4.

65   Beek, op. cit., p. 7.

66   Johan Huizinga, 'Erasmus', 1924 (Haarlem: H. D. Tjeenk Willink, 1936, 13th edn) p. 81. This is a Dutch elaboration of an English short biography written by Huizinga for a series 'Great Hollanders' (New York: Charles Scribner, 1924).

67   The Dutch historian and expert on this period of time, D. Th. Enklaar, claims correctly in a footnote that no distinction was made in the Middle Ages between folly and mental illness: 'Varende Luyden', 1937 (Arnhem: Gysbers & Van Loon, 1975, 3rd edn), p. 66.
      For an excellent account of the notion of folly among the humanists see Barbara Könneker, 'Wesen und Wandlung der Narrenidee im Zeitalter des Humanismus' (Wiesbaden: Franz Steiner Verlag, 1966). On Erasmus and his 'Praise of Folly', pp. 248-329.

68   Beek, op. cit., p. 151f. The famous (and, later, also infamous) institution Bedlam in London was originally also an undifferentiated asylum where both the physically and the mentally ill were kept. The differentiation into an asylum for the insane was completed in the fifteenth century. Beek claims that this differentiation occurred in Europe generally in the fourteenth and fifteenth centuries, op. cit., p. 151.

69   Foucault, op. cit., p. 19. The historical literature cited by Foucault stems from the nineteenth century and is generally not reliable because it uses a biased, medical frame of reference without any knowledge of the symbolic nature of medieval folly.

70   Although this date is suspicious (Shrove Tuesday being a day of abundant folly celebrations), we may trust that Gelabert wanted to be serious.

71   Beek, op. cit., pp. 154f.

72   Ibid., pp. 173-210. On St Dimphna and Geel see M. H. Koyen and M. de Bont, 'Geel door de Eeuwen heen' (Geel: Comité Sint Dimphna jaar, 1975), in particular chapters 1 and 10, pp. 9-22, 122-30. See also M. H. Koyen, Krankzinnigenzorg. St. Dimphna en Geel, in 'Spiegel Historiael' (1974: 9, 10), pp. 514-21. Also Beek, op. cit., pp. 217f, 245f. The name of the saint is spelled both as Dimphna and Dimpna. On a tile found in her sarcophagus the name was spelled as Dipna (AD 700-800). Cf. Koyen and De Bont, op. cit., p. 17. These authors relate on p. 13 that Dimphna fled from Ireland

in the company of her confessor, Gerebernus, and the court jester. The latter remains anonymous, and his fate after the death of Dimphna and her priest is unknown.
73 Beek, op. cit., p. 170
74 Ibid. The number of patients in these asylums was initially very small. The famous house Reinier van Arkel, at Den Bosch (the Netherlands), for instance, started in 1442 with facilities for five patients, and this number had only increased to nine in 1474. In the sixteenth century this number was about twenty, in the seventeenth century, thirty. The Amsterdam institution began in 1562 with eleven patients, which grew to forty-two soon after. Cf. G. T. Haneveld, 'Oude Medische Gebouwen van Nederland' (Amsterdam: R. Meesters & Ass., 1976), p. 24.
75 Max Weber used this concept regularly as a sociological type. Cf. for example his 'Ancient Judaism', trans. H. H. Gerth and D. Martindale (Chicago: Free Press, 1952), pp. 336ff.
76 On the social and legal consequences of infamy, see Otto Beneke, 'Von Unehrlichen Leuten' (Halburg: Perthes, Besser und Manke, 1863); W. Danckert, 'Unehrliche Leute. Die verfemten Berufe' (Bern-München: Francke Verlag, 1963). A typical example of an infamous profession was, of course, that of the executioner. See C. L. Kruithof, De Beul als Paria, 'Mens en Maatschappij' (1979: 54), pp. 62-75.
77 Beek, op. cit., pp. 147f.
78 Sometimes mental patients were punished physically, but, as Beek points out, this was not done 'therapeutically' because they were 'mad', but 'pedagogically' because they were unruly. Beek, op. cit., p. 148.
79 On the pillory, see G. Bader-Weisz and K. Bader, 'Der Pranger. Ein Strafwerkzeug und Rechtswahrzeichen des Mittelalters' (Freiburg, 1935).
80 In 1562 the city of Amsterdam placed several of these 'fools' houses' together in one place, thus starting the first asylum for the insane of this city. Beek, op. cit., pp. 147f.
81 Eugen Holländer, 'Die Medizin in der klassischen Malerei' (Stuttgart: Encke Verlag, 1903), p. 211.
82 Ibid., pp. 206f.
83 Beek believes erroneously that these fools, depicted in the margins of psalm 53, chew on bread. Beek, op. cit., pp. 28, 31.
84 On medieval folly and magic, cf. Beek, op. cit., pp. 57-63.
85 Ronald Sheridan and Anne Ross, 'Gargoyles and Grotesques, Paganism in the Medieval Church' (Boston: New York Graphic Society, 1975).
86 Peter Gay, op. cit. (cf. note 49).

2 TWISTERS OF REALITY
1 Norbert Elias, 'Ueber den Prozess der Zivilization', 2 vols, 1936 (Bern-München: Francke Verlag, 1969, 2nd edn).
2 Cf. Alvin Redman (ed.), 'The Wit and Humor of Oscar Wilde' (New York: Dover Publications, 1959).
3 Dandyism will be discussed in chapter 3 (pp. 127-9).
4 Cf. Etienne Gilson, 'Reason and Revelation in the Middle Ages', 1938 (New York: Scribners' Sons, n.d.), in particular chapter 2, The Primacy of Reason, pp. 37-66.
5 Scholastic dialectic, to give one example, was once called irreverently 'quique le quique', i.e. cockadoodledoo. Cf. Helen Waddell, 'The Wandering Scholars' (London: Constable, 1927), p. 123.
6 See for a detailed study of late-medieval popular culture of which folly was an essential component, Peter Burke, 'Popular Culture in Early Europe' (New York-London: Harper Torchbooks, 1978). For a very fine analysis of the popular culture of early-modern France: Nathalie Zemon Davis, 'Society and Culture in Early Modern France' (Stanford University Press, 1975).
7 A standard description of these entertainers is contained in E. K. Chambers, 'The Medieval Stage', vol. 1 (Oxford University Press, 1903), Book I, chapters 1 to 4, Minstrelsy, pp. 1-88. See also the Dutch essays of D. Enklaar, 'Varende Luyden', 1937 (Arnhem: Gysbers & Van Loon, 1975, 3rd edn).

The focus is mainly on the Netherlands. On the musicians among these wandering entertainers cf. J. E. Spruit, 'Van Vedelaars, Trommers en Pijpers' (Utrecht: Oosthoek's Uitgeversmaatschappij, 1969).

8 Robert Briffault, 'The Troubadours', ed L. F. Koons (Bloomington: Indiana University Press, 1965), in particular chapter 3, Armour Courtois, pp. 80-101.

9 W. Dankert, 'Unehrliche Leute. Die verfemten Berufe' (Bern-München: Francke Verlag, 1963).

10 Sociologically speaking these entertainers lacked the characteristics of ethnicity. Cf. Nathan Glazer and Daniel P. Moynihan (eds), 'Ethnicity. Theory and Experience' (Cambridge, Mass.: Harvard University Press, 1976).

11 William Langland, 'Piers the Ploughman', trans. into modern English by J. F. Goodridge (London: Penguin Books, 1978), p. 26.

12 The name 'goliard' was often connected with the Philistine Goliath of the Old Testament, who was generally identified with the devil in the Middle Ages. Cf. C. H. Haskins, 'The Renaissance of the Twelfth Century' (Cambridge, Mass.: Harvard University Press, 1939). Others derive it from the Latin 'gula' which means 'gluttony'. Cf. Edwin H. Zeydel (ed.), 'Vagabond Verse' (Detroit: Wayne State University Press, 1966), p. 17. Actually, both these derivations are substantially adequate, as goliards behaved like 'Devil's Angels' and were notorious as great gluttons. The name 'eberhardini' is harder to reconstruct. Waddell, op. cit., p. 216, believed it to be a nick-name after Eberhard, Archbishop of Salzburg (1200-49) who was once paro-died by a wandering scholar, although he seemed to have favoured the 'vagantes' a great deal. Cf. Enklaar, op. cit., p. 144. In the Netherlands they were called 'Everaertsbroeders', which is clearly a Dutch translation of 'eberhardini'.

13 The standard study of the 'vagantes' is Waddell, op. cit. See in particular the valuable collection of goliardic poetry ed and trans. Zeydel, op. cit.

14 Cf. Waddell, op. cit., Appendix E, Councils on the Clericus Vagus or Joc-ulator, pp. 244-70.

15 Ibid., p. 217.

16 Ibid., p. 175.

17 Ibid., p. 176.

18 Ibid., pp. 170f.

19 Cf. Marc Bloch, 'Feudal Society', vol. 1, trans. L. Manyon (University of Chicago Press, 1970, 8th edn), Part 1, The Environment: the Last Invasions, pp. 3-58. See also Geoffrey Barraclough, 'The Crucible of Europe' (Berke-ley, LA: University of California Press, 1976), chapter 4, The Impact of Invasions, pp. 74-83.

20 See Zeydel, op. cit., in particular the introduction, pp. 14-44.

21 E. J. Hobsbawm, 'Bandits', 1969 (London: Penguin Books, 1972). He em-phasizes the ambiguity of the bandit which is similar to the ambiguity of the fool:

> He is an outsider and a rebel, a poor man who refuses to accept the normal roles of poverty, and establishes his freedom by means of the only resources within reach of the poor, strength, bravery, cunning and determination. This draws him close to the poor. ... At the same time the bandit is, inevitably, drawn into the web of wealth and power, because, unlike other peasants, he acquires wealth and exerts power (pp. 87f).

The fool usually lacked the social conscience Hobsbawm adjudicates to the 'social bandit'. There never was something like 'social folly', nor was there a 'noble fool' comparable to the 'noble robber'. If the fool of Henry VIII, Will Sommers, was compassionate, he still was a far cry from a social bandit like Robin Hood. Cf. Hobsbawm on social bandits, pp. 17-29, 41-57.

22 Waddell, op. cit., p. 263.

23 Ibid., p. 187.

24 Ibid., p. 162.

25 Ibid., p. 165.

26 Chambers, op. cit., pp. 54f.

27 Ibid., p. 55.
28 Enklaar, op. cit., p. 70.
29 Cf. Introduction of Fr. Zarncke to his edition of Sebastian Brant's 'Narrenschiff' (Darmstadt: Wissenschaftliche Buchgesellschaft, 1973), pp. lxviif.
30 Cf. Haskins, op. cit.
31 Cf. Peter Gay, 'The Enlightenment: An Interpretation. The Rise of Modern Paganism', 1966 (New York: Random House Vintage Books, 1968).
32 Next to the so-called Cambridge Songs, a manuscript that dates from approximately 1050, the Carmina Burana (c. 1250) are the main source of goliardic poetry. The latter were discovered in a Bavarian monastery in 1803 and were widely distributed in our century through the popular composition of Carl Orff. These very earthy and paganistic songs were obviously copied studiously by monks, which may prove how deeply this kind of worldly vitalism had penetrated into the medieval church. See again Zeydel, op. cit., for these and several other goliardic songs.
33 There was, for instance, a 'Mass of Drinkers', an 'Office of Gamblers', a 'Gospel according to Ovid' - the latter, incidentally, being a favourite among the goliards.
34 One goliard rhymed a mock Credo: 'Credo in wine that's fair to see, And in a barrel of my host, More than *in the Holy Ghost*, The Tavern is my sweetheart, yea, *And Holy Church* is not for me.'
    The blasphemy went mostly not much further than this, unlike the behaviour of learned men, scolded by Langland, because together with fools and ignorant jesters they 'will crack a joke or two about the Trinity.' Langland, op. cit., p. 114.
35 J. Huizinga, 'Erasmus', 1924 (Haarlem: H. D. Tjeenk Willink, 1936, 13th edn), p. 21.
36 Andrew Boorde, or Borde (c. 1490-1549), was in this respect an interesting case. After twenty years of rigorous asceticism in the Carthusian order, he requested a dispensation from his prior: 'I am nott able to byd the rigorisite off your relygyon,' he wrote. He travelled widely throughout Europe as a student of medicine, acquired fame at home as the author of a few popular books on health and illness, and even came into contact with Henry VIII and his adviser Cromwell. But his career came to a sad end. In 1549 he was accused of keeping three prostitutes, convicted as souteneur, and thrown in jail on 9 April. He died soon after. See: 'Dictionary of National Biography', vol. 5 (London: 1886), pp. 371-3 s.v. Boorde (author: F. J. Furnivall). See also the Prologue to 'The First and Best Part of Scoggins Iests', gathered by Andrew Boord, Doctor of Physicke (London: printed for Francis Williams, 1626). That he did possess a goliardic streak is testified by the following words: 'I doe advertise every man in avoiding pensiveness, or too much study of melancholie, to be merrie with honesty in God, and for God, whom I humbly beseach to send us the mirth of Heaven. Amen.' It is, however, questionable if Boorde really was the author of this little booklet, of which there are two handsome editions in the British Library.
37 Zeydel, op. cit., p. 61.
38 Ibid., p. 101.
39 J. Burckhardt, 'Die Kultur der Renaissance', 1860 (Stuttgart: Kröner Verlag, 1976), p. 154.
40 As to the social criticism of the goliards, one usually refers in the literature to 'De Nugis Curialium' (Zeydel, 'On Courtly Folderol'), by Walter Mapes (d. 1210). Cf. M. R. James (ed) (Oxford, 1914). It is a satirical treatise on the trivialities of British court life and a sharp critique of the scholastic veneration of 'antiquitas'. This adoration of the past in scholasticism was paired to a rejection of the present, i.e. 'modernitas'. Cf. A. H. Bredero, 'Oratio pro Domo: Tegen een misverstaan der Middeleeuwen' (Amsterdam: Free University, 1976. Inaugural address), pp. 9f. Mapes may have sympathized with the goliards as a young man, but he certainly was not a genuine 'vagus'. After he studied in Paris, he served at the British court under Thomas à Becket. In 1179 he participated in the Lateran Council which ruled, among other things, that monks who had deserted their mon-

astery should be forced to return (Waddell, op. cit., p. 258). He next functioned as archdeacon in Oxford (Zeydel, op. cit., pp. 33f). According to Zeydel, a few goliardic songs were falsely attributed to Mapes. In sum, Mapes's social criticism should not too easily be identified with the goliardic 'movement'. A Viennese police ordinance of 1552 complains about the opportunism of those impetuous entertainers who insult both worldly and religious estates. But when they socialize with clergy they sing about secular people and when they are with the latter they sing at the expense of the former. This often causes irritation, discord, and disobedience. They should be punished by the authorities. However, the regulation adds, in all fairness, those who perform 'Magistergesang' are to be excluded from such measures. J. E. Schlager, 'Wiener Skizzen aus dem Mittelalter', Neue Folge (Vienna, 1839), p. 206.

41 Waddell, op. cit., Appendix C, pp. 239-41. Cf. Also Lydgate's satirical poem The Order of Fools. Barbara Swain, 'Fools and Folly in the Middle Ages and the Renaissance' (New York: Columbia University Press, 1952), pp. 49-51.

42 Ibid., p. 165.

43 Zeydel, op. cit., p. 59.

44 Ibid., p. 61.

45 Ibid., p. 63.

46 Ibid., pp. 70f.

47 J. Huizinga, 'Homo Ludens. A Study of the Play-Element in Culture', 1938 (Boston: Beacon Press, 1964, 4th edn), p. 179.

48 Ibid.

49 For a sociological discussion of 'low' and 'high' culture, see Herbert J. Gans, 'Popular Culture and High Culture' (New York: Basic Books, 1974).

50 Voltaire, 'Dictionnaire Philosophique', s.v. 'Amité' (Paris: Garnier-Flammarion, 1964), p. 33.

51 Cf. Chambers, op. cit., in particular pp. 116-45.

52 Ibid., pp. 95f.

53 This makes sense indeed because it could explain the present-day carnival festivities (mardi gras) as a remnant of the medieval Festival of Fools with which it has much in common. Pleij argues in his dissertation that we are dealing here with one long festive period from 11 November (St Martin) until Easter, consisting of various carnivalesque celebrations. Cf. Herman Pleij, 'Het Gilde van de Blauwe Schuit' (Amsterdam: Meulenhoff, 1979), p. 15.

54 Du Tilliot, 'Mémoires pour servir à l'histoire de la fête des foux' (Lausanne-Genève, 1751), pp. 10f.

55 Chambers, op. cit., chapters 13 and 14, Feast of Fools, pp. 275-335; chapter 15, The Boy Bishop, pp. 337-71.

56 See, for these names, Chambers, op. cit., p. 275; Du Tilliot, passim. Next to Chambers and Du Tilliot, I made use of the following literature: G. M. Dreves, Zur Geschiche der fête des fous, 'Stimmen aus Maria-Laach' (1894: 47), pp. 571-87; M. J. Rigollot and C. L. Leber, 'Monnaies Inconnues des Evèques des Innocenx, des Fous' (Paris: Merlin, 1837). (Among other things, this book presents a numismatic analysis of the lead coins without monetary value which were distributed abundantly during the Festival of Fools. This usage occurred also in the ancient Roman Saturnalia: the king chosen from among the domestic slaves distributed lead coins which bore the emblem of the lord of the household, or a picture of the 'king's' favourite god, or some laughter-provoking words. In addition, during the Festival, a couple of days, called the Sagillaria, were devoted to the exchange of small gifts without much value, see pp. 9f.) See for the religion and magical nature of gift-exchange: Marcel Mauss, 'The Gift', 1925, trans. I. Cunnison (New York: Norton, 1967). Cf. also H. Villetard, A Propos de la fête des fous au Moyen Age, 'Bulletin de la société des sciences historiques et naturelles de l'Yonne', 1910, vol. 64 (Auxerre, 1911), pp. 205-28.

57 Vilfredo Pareto, 'The Mind and Society. A treatise on General Sociology', Vol. I, trans. A. Bongiorno and A. Livingston (New York: Dover Publications, 1963), para. 737, note 2, p. 446.

58 Chambers, op. cit., p. 294; Du Tilliot, op. cit., pp. 51f.
59 J. G. Frazer, 'The Golden Bough', 1922, 1-vol. abbr. edn (New York: Macmillan, 1941), p. 584.
60 Ibid., pp. 281f.
61 Ibid., pp. 587-9.
62 Pareto, op. cit., para. 736, p. 445.
63 John G. Bourke, 'Scatalogical Rites of All Nations' (Washington, DC: W. H. Howdermilk, 1891), chapter 3, The Feast of Fools in Europe, pp. 11-23.
64 Ibid., p. 12.
65 Frazer, op. cit., p. 583. Marx's brief description of the communist community in 'Die Deutsche Ideologie' (1845-6) bears strong Saturnalian features. There is also a strong similarity between political revolutions and Saturnalian festivities. Cf. M. de Ferdinandy, Carnival and Revolution, 'Atlas' (February 1964), pp. 98-104.
66 Frazer, op. cit., p. 584.
67 C. G. Jung, On the Psychology of the Trickster Figure, in Paul Radin, 'The Trickster. A Study in American Indian Mythology' (London: Routledge & Kegan Paul, 1956), pp. 195-211. Quotation, p. 198. Cf. also Chambers, op. cit., p. 275.
68 Villetard, op. cit., passim.
69 Chambers, op. cit., p. 283.
70 Cf. superb discussion, ibid., pp. 279-84. Chambers discusses a second fools' missal, the Office of Beauvais (c. 1227-34), ibid., pp. 284-8.
71 Ibid., p. 281.
72 Cf. E. van Erven, Particularitées inconnues sur quelques fous en titre d'office, in 'Messager des sciences historiques' (Gand, 1858), pp. 314-31, in particular pp. 316f.
73 Barbara Swain, op. cit., p. 76.
74 Chambers, op. cit., p. 296.
75 Ibid., p. 297.
76 Enklaar, op. cit., p. 51.
77 Most authors give March 1444 as the date of this letter. Chambers, however, gives the precise date, namely 12 March 1444/5, op. cit., p. 294, note 1. In a letter, dated 17 April 1445, King Charles VII reminds the city of Troyes of the arguments against the Festival of Fools put forward by the Parisian theologians. They condemned the horrid festival as being superstitious and paganistic (Rigollot, op. cit., p. 8).
78 Du Tilliot, op. cit., pp. 51f.
79 Ibid., p. 52.
80 Chambers, op. cit., pp. 294f.
81 H. Kramer and J. Sprenger, 'Malleus Maleficarum', 1486, trans. from Latin by M. Summers (London: Arrow Books, 1971).
82 Swain, op. cit., p. 112: 'You tell me Dame Folly is dead? Good Lord, what a lie! I never saw her so well and so powerful as she is at present.'
83 Cf. Du Tilliot, op. cit., second part, pp. 79-183; Chambers, op. cit., pp. 372-82; Enklaar, op. cit., pp. 49-59.
84 Nathalie Zemon Davis, The Reasons for Misrule, in 'Society and Culture in Early Modern France' (Stanford University Press, 1975), pp. 97-123.
85 Swain, op. cit., p. 79.
86 Cf. R. Busquet, 'Farces du Moyen-Age' (Paris: F. Lanore, 1973). One of the most popular farces of the fifteenth century was 'Maistre Pierre Pathelin', the cloth-merchant. Cf. Richard T. Holbrook (ed.), 'Maistre Pierre Pathelin' (Paris: Librarie Honoré Champion, 1970). Cf. Chambers, op. cit., pp. 380-2; Swain, op. cit., pp. 91-113. The German pendant was the 'Fastnachtspiel'. Cf. Könneker, 'Wesen und Wandlung der Narrenidee im Zeitalter des Humanismus' (Wiesbaden: Franz Steiner Verlag, 1966), pp. 56-74.
87 The following discussion borrows primarily from Davis, op. cit.
88 Ibid., pp. 104f.
89 The word is certainly an onomatopoeia, as it refers to the rattling noise produced on pots, pans, drums and other 'instruments' by which a chosen

victim is teased. Cf. Chambers, op. cit., pp. 153f., where he also discusses the English pendant.
90   Davis, op. cit., p. 114.
91   Du Tilliot, op. cit., p. 96.
92   Swain, op. cit., p. 211, note 26. Cf. Chambers, op. cit., p. 376.
93   Swain, op. cit., p. 81.
94   Davis, op. cit., p. 116.
95   Enklaar, op. cit., pp. 41-98.
96   Pleij, op. cit., pp. 187ff.
97   Ibid., pp. 15f. Pleij gives the full text of this curious document (pp. 237-44).
98   Abbé de Bellegarde, 'Reflexions sur le ridicule et sur les moyens de l'éviter' (The Hague: G. de Voys, 1729, 9th edn).
99   M. J. Rigollot, op. cit., Introduction by C. Leber in which the colour symbols of folly are discussed: pp. lxx-lxxiv. The colour yellow symbolized infamy and was the colour of lackeys and prostitutes, also of Jews. The Council of Arles (1234) ruled that Jews ought to wear a round mark on their stomachs, in order to distinguish them from the Christians! In 1269 it was ordained that this mark should be made of yellow fabric. On the miniatures of the fourteenth and fifteenth centuries, heretics, entertainers, fools and notoriously unfaithful spouses were depicted in yellow clothes. The colour green not only symbolized hope and faith, but, strangely enough, also dishonour. In cases of bankruptcy, for example, people were often made to wear green caps (pp. lxxi-lxxiii).
A semi-official record of 1605 gives the following description of a jester's outfit:
[The suit] is made from strips of serge, half green and half yellow and where there are yellow strips, there is green trimming; between the strips there is also yellow and green taffeta, which is stitched to the said strips and trimming. The hose is sewed to the breeches, one [leg] all of green serge and the other of yellow, and the cap also, half yellow half green, with ears (Robert H. Goldsmith, 'Wise Fools in Shakespeare' (Liverpool University Press, 1958), p. 3).
100 For the following see Enklaar, op. cit., pp. 61ff.
101 Cf. Swain, op. cit., p. 120.
102 Enklaar, op. cit., p. 62.
103 Ibid., p. 65.
104 Ibid., p. 67.
105 Ibid., p. 64.
106 Zarncke, op. cit., p. lvi.
107 See Joel Lefebvre, 'Les Fols et la folie' (Paris: Librairie C. Klinksieck, 1968), p. 78.
108 See, for a part of this text, Zarncke, op. cit., pp. lxif.
109 Cf. D. Th. Enklaar, 'Uit Uilenspiegel's Kring' (Assen: Van Gorcum, n.d.), p. 29.
110 Brant, as Zarncke remarked, was driven by the desire to teach and to improve (op. cit., p. xli). The literary background of Brant's 'Ship of Fools' consisted mainly of morality plays and moralizing poems. Cf. Könneker, op. cit., in particular pp. 28-55, 75-132.
111 Sebastian Brant (1457-1521) studied law and 'humaniora' in Basle from 1475, and became university lecturer in law in 1489. He then moved to Strassburg in 1501, where he became secretary of the city in 1503. Könneker places emphasis upon his remarkably secular way of thinking which came close to the stoic philosophy of the 'vir bonus', and seemed to prelude the Enlightenment. As to the latter, Könneker speaks in his case of a faith in reason, 'Vernunftglauben' (op. cit., pp. 125-32).
112 Zarncke (op. cit., p. lxxvi).
113 Cf. also ibid., pp. cxxf.
114 Cf. K. G. Knight, Seventeenth-Century Views of Human Folly, in E. F. Norman (ed.), 'Essays in German Literature I' (London: Institute of Germanic Studies, University of London, 1965), pp. 52-71.

115 Ibid., p. 58.
116 Ibid., p. 67.
117 Thomas Lodge, 'Wits Miserie and the Worlds Madnasse: Discovering the Devils Incarnat of this Age' (London: C. Burby, 1596), pp. 84f. For Lodge's biography see Dictionary of National Biography, vol. XXIV (London, 1893) s.v. Lodge (author: L. Cust), pp. 60-7.
118 Swain, op. cit., pp. 172ff, 184.
119 Ilse-Marie Bostelmann, 'Der niederdeutsche Ulenspiegel und seine Entwicklung in den Niederlanden' (Hamburg University Press, 1940), p. 9.
120 Nazreddin was also mentioned as the court jester of Timurleng. Cf. Enid Welsford, 'The Fool. His Social and Literary History', 1935 (Gloucester, Mass.: Peter Smith, 1966), p. 30. But it is quite probable that different individuals bore this legendary name. Karl F. Flögel, 'Geschichte der Hofnarren' (Leipzig: Barth, 1789), p. 177, mentions this name as an official emissary. On Ash'ab, see F. Rosenthal, 'Humor in Early Islam' (Leiden: Brill, 1956), pp. 22-4.
121 Cf. the theological debates on the so-called 'historical Jesus'. For example, James M. Robinson, 'Kerygma und historischer Jesus' (Zurich: Zwingli Verlag, 1960).
122 For an analysis of Eulenspiegel within the general climate of folly, see D. Th. Enklaar, 'Uit Uilenspiegel's Kring' (Assen: Van Gorcum, 1940).
123 A booklet was bought, the account states, 'quod intitulatur Ulenspiegel'. Bostelmann, op. cit., p. 7.
124 Ibid., pp. 10f.
125 Ibid., p. 24. This political motive was used by the Flemish novelist Charles de Coster (1827-79) in his 'La Légende d'Ulenspiegel', 1867.
126 Cf. Bostelmann, op. cit. The relationship between satire and the up-and-coming bourgeoisie of the fifteenth and sixteenth centuries is a very complex one, which cannot be discussed here. Cf. Jean V. Alter, 'Les Origines de la satire anti-bourgeoise en France. Moyen âge-XVIe siècle' (Geneva: Librairie Droz, 1966).
127 C. G. Jung, On the Psychology of the Trickster Figure, in Paul Radin, 'The Trickster. A Study in American Indian Mythology' (London: Routledge & Kegan Paul, 1956), pp. 195-211.
128 Cf. Léon Poliakov, 'The History of Anti-Semitism', 1956, trans. R. Howard (New York: Schocken Books, 1974), in particular pp. 17-25.
129 Cf. Alexander N. St Clair, 'The Image of the Turk in Europe' (New York: Metropolitan Museum of Art, 1973). During the Renaissance in Italy, the Turks were looked at more in terms of awe and even some admiration. Cf. Jacob Burckhardt, 'Die Kultur der Renaissance in Italien', 1860 (Stuttgart: Kröner Verlag, 1976), pp. 86ff, 469f.
130 Swain, op.cit, p. 46.
131 François Villon, 'Le Testament', XXXIX. Cf. Villon, 'Oeuvres', vol. 1, trans. into modern French and annotated by A. Lanly (Paris: Librairie H. Champion, 1974), p. 81. In a footnote Lanly surmises that Villon had knowledge of the frescos of the 'Cimetière des Innocents' which show a famous death-dance.
132 Swain, op. cit., p. 203, note 58.
133 Cf. James M. Clark, 'The Dance of Death in the Middle Ages and the Renaissance' (Glasgow: Jackson, 1950). The famous Lubeck death-dance in the Marienkirchen (1463) was destroyed during the Second World War. See Clark, op. cit., pp. 78ff. An excellent example of a literary death-dance stems also from Lubeck and had its first printings in 1489 and 1496. See the fine edition of Hermann Baethcke, published in Tübingen in 1876, reprinted by the Wissenschaftliche Buchgesellschaft at Darmstadt in 1968: 'Des Dodes Danz'.
134 D. Th. Enklaar, 'De Dodendans, Een cultuur-historische Studie' (Amsterdam: Veen, 1950), pp. 23, 31.
135 Edelgard Dubruck, 'The Theme of Death in French Poetry of the Middle Ages and the Renaissance' (The Hague: Mouton, 1964), pp. 57-9. Cf. J. Huizinga, 'Herfsttij der Middeleeuwen' 1919 (Haarlem: Tjeenk Willink, 1957, 9th edn), p. 142.

3 PARASITES OF POWER
 1 The literature on the history of court fools is very extensive, although
    since Flögel's classic work very repetitive. Most of this literature is also
    rhapsodic and anecdotal, Cf. Karl F. Flögel, 'Geschichte der Hofnarren'
    (Liegnitz, Leipzig: David Siegert, 1789). Much of this book was incorpor-
    ated in Fr. Nick, 'Hof- und Volksnarren', 2 vols (Stuttgart: J. Scheible,
    1861). Very good on French court fools is A. Canel, 'Recherches historiques
    sur les fous des rois de France' (Paris: A. Kemerre, 1873). Cf. also
    M. A. Gazeau, 'Les Bouffons' (Paris: Hachette, 1882). Very well docu-
    mented, particularly with regard to English court fools, is Enid Welsford,
    'The Fool. His Social and Literary History', 1935 (Gloucester, Mass.: Peter
    Smith, 1966). Written in a popular vein with much less historical reliability
    is John Doran, 'The History of Court Fools', 1858 (New York: Haskell
    House, 1966).
 2 I shall not distinguish between 'court fool' and 'court jester'.
 3 Welsford claims that this distinction goes back at least to the twelfth cen-
    tury. Welsford, op. cit., p. 119.
 4 Robert Armin, 'Nest of Ninnies', 1608 (London: printed for the Shakes-
    peare Society by F. Shoberl, 1842), p. 12. Armin records a little song
    which begins thus: 'Naturall fooles are prone to selfe conceipt: Fooles are
    artificiall, with their wits lay wayte To make themselves fools, liking the
    disguise, To feede their own mindes, and the gazers eyes' (p. 12).
 5 To Moreau all court and domestic fools were pathological creatures. He is
    of course not able to substantiate this careless generalization. Cf. Paul
    Moreau, 'Fous et bouffons. Etude physiologique, psychologique et histor-
    ique' (Paris: J.-B. Ballière, 1888).
 6 Caillette, natural fool at the court of François I next to Triboulet, was
    once nailed to a wooden pole by the ear, until released by an older courtier
    who pitied him. Some pages were questioned about this cruelty but when
    one of the suspects said: 'I had nothing to do with this,' the fool repeated
    his words literally. The case was then dismissed. Cf. Canel, op. cit., pp.
    94-6; Doran, op. cit., p. 249. Also André Stegmann, Sur Quelques Aspects
    des fous en titre d'office dans la France du XVIe siècle, in 'Folie et
    Déraison à la Renaissance', colloque international tenu en Novembre 1973
    (Brussels: Editions de l'Université de Bruxelles, 1976), p. 62; and M. A.
    Gazeau, op. cit., pp. 67-72.
 7 Cf. for example Le Vicomte who passed through the court of the young
    Louis XII 'like a shadow' (Canel) and was mentioned in the royal accounts
    as a person who received some clothes. Canel, op. cit., p. 98. Countless
    examples of such briefly mentioned fools can be added.
 8 Cf. A. Jal, 'Fous en titre d'office', in 'Dictionnaire critique de biographie
    et d'histoire' (Paris: Henri Plon, 1867), p. 598; ' A ung povre fol nommé
    Dago, suivant la cour, ung escu on 27 s.6 deniers tournois le 2. nov. 1454'.
    And: 'A ung povre fol nommé Robinet, aussi suivant la cour, le 10 nov.
    1454, 10 s. tourn.' The former might be the same fool who served in Brit-
    tany as domestic fool of Arthur de Richemont first and as a 'fou en titre
    d'office' of the Duc de Bretagne from November 1457. Cf. J. Trévédy,
    'Fous, folles et astrologues à la cour de Bretagne' (Paris: Quimper-Rennes,
    1891), pp. 8f.
 9 This was the professional soldier and court fool Chicot who served Henri
    III, Henri IV and Charles IX of France. Cf. Jal, op. cit., p. 602. His
    ennoblement did cause quite some opposition from the Chambre des Comptes,
    but he received his certificate in March 1584 from Henri III: J. Mathorez,
    'Histoire de Chicot. Bouffon de Henri III' (Paris: Henri Leclerc, 1914),
    p. 23.
10 The role of attendant or keeper of fools will be discussed later.
11 Norris W. Yates, 'The American Humorist' (Iowa State University Press,
    1964), p. 22.
12 The comparison is historically correct. Fools have always been mentioned
    in one breath with dogs, falcons and monkeys.
13 Cf. Armin, op. cit., pp. 41-8.

14 Ibid., p. 41. Armin himself was a student of the actor and fool Tarlton,
    cf. the Introduction to his book by J. P. Collier, p. xi. On Tarlton see:
    J. O. Halliwell, 'Tarlton's Jests and News out of Purgatory' (London:
    printed for the Shakespeare Society, 1848); E. I. Carlyle, 'Richard Tarl-
    ton', in 'Dictionary of National Biography', S. Lee (ed.), vol. 55 (London,
    1898), pp. 369-71. Tarlton, who died in 1588, was such a famous clownish
    comedian that the verb 'tarletonizing' was used in 1592. Ibid., p. 370.
15 Canel, op. cit., pp. 252, 254. See also Jacob Bibliophile (Paul Lacroix),
    Essai historique sur les fous des rois de France, in 'Les Deux Fous', 2
    vols (Paris: Delloye & Lecon, 1837), p. 141. The essay is an historical
    introduction to a novel and should be used with a critical sense, as Lacroix
    is prone to follow his own fantasy more than the facts.
16 Canel, op. cit., p. 253. Jacob Bibliophile (op. cit., p. 141), 'Tout le
    monde le craignait tant sa langue était piquante et envenimée'. Jal claims
    that L'Angéli was eventually thrown out of court under the pressure of
    frequently insulted courtiers (op. cit., p. 603).
17 His real name was Guillaume Marchand. See for this very famous virtuoso:
    J. Mathorez, 'Notes sur Maître Guillaume, fou de Henri IV et de Louis XIII'
    (Paris: Fontemoing & Cie, 1913). Cf. also Canel, op. cit., pp. 207-21.
18 Cf. C. Leber, Introduction to M. J. Rigollot, 'Monnaies inconnues des
    évêques, des innocens, des fous et de quelques autres associations singu-
    lières du même temps' (Paris: Merlin, 1837), p. cxliii. Cf. also William J.
    Thomas, 'Anecdotes and Traditions' (London: printed for the Camden
    Society by John Bowyer Nichols, 1839), p. 56; and Welsford, op. cit.,
    p. 115.
19 Marc Bloch, 'Feudal Society', 2 vols, trans. L. A. Manyon, 1961 (Univer-
    sity of Chicago Press, 1970), vol. I, 'The Growth of Ties of Dependence'.
20 Canel, op. cit., pp. 29f. Strangely enough it was also said of this man
    Corneille that he was a banker and quite rich (ibid., p. 30). City fools
    entertained the people of their own town during festive occasions, such as
    religious processions or the solemn entrance into town of a famous ruler.
    On procession fools, see Canel, op. cit., p. 30. Cf. W. van de Poll, 'Hof-
    narren en Stadsgekken in Gelderland', 1898, in 'Geldersche Volksalmanak'
    (Arnhem: P. Gouda-Quint, 1900), p. 180, about two town fools entertain-
    ing the waiting crowd prior to the entrance of emperor Charles V in
    Nijmegen, the Netherlands. On city fools in Gelderland in the sixteenth
    century, see ibid., pp. 179f.
21 Flögel, op. cit., pp. 90-162, gives an extensive survey of fools and folly in
    antiquity. Other names for these parasites were indicative of the treatment
    they received: 'umbra' = shadows; 'flagrones' = people who are constantly
    beaten; 'capitones' = thickheads; 'klimakides' = little ladders, e.g. women
    who had to kneel down in order for their female and male owners to step on
    them into a carriage (ibid., p. 120; cf. also Doran, op. cit., pp. 1-41
    which borrows mainly from Flögel).
22 Ibid., p. 62.
23 William H. Prescott, 'History of the Conquest of Mexico', 1886, new and
    rev. edn by J. F. Kirk (London: Allen & Unwin, 1925), p. 290, footnote
    5. These jesters 'greatly astonished the Europeans by the marvellous facil-
    ity of their performances, and were thought a suitable present for his
    Holiness the Pope' (p. 607). Cf. Bernal Diaz, 'The Conquest of New Spain',
    c. 1570, trans. J. M. Cohen (London: Penguin Books, 1967), pp. 227-30
    for an eye-witness report on the entertainers of Montezuma. For information
    about Cortés's own fool, cf. Prescott, op. cit., p. 119.
24 Flögel, op. cit., p. 433.
25 Cf. Canel, op. cit., p. 230.
26 See Trévédy, op. cit., and Canel, op. cit., pp. 231, 180f. Some of them
    had a female guardian, called in France 'gouvernante'. See ibid., pp. 180f.
27 Ibid., p. 183.
28 Ibid., p. 231. Also Welsford, op. cit., p. 156.
29 On Mathurine see Canel, op. cit., pp. 189ff; J. Mathorez, 'Mathurine et
    les Libelles publiées sous son nom' (Paris: Henri Leclerq, 1922); Welsford,
    op. cit., pp. 153f.

30 Cf. note 17.
31 Mathorez, op. cit., p. 7: 'aussi malicieuse qu'un vieux singe.'
32 Ibid., p. 8.
33 Ibid., p. 12.
34 Ibid., p. 13. These often quoted words of Mathurine stem from a pamphlet of 1605 called 'Le Lunatique à Maître Guillaume'. Cf. Canel, op. cit., p. 233. Angoulevent, whose full name was Nicolas Joubert, sieur d'Angoulevent, was not a 'fou en titre d'office' but in all probability 'un fou suivant la cour' who allegedly presided as 'Prince des Sots' the joyous society 'Basoche' of Paris. Cf. Canel, op. cit., pp. 233-8. According to Leber, 'Angoulevent' was the name of the joyous society in which Joubert performed as 'farceur'. Rigollot, op. cit., p. lii. This seems to be incorrect.
35 This perverse curiosity was also focused on giants, as well as on other physical deformities. Cf. E. J. Wood, 'Giants and Dwarfs' (London: Richard Bentley, 1868). On the psychology of this curiosity see Leslie Fiedler, 'Freaks. Myths and Images of the Secret Self' (New York: Simon & Schuster, 1978). Under an old portrait of a dwarf was written: 'Gaze on with wonder, and discerne in me; The abstract of the world's epitome' (Wood, op. cit., p. 282).
36 Wood, op. cit., p. 256. Doran, op. cit., p. 40.
37 Flögel, op. cit., p. 514.
38 Dorothy Anne Liot Backer, 'Precious Women' (New York: Basic Books, 1974), p. 82.
39 Ibid., p. 108.
40 Ibid., p. 104.
41 Flögel, op. cit., p. 516.
42 See on minstrelization of little people Marcello Truzzi, Lilliputians in Gulliver's Land: The Social Role of the Dwarf, in Marcello Truzzi (ed.), 'Sociology and Everyday Life' (Englewood Cliffs, N.J.: Prentice-Hall, 1968), pp. 197-211.
43 Lewis A. Coser, 'Greedy Institutions. Patterns of Undivided Commitment' (New York: Free Press; London: Collier-Macmillan, 1974).
44 See J. Wardroper (ed.), 'Jest upon Jest' (London: Routledge & Kegan Paul, 1970).
45 Jacob Bibliophile (Paul Lacroix), op. cit., p. 144.
46 The 'sarcastic' interpretation of 'The Prince' was already in the sixteenth century proposed by Alberico Gentile. It was repeated later by Spinoza, Rousseau and Macaulay. See the Introduction by L. G. Crocker to Niccolo Machiavelli, 'The Prince', trans. C. Detmold (New York: Washington Square Press, 1968), p. xviii. The interpretation is very hazardous, particularly if one keeps Machiavelli's dictum in mind: 'I never believe what I say, or say what I believe.' Cf. J. R. Hale, 'Machiavelli and Renaissance Italy', 1961 (London: Penguin Books, 1972), p. 4.
47 Cf. Neville Williams, 'Henry VIII and his Court', 1971 (London: Sphere Books, 1973). On p. 182 Williams mentions Will Sommer who 'kept behind the scenes, serving his master with adroit circumspection, becoming almost a confessor. Wives changed, ministers fell, palace officials incurred the royal displeasure, but Will Sommers went on for ever. In the last ten years of the reign he was perhaps the man nearest Henry's thoughts and he never wittingly allowed himself to be exploited by factions at court.'
48 Cf. for example Flögel, op. cit., p. 89. See also Franz Rosenthal, 'Humour in Early Islam' (Leiden: Brill, 1956).
49 Robert Briffault, 'The Troubadours', ed. L. F. Koons (Bloomington: Indiana University Press, 1965), pp. 24-80.
50 Canel, op. cit., pp. 127f.
51 Cf. Flögel, op. cit., p. 423. On the scalds, see ibid., pp. 418-25.
52 See Welsford, op. cit., p. 88, 92f. The original meaning of 'fili' is, according to Welsford (p. 92), 'seer'. See also Flögel, op. cit., pp. 385f.
53 Jacob Bibliophile, op. cit., p. 11.
54 Welsford, op. cit., p. 157.
55 Canel, op. cit., pp. 174f, 185.

56 Jacob Bibliophile, op. cit., p. 12.
57 Flögel, op. cit., p. 9; Leber, op. cit., p. xlii, footnote 2; Canel, op. cit., p. 56; Gazeau, op. cit., p. 58.
58 Canel quotes a historian who strongly rejects the authenticity of this letter and even speaks in despair of 'cette maudite lettre' (ibid., p. 57).
59 Briffault, op. cit., p. 81.
60 The profession of executioner did not always stay in one family. An interesting method of recruitment was to grant pardon to a convicted criminal on the condition that he would take on the infamous profession. See Finn Hormann, The Executioner; His Role and Status in Scandinavia, in M. Truzzi (ed.), 'Sociology and Everyday Life' (Englewood Cliffs, N.J.: Prentice-Hall, 1968), pp. 125-37.
61 Welsford, op. cit., pp. 340f. See also Otto Pächt, 'Die Autorschaft des Gonella-Bildnisses' (Vienna: Verlag A. Schroll, 1974), which discusses the beautiful Gonella portrait in the Viennese Kunsthistorisches Museum.
62 This fact is too much overlooked in the literature on court fools. For instance, the famous Brusquet was drawn once as a dwarf next to a huge dog (cf. Gazeau, op. cit., p. 87). But in most descriptions of the man he is not at all referred to as a little man. Possibly more than one individual bore this funny name. This fool started as quack physician in the army, next moved up at the Parisian court as 'valet de garde-robe', 'valet de chambre' and finally 'maître de la poste de Paris' while being appointed court fool at the same time (Canel, op. cit., p. 204). In addition, Raimbault claims that he acted as officially appointed country-judge – 'viguier' – at Antibes also (cf. M. Raimbault, 'Jean-Antoine Lombard, Dit Brusquet, Viguier d'Antibes en 1548' (Paris: Imprimerie Nationale, 1905). One begins to suspect that all these functions were not in the power of one single man (cf. also van Erven: Particularités inconnues sur quelques fous en titre d'office du moyen-âge, in 'Messagers des sciences historiques', Gand, 1858, pp. 314-31, in particular p. 325).
63 Welsford, op. cit., p. 148; Gazeau, op. cit., pp. 114-18.
64 Brantôme (Pierre de Corbeille, abbé séculier de Brantôme), 'Vie des grands capitains' in 'Oeuvres Complètes', vol. I (Paris: R. Sabe, 1848), pp. 329f.
65 Welsford, op. cit., p. 148.
66 Doran is too quick to surmise from Roper's story that More was in danger of becoming a court jester. He quotes Roper (incorrectly) without mentioning his name or giving any reference (Doran, op. cit., p. 147).
67 William Roper, 'A Man of Singular Virtue', c. 1540, ed A. L. Rowse (London: The Folio Society, 1980), pp. 34f.
68 Canel, for instance, mentions the poor 'folle' Lisette, owned by a princess of Conti. She tried to imitate the noted Mathurine but was never very successful at it (Canel, op. cit., p. 245).
69 See for an excellent survey E. Tietze-Conrat, 'Dwarfs and Jesters in Art' (London: Phaidon Press, 1957).
70 Doran, op. cit., p. 135.
71 Cf. H. H. Beek, 'Waanzin in de Middeleeuwen', 1969 (Hoofddorp: De Toorts, 1974), pp. 28f.
72 See Francis Douce, 'Illustrations of Shakespeare and of Ancient Manners' (London: printed for Longman, Harst, Rees & Orme, 1807), pp. 325f.
73 Doran, op. cit., p. 210f.
74 Flögel, op. cit., pp. 312-14; Welsford, op. cit., pp. 10f.
75 Flögel, op. cit., p. 174. See H. D. Barnham, 'Tales of Nasr-er-Din Khoja' (London, 1923); Rosenthal, op. cit., passim; Welsford, op. cit., pp. 29-311.
76 Flögel, op. cit., p. 408.
77 Ibid., p. 409.
78 Cf. my 'Humor und Gesellschaft' (Wien-Graz-Köln: Styria Verlag, 1976) which is a sociological analysis of humour and laughter.
79 Flögel, op. cit., p. 308.
80 Welsford, op. cit., p. 178; Doran, op. cit., p. 204.
81 Flögel, op. cit., pp. 366f.

82 Ibid., p. 288; Doran, op. cit., p. 343. The incident is briefly mentioned by Roland H. Bainton, 'Here I stand. A Life of Martin Luther' (New York, 1950), p. 92. He deems the whole event 'revealing of the coarseness and insensitivity of that whole generation'.
83 Canel, op. cit., pp. 123f.
84 Brantôme, op. cit., pp. 166-79. The Brusquet-Strozzi story is after Brantôme repeated by many historians.
85 Canel, op. cit., pp. 162-64.
86 Flögel, op. cit., p. 448.
87 Doran, op. cit., p. 264. Brantôme describes Thoni as a man of all seasons: 'Il s'accomodit selon les saisons et le temps' (op. cit., p. 330).
88 Cf. W. Danckert, 'Unehrliche Leute. Die verfemten Berufe' (Bern-München: Francke Verlag, 1963); Otto Beneke, 'Von unehrlichen Leuten' (Hamburg: Perthes, Besser & Manke, 1863).
89 Cf. Canel, op. cit., pp. 281ff.
90 Robert Armin, op. cit., p. 46: 'and Will laid him down among the spaniels to sleepe.' Also p. 48.
91 'Whitehall, March 11, 1637. It is this day ordered by his Majesty, with the advice of the board, that Archibald Armstrong, the King's Fool, for certain scandalous words of a high nature, spoken by him against the Lord Archbishop of Canterbury, his Grace, and proved to be uttered by him, by two witnesses, shall have his coat pulled over his head, and be discharged of the King's service, and banished from the court, for which the Lord Chamberlain of the King's household is prayed and required to give order to be executed. And immediately the same was put in execution' (Doran, op. cit., p. 205).
92 A. Armstrong, 'Archy's Dream' - 'sometimes Iester to his Maiestie; but exiled the court by Canterburies malice. With relation for whom an odde chaire stood voided in Hell. Printed in the yeare 1641' (London: John Tuckett, 1868). Archie once received reportedly an estate of 1,000 acres in Ireland and became a rich landowner in Arthuret, Cumberland after his eviction from court. It was written of him with good reason that 'Archee, by kings and princes graced of late, jested himself in a fair estate' (Lee, op. cit., pp. 90f).
93 Doran, op. cit., p. 279. See, for Armstrong, Welsford, op. cit., pp. 172-83.
94 Doran, op. cit., p. 305. Flögel, op. cit., pp. 412f.
95 See Lewis A. Coser, The Alien as Servant of Power: Court Jews and Christian Renegades, in 'Greedy Institutions', pp. 32-47.
96 Canel, op. cit., p. 204. The same king was addressed as 'Monsieur mon bon ami' by Maître Guillaume (ibid., p. 214).
97 J. Mathorez, 'Histoire de Chicot', op. cit., pp. 22f.
98 Chicot was referred to as 'bouffon quand il voulait', fool when he felt like being one, Canel, op. cit., p. 200; Welsford, op. cit., p. 153. But he was also called 'bouffon du roi', the king's fool (p. 200).
99 Canel, op. cit., p. 243.
100 Geoffrey Barraclough, 'The Crucible of Europe' (Berkeley, Los Angeles: University of California Press, 1976).
101 G. Kalff, 'Opkomst, bloei en verdwijning van de hofnar' (Amsterdam: De Poortpers, 1954), p. 159.
102 See Lewis A. Coser, The Royal Mistress as an Instrument of Rule, in 'Greedy Institutions', pp. 47-66.
103 W. Lepenies, 'Melancholie und Gesellschaft' (Neuwied-Berlin: Luchterhand, 1969), pp. 55-68.
104 Flögel, op. cit., p. 441.
105 See for a lively description of this journey; 'A True Relation and Journall of the Manners of the Arrival and Magnificent Entertainment given to the High and Mighty Prince Charles, Prince of Great Britain, by the King of Spaine in his Court at Madrid' (London: printed by John Haviland for William Barret, 1623); and 'A Continuation of a former Relation Concerning the Entertainment given to the Prince His Highnesse by the King of Spaine

at his Court at Madrid' (London: printed by John Haviland for William
Barret, 1623). According to S. L. Lee this journey was the summit of
Archie's career. Although an opponent of 'the Spanish match' he travelled
with Prince Charles and Buckingham to the Spanish court, for the occasion
of which he received an 'extraordinarie rich coate' (cf. S. L. Lee, Archibald Armstrong, in 'Dictionary of National Biography', L. Stephen (ed.),
vol. 2 (London: Smith, Elder & Co., 1885), p. 89.

106   See for this letter Welsford, op. cit., pp. 157f, and Doran, op. cit., pp.
      199f. The letter can be found in the British Library, Add. MS. 19.402.
      fol. 79. The fool, by the way, is not bragging about his close contacts with
      the Spanish king. James Howell writes 10 July 1623 that 'our cousin Archie
      hath more privilege than any', and that he is often sent for by the 'Infanta'
      to amuse her. Yet, he behaved quite impossibly towards the other mem-
      bers of the delegation and even got into a verbal fight publicly with
      Buckingham. He dared to criticize the duke's handling of the negotiations
      with regard to the marriage, whereupon the mighty courtier ordered him to
      be silent, lest he had him hanged. Archie riposted mockingly: 'No one has
      ever heard of a fool being threatened for talking, but many dukes have
      been beheaded for their insolence' (Lee, op. cit., pp. 89f).

107   Doran, op. cit., p. 261.
108   Welsford, op. cit., p. 17.
109   Anthony Ashley Cooper, Earl of Shaftesbury, was probably the first to
      bring up the safety-valve argument, although he did not link it to absolut-
      ism and court fools. See his 'Characteristics', 1711, Treatise 2 on the
      freedom of Wit and Humour (New York: Bobbs-Merrill, 1964), pp. 50f. See
      also Flögel, op. cit., p. 83.
110   J. Mathorez, 'Notes sur Maître Guillaume', vide note 17, above, and
      J. Mathorez, 'Mathurine et les Libelles pubilées sous son nom' (Paris: Henri
      Leclerq, 1922).
111   J. Mathorez, 'Notes sur Maître Guillaume', p. 25.
112   Cf. Norbert Elias, 'Die höfische Gesellschaft', 1969 (Darmstadt-Neuwied:
      Luchterhand, 1975).
113   This is a crucial theme in the study of Lepenies, op. cit.
114   See e.g. Doran, op. cit., p. 351.
115   On Taubmann, see Friedrich Ebeling, 'Zur Geschichte der Hofnarren', 1882
      (Leipzig: Joh. Lehmann, 1884) and Gunther Zehm, Der Hofnarr und seine
      Nachkommen, 'Die Welt', 28 August 1965 (199: III).
116   Flögel, op. cit., p. 223.
117   Ibid., pp. 226-8.
118   Ibid., pp. 235-40.
119   Ibid., pp. 242f.
120   Nick, op. cit., p. 63.
121   Ralf Dahrendorf, Der Intellektuelle und die Gesellschaft. Ueber die soziale
      Funktion des Narren im 20. Jahrhundert, 'Die Zeit', 24 March 1963 (18: 13),
      p. 9. For a summary see Lewis A. Coser, 'Men of Ideas' (New York: Free
      Press, 1965), p. ix.
122   Lepenies, op. cit., pp. 79-99.
123   Georges Lefebre, 'The Coming of the French Revolution', 1939, trans.
      R. R. Palmer (Princeton University Press, 1969).
124   Canel, op. cit., pp. 245f.
125   Backer, op. cit., p. 72.
126   See Cesar Grana, 'Modernity and its Discontents', 1964 (New York: Harper
      Torchbooks, 1967).
127   Backer, op. cit., p. 74.
128   Grana, op. cit., p. 192. See in particular, pp. 148-54.
129   For modern narcissism see Christopher Lasch, 'The Culture of Narcissism'
      (London: Abacus, 1980).
130   Grana, op. cit., p. 148.
131   Ibid., p. 129.
132   Otto Mann, 'Der Dandy. Ein Kulturproblem der Moderne', 1925. (Heidel-
      berg: W. Rothe Verlag, 1962), p. 111.

133   Cf. Donald Day, 'Will Rogers. A Biography' (New York: David McKay, 1962).
134   Yates, op. cit., p. 119.
135   D. Hobson, The Hollywood Flack, 'TV Guide' (April 1969), pp. 6-11.
136   Canel, op. cit., p. 221. 'I have been declared dead, but that's an error, because my folly stays alive.'

4 ENCHANTERS FROM BEYOND
  1   The concept 'primitive' with regard to non-Western, pre-modern cultures should be used, of course, with great care. The following remark of Dick Gregory ought to be taken to heart 'You gotta say this for the white race, its self-confidence knows no bounds. Who else should go to a small island in the South Pacific where there is no poverty, no unemployment, no war, and no worry - and call it a "primitive society" ' (Langston Hughes (ed.): 'The Book of Negro Humor' (New York: Dodd, Mead & Co., 1966), p. 10).
  2   Mircea Eliade, 'Schamanismus und Archaische Ekstasetechnik', trans. from the French by I. Köck (Zürich - Stuttgart: Rascher Verlag, 1947); Hans Findeisen, 'Schamanentum' (Stuttgart: W. Kohlhammer, 1957).
  3   F. Sierksma, 'Tibet's Terrifying Deities' (The Hague: Mouton, 1966), p. 14.
  4   Cf. Ernst Schäfer, 'Fest der weissen Schleier' (Braunschweig: Im Vieweg-Verlag, 1952, 3rd edn), in particular pp. 108-22. Schäfer's expedition to Tibet took place in 1938-9.
  5   William H. Prescott, 'History of the Conquest of Mexico', 1886, new and rev. edn by J. F. Kirk (London: Allen & Unwin, 1925), p. 290.
  6   Bernal Diaz, 'The Conquest of New Spain', c. 1570, trans. J. M. Cohen (London: Penguin Books, 1967), p. 227.
  7   Franz Boas, 'The Social Organization and the Secret Societies of the Kwakiutl Indians', Report of the United States National Museum, under the Direction of The Smithsonian Institution for the Year ending 30 June 1895 (Washington: Government Printing Office, 1897), p. 637.
  8   Anon, 'The Captive of Nootka or the Adventures of John T. Jewett' (Philadelphia: Henry F. Anners, 1841), pp. 202f. Cf. also pp. 219, 155.
  9   Cf. R. H. Blyth, 'Japanese Humor' (Tokyo: Japan Travel Bureau, 1957), p. 73 on Sorori (Sugimoto Shinzaemon) fool of Hideyoshi in the Muromachi Period, 1393-1573.
 10   See Karl F. Flögel, 'Geschichte der Hofnarren' (Liegnitz und Leipzig: David Siegert, 1789), pp. 170-89. See also Franz Rosenthal, 'Humor in Early Islam' (Leiden: Brill, 1956), passim.
 11   Cf. Captain John G. Bourke, 'Scatological Rites of all Nations' (Washington, DC: W. J. Lowdermilk, 1891), pp. 4-10, The Urine Dance of the Zunis. This chapter is followed immediately by one on the Festival of Fools in Europe.
 12   Paul Radin, 'The Trickster. A Study in American Indian Mythology' (New York: Philosophical Library, 1956).
 13   Huizinga, 'De Vidûsaka in het Indisch Tooneel' (Groningen: Noordhoff, 1897) pp. 84, 139. For a recent analysis of the vidûsaka role cf. F. B. J. Kuiper, 'Varuna and Vidûsaka. On the Origin of the Sanskrit Drama' (Amsterdam: North-Holland Publishing, 1979). For more references on this subject, cf. ibid., p. 199.
 14   Geoffrey Gorer, 'Africa Dances' (London: John Lehmann, 1949), p. 125.
 15   E. Adamson Hoebel, 'The Cheyennes. Indians of the Great Plains' (New York: Holt, Rinehart & Winston, 1960), pp. 96f.
 16   Ruth Benedict, 'Patterns of Culture', 1934 (New York: Mentor Books, 1959), p. 95.
 17   Ibid., p. 114.
 18   Ibid., p. 116.
 19   Ruth Bunzel, Introduction to Zuni Ceremonialism, in 'Bureau of American Ethnology: Annual Report' 47 (1929-30), Washington, 1932, pp. 467-1086.
 20   Ibid., p. 251.
 21   Elsie Clews Parsons and Ralph L. Beals, The Sacred Clowns of the Pueblo and Mayo-Yaqui Indians, 'American Anthropologist', 36: 4 (1934), pp. 491-514.
 22   Ibid., p. 491.

23 Quoted by Lucille H. Charles, The Clown's Function, 'Journal of American Folklore', 58 (1945), p. 30.
24 Bourke, op. cit., p. 6.
25 Parsons and Beals, op. cit., p. 491.
26 Ibid., p. 497.
27 Ibid., p. 500.
28 Ibid.
29 Ibid., p. 506.
30 Julien H. Steward, The Ceremonial Buffoon of the American Indian, 'Papers of the Michigan Academy of Science, Arts and Letters', 14 (Ann Arbor: University of Michigan Press, 1931), p. 194.
31 N. Ross Crumrine, Capakoba, the Mayo Easter Ceremonial Impersonator: Explanations of Ritual Clowning, 'Journal of the Scientific Study of Religion', 8:1 (1969), p. 3.
32 Ibid., p. 7.
33 Ibid.
34 Cf. p. 25-7.
35 Bunzel, op. cit., p. 521.
36 Parsons and Beals, op. cit., p. 505.
37 Jacob Levine, Regression in Primitive Clowning, 'Psychoanalytic Quarterly', 30 (1961), p. 80.
38 Ibid., p. 72.
39 John J. Honigmann, An Interpretation of the Socio-Psychological Functions of the Ritual Clown, 'Character and Personality' ('Journal of Personality'), 10 (1942), p. 221. Cf. also Edward Norbeck, African Rituals of Conflict, 'American Anthropologist', 65 (1963), pp. 1254-78.
40 Charles, op. cit., p. 32.
41 Max Gluckman, 'Custom and Conflict in Africa', 1956 (Oxford: Basil Blackwell, 1970), p. 109.
42 Cf. Vusamazulu Credo Mutwa, 'Africa is My Witness' (Johannesburg: Blue Crane Books, 1966), pp. 195-207, The Rebellion of the Women.
43 Gluckman, op. cit., p. 119.
44 W. F. Wertheim, 'East-West Parallels' (Chicago: Quadrangle Books, 1964), p. 31.
45 G. van der Leeuw, 'Religion in Essence and Manifestation', 1938, 2 vols, trans. J. E. Turner (New York: Harper & Row, 1963), vol. 2, pp. 671-95.
46 Ibid., pp. 23-190. Cf. for what follows also Mircea Eliade, 'The Sacred and the Profane. The Nature of Religion', trans. from the French by W. R. Trask (New York: Harcourt, Brace & World, 1959).
47 See Marcel Mauss, 'The Gift', trans. I. Cunnison (New York: Norton, 1967).
48 Mircea Eliade, 'Cosmos and History. The Myth of the Eternal Return', 1949, trans. W. R. Trask (New York: Harper Torchbooks, 1959).
49 Crumrine, op. cit., p. 18.
50 Radin, op. cit., pp. ix-xi.
51 Flögel, op. cit., pp. 166f. John Doran, 'The History of Court Fools', 1858 (New York: Haskell House, 1956), pp. 81-3. The spider is called Nanni, according to Flögel. Doran claims that the trickster Nanni was the son of a mythological spider.
52 On the spider 'ikto-mi' among the Dakota Sioux, see Radin, op. cit., p. 132. Apparently the spider is somehow the mythological symbol of magical folly.
53 Radin, op. cit., p. ix.
54 Ibid., p. 168.
55 Ibid., p. 133.
56 Ibid., episode no. 4.
57 Ibid., p. 152.
58 Ibid., p. x.
59 Ibid., pp. 173-201.
60 Ibid., p. 200. See also pp. 65f. of this book.
61 Huizinga, op. cit., p. 21.

62   Ibid., pp. 22-40.
63   Ibid., p. 29.
64   Ibid.
65   Ibid., p. 37.
66   Ibid., p. 41. Trans. Kuiper, op. cit., p. 206.
67   Huizinga, op. cit., p. 38.
68   Kuiper, op. cit., pp. 23f.
69   Clifford Geertz, 'The Interpretation of Cultures' (New York: Basic Books, 1973), p. 34.
70   Ibid., pp. 139f.
71   Ibid., p. 140.
72   Elsie C. Parsons, Notes on Zuni, Part 2, 'Memoirs of the American Anthropological Association', 4 (1917), pp. 244f.

5   CONCLUSION: FOLLY AND MODERNITY
 1   See my 'The Abstract Society', 1970 (London: Penguin Books, 1972).
 2   Enid Welsford, 'The Fool. His Social and Literary History', 1935 (Gloucester, Mass.: Peter Smith, 1966).
 3   See my 'On Clichés. The Supersedure of Meaning by Function in Modernity' (London: Routledge & Kegan Paul, 1979).
 4   See my The Anti-Institutional Mood, 'Worldview', 15:9 (September 1972), pp. 32-6.
 5   See Richard Sennet, 'The Fall of Public Man', 1974 (Cambridge University Press, 1977); Christopher Lasch, 'The Culture of Narcissism', 1979 (London: Abacus, Sphere Books, 1980).
 6   See my sociology of humour and laughter, 'Humor und Gesellschaft', 1971 (Graz, Vienna, Cologne: Styria Verlag, 1976). Although I have not been able to verify this historically, I believe that the telling of jokes as funny stories within informal, social settings did not occur in the days of traditional folly. Whereas we in modern society create a (rather ephemeral) looking-glass reality in our jokes, traditional people played the fool on various occasions or watched jesters at work as domestic, court or popular fools or as ceremonial clowns. In this sense the humour of our jokes is a rather generalized successor to the folly of these traditional people and their numerous jesters.

NAME INDEX

Goodridge, J.F., 176
Gorer, G., 135, 138, 188
Grana, C., 171, 187
Greeley, A., 172
Gregory, Dick, 188
Gregory the Great, Pope, 59
Grock (circus clown), 24
Groue, Louis de la, see Farce, la
Guazzalotti, Andrea, 78
Guérin (court fool), 96
Gundling, J. Freiherr von (learned
  fool), 124

Hale, J.R., 184
Halliwell, J.O., 183
Haneveld, G.I., 175
Harcourt, Comte d', 73
Harpaste (domestic 'folle'), 95
Haskins, C.H., 176
Hegel, G.W.F., 13
Heidegger, M., 13
Henri II (France), 104
Henri III (France), 96, 103, 182
Henri IV (France), 94, 96, 115, 182,
  183
Henry VIII, 86, 94, 101, 103, 104,
  105, 106, 113, 114, 116, 176, 177,
  184
Herder, J.G., 18
Hideyoshi, 188
Hobsbawm, E.J., 176
Hobson, D., 188
Hoebel, A., 188
Holbroots, R.T., 179
Hölderlin, E., 13
Holländer, E., 175
Honigmann, J., 142, 189
Hood, Robin, 87, 176
Hope, Bob, 24
Hormann, F., 185
Howard, R., 181
Howell, J., 187
Hughes, L., 188
Hugh of Orléans (goliard), 57
Huizinga, J., 35, 41, 53, 57, 135,
  151, 153, 174, 177, 178, 181, 188,
  189
Hus, J., 80, 109

Ibn Kaldun, 16
Illich, I., 172
Innocent X, Pope, 98
Isidor of Seville, 51, 56
Ivan Vasilovitch, Czar, 107

Jacopone da Todi, 87
Jacquette (court 'folle'), 96
Jal, A., 182, 183
James I (England), 119
James, M.R., 177
Jewett, John R., 133, 188

Johannes Adelphus, 81
Joubert, Nicolas, see Angoulevent
Jung, C.G., 65, 66, 85, 150, 179,
  181

Kalff, G., 186
Kaye, Danny, 24
Keckskemeti, P., 171
Kerenyi, K., 150
King Archie, see Armstrong, Archie
King, P.G., 173
Kinneklimmets (ceremonial clown), 134
Kirk, J.F., 183, 188
Klapp, O.E., 29, 173
Knight, K.G., 82, 180
Köck, I. 174, 188
Könneker, B., 81, 174, 179, 180
Koyen, M.H., 174
Kramer, H., 179
Kruithof, C.L., 176, 184
Kuiper, F.B.J., 151, 188, 189

Lackland, John, 94
Lacroiz, Paul, see Bibliophile, Jacob
La Jardinière (court 'folle'), 96
La More (court 'folle'), 96
Langland, W., 47, 176, 177
Lanly, A., 181
Lasch, C., 160, 171, 187, 190
La Turque (court 'folle'), 96
Laud, Archbishop, 109, 141, 186
Leber, C.L., 178, 180, 183, 184, 185
Lee, S., 183, 186, 187
Leeuw, G. van der, 145, 170, 189
Lefèbvre, G., 180, 187
Lefèbvre, J., 127
Leo X, Pope, 55, 86, 120
Lepenies, W., 126, 186, 187
Le Vicomte (fool), 182
Levine, J., 142, 189
Lieber, H.J., 174
Lippman, Walter, 93
Lisette (court 'folle'), 185
Livingston, A., 178
Locher, J., 79
Lodge, T., 82, 181
Lombard, J.A., see Brusquet
Lord Allan (dandy), 129
Louis XI, 68
Louis XII, 182
Louis XIII, 94, 96, 183
Louis XIV, 34, 94, 101, 105, 116, 117,
  120, 121, 126, 127
Louis XVI, 101, 127
Louis Philippe, 127
Luckács, G., 9, 14, 171
Luckmann, T., 170
Luther, M., 109, 121, 186
Lydgate, 178

Machiavelli, N., 55, 100, 101, 116,
  184

SUBJECT INDEX

Routledge Social Science Series

Routledge & Kegan Paul   London, Henley and Boston

39 Store Street,
London WC1E 7DD
Broadway House,
Newtown Road,
Henley-on-Thames,
Oxon RG9 1EN
9 Park Street,
Boston, Mass. 02108

Contents

*Authors wishing to submit manuscripts for any series
in this catalogue should send them to the Social Science Editor,
Routledge & Kegan Paul Ltd, 39 Store Street,
London WC1E 7DD.*
● *Books so marked are available in paperback.*
○ *Books so marked are available in paperback only.*
*All books are in metric Demy 8vo format (216 × 138mm approx.)
unless otherwise stated.*

2

International Library of Sociology
General Editor John Rex

GENERAL SOCIOLOGY

Barnsley, J. H. The Social Reality of Ethics. *464 pp.*
Brown, Robert. Explanation in Social Science. *208 pp.*
● Rules and Laws in Sociology. *192 pp.*
Bruford, W. H. Chekhov and His Russia. *A Sociological Study. 244 pp.*
Burton, F. and **Carlen, P.** Official Discourse. *On Discourse Analysis, Government Publications, Ideology. About 140 pp.*
Cain, Maureen E. Society and the Policeman's Role. *326 pp.*
● **Fletcher, Colin.** Beneath the Surface. *An Account of Three Styles of Sociological Research. 221 pp.*
Gibson, Quentin. The Logic of Social Enquiry. *240 pp.*
Glassner, B. Essential Interactionism. *208 pp.*
Glucksmann, M. Structuralist Analysis in Contemporary Social Thought. *212 pp.*
Gurvitch, Georges. Sociology of Law. *Foreword by Roscoe Pound. 264 pp.*
Hinkle, R. Founding Theory of American Sociology 1881–1913. *About 350 pp.*
Homans, George C. Sentiments and Activities. *336 pp.*
Johnson, Harry M. Sociology: *A Systematic Introduction. Foreword by Robert K. Merton. 710 pp.*
● **Keat, Russell** and **Urry, John.** Social Theory as Science. *278 pp.*
Mannheim, Karl. Essays on Sociology and Social Psychology. *Edited by Paul Keckskemeti. With Editorial Note by Adolph Lowe. 344 pp.*
Martindale, Don. The Nature and Types of Sociological Theory. *292 pp.*
● **Maus, Heinz.** A Short History of Sociology. *234 pp.*
Myrdal, Gunnar. Value in Social Theory: *A Collection of Essays on Methodology. Edited by Paul Streeten. 332 pp.*
Ogburn, William F. and **Nimkoff, Meyer F.** A Handbook of Sociology. *Preface by Karl Mannheim. 656 pp. 46 figures. 35 tables.*
Parsons, Talcott and **Smelser, Neil J.** Economy and Society: *A Study in the Integration of Economic and Social Theory. 362 pp.*
Payne, G., Dingwall, R., Payne, J. and **Carter, M.** Sociology and Social Research. *About 250 pp.*
Podgórecki, A. Practical Social Sciences. *About 200 pp.*
Podgórecki, A. and **Łos, M.** Multidimensional Sociology. *268 pp.*
Raffel, S. Matters of Fact. *A Sociological Inquiry. 152 pp.*
● **Rex, John.** Key Problems of Sociological Theory. *220 pp.*
Sociology and the Demystification of the Modern World. *282 pp.*
● **Rex, John.** (Ed.) Approaches to Sociology. *Contributions by Peter Abell, Frank Bechhofer, Basil Bernstein, Ronald Fletcher, David Frisby, Miriam Glucksmann, Peter Lassman, Herminio Martins, John Rex, Roland Robertson, John Westergaard and Jock Young. 302 pp.*
Rigby, A. Alternative Realities. *352 pp.*
Roche, M. Phenomenology, Language and the Social Sciences. *374 pp.*
Sahay, A. Sociological Analysis. *220 pp.*
Strasser, Hermann. The Normative Structure of Sociology. *Conservative and Emancipatory Themes in Social Thought. About 340 pp.*
Strong, P. Ceremonial Order of the Clinic. *267 pp.*
Urry, John. Reference Groups and the Theory of Revolution. *244 pp.*
Weinberg, E. Development of Sociology in the Soviet Union. *173 pp.*

FOREIGN CLASSICS OF SOCIOLOGY

● **Gerth, H. H.** and **Mills, C. Wright.** From Max Weber: *Essays in Sociology. 502 pp.*

● **Tönnies, Ferdinand.** Community and Association *(Gemeinschaft und Gesell-schaft).|Translated and Supplemented by Charles P. Loomis. Foreword by Pitirim A. Sorokin. 334 pp.*

SOCIAL STRUCTURE

Andreski, Stanislav. Military Organization and Society. *Foreword by Professor A. R. Radcliffe-Brown. 226 pp. 1 folder.*

Broom, L., Lancaster Jones, F., McDonnell, P. and **Williams, T.** The Inheritance of Inequality. *About 180 pp.*

Carlton, Eric. Ideology and Social Order. *Foreword by Professor Philip Abrahams. About 320 pp.*

Clegg, S. and **Dunkerley, D.** Organization, Class and Control. *614 pp.*

Coontz, Sydney H. Population Theories and the Economic Interpretation. *202 pp.*

Coser, Lewis. The Functions of Social Conflict. *204 pp.*

Crook, I. and **D.** The First Years of the Yangyi Commune. *304 pp., illustrated.*

Dickie-Clark, H. F. Marginal Situation: *A Sociological Study of a Coloured Group. 240 pp. 11 tables.*

Giner, S. and **Archer, M. S.** (Eds) Contemporary Europe: *Social Structures and Cultural Patterns, 336 pp.*

● **Glaser, Barney** and **Strauss, Anselm L.** Status Passage: *A Formal Theory. 212 pp.*

Glass, D. V. (Ed.) Social Mobility in Britain. *Contributions by J. Berent, T. Bottomore, R. C. Chambers, J. Floud, D. V. Glass, J. R. Hall, H. T. Himmelweit, R. K. Kelsall, F. M. Martin, C. A. Moser, R. Mukherjee and W. Ziegel. 420 pp.*

Kelsall, R. K. Higher Civil Servants in Britain: *From 1870 to the Present Day. 268 pp. 31 tables.*

● **Lawton, Denis.** Social Class, Language and Education. *192 pp.*

McLeish, John. The Theory of Social Change: *Four Views Considered. 128 pp.*

● **Marsh, David C.** The Changing Social Structure of England and Wales, 1871–1961. *Revised edition. 288 pp.*

Menzies, Ken. Talcott Parsons and the Social Image of Man. *About 208 pp.*

● **Mouzelis, Nicos.** Organization and Bureaucracy. *An Analysis of Modern Theories. 240 pp.*

● **Ossowski, Stanislaw.** Class Structure in the Social Consciousness. *210 pp.*

● **Podgórecki, Adam.** Law and Society. *302 pp.*

Renner, Karl. Institutions of Private Law and Their Social Functions. *Edited, with an Introduction and Notes, by O. Kahn-Freud. Translated by Agnes Schwarzschild. 316 pp.*

Rex, J. and **Tomlinson, S.** Colonial Immigrants in a British City. *A Class Analysis. 368 pp.*

Smooha, S. Israel: Pluralism and Conflict. *472 pp.*

Wesolowski, W. Class, Strata and Power. *Trans. and with Introduction by G. Kolankiewicz. 160 pp.*

Zureik, E. Palestinians in Israel. *A Study in Internal Colonialism. 264 pp.*

SOCIOLOGY AND POLITICS

Acton, T. A. Gypsy Politics and Social Change. *316 pp.*

Burton, F. Politics of Legitimacy. *Struggles in a Belfast Community. 250 pp.*

Crook, I. and **D.** Revolution in a Chinese Village. *Ten Mile Inn. 216 pp., illustrated.*

Etzioni-Halevy, E. Political Manipulation and Administrative Power. *A Comparative Study. About 200 pp.*

Fielding, N. The National Front. *About 250 pp.*

● **Hechter, Michael.** Internal Colonialism. *The Celtic Fringe in British National Development, 1536–1966. 380 pp.*

Kornhauser, William. The Politics of Mass Society. *272 pp. 20 tables.*

4

Korpi, W. The Working Class in Welfare Capitalism. *Work, Unions and Politics in Sweden. 472 pp.*

Kroes, R. Soldiers and Students. *A Study of Right- and Left-wing Students. 174 pp.*

Martin, Roderick. Sociology of Power. *About 272 pp.*

Merquior, J. G. Rousseau and Weber. *A Study in the Theory of Legitimacy. About 288 pp.*

Myrdal, Gunnar. The Political Element in the Development of Economic Theory. *Translated from the German by Paul Streeten. 282 pp.*

Varma, B. N. The Sociology and Politics of Development. *A Theoretical Study. 236 pp.*

Wong, S.-L. Sociology and Socialism in Contemporary China. *160 pp.*

Wootton, Graham. Workers, Unions and the State. *188 pp.*

CRIMINOLOGY

Ancel, Marc. Social Defence: *A Modern Approach to Criminal Problems. Foreword by Leon Radzinowicz. 240 pp.*

Athens, L. Violent Criminal Acts and Actors. *104 pp.*

Cain, Maureen E. Society and the Policeman's Role. *326 pp.*

Cloward, Richard A. and **Ohlin, Lloyd E.** Delinquency and Opportunity: *A Theory of Delinquent Gangs. 248 pp.*

Downes, David M. The Delinquent Solution. *A Study in Subcultural Theory. 296 pp.*

Friedlander, Kate. The Psycho-Analytical Approach to Juvenile Delinquency: *Theory, Case Studies, Treatment. 320 pp.*

Gleuck, Sheldon and **Eleanor.** Family Environment and Delinquency. *With the statistical assistance of Rose W. Kneznek. 340 pp.*

Lopez-Rey, Manuel. Crime. *An Analytical Appraisal. 288 pp.*

Mannheim, Hermann. Comparative Criminology: *A Text Book. Two volumes. 442 pp. and 380 pp.*

Morris, Terence. The Criminal Area: *A Study in Social Ecology. Foreword by Hermann Mannheim. 232 pp. 25 tables. 4 maps.*

Rock, Paul. Making People Pay. *338 pp.*

● **Taylor, Ian, Walton, Paul** and **Young, Jock.** The New Criminology. *For a Social Theory of Deviance. 325 pp.*

● **Taylor, Ian, Walton, Paul** and **Young, Jock.** (Eds) Critical Criminology. *268 pp.*

SOCIAL PSYCHOLOGY

Bagley, Christopher. The Social Psychology of the Epileptic Child. *320 pp.*

Brittan, Arthur. Meanings and Situations. *224 pp.*

Carroll, J. Break-Out from the Crystal Palace. *200 pp.*

● **Fleming, C. M.** Adolescence: Its Social Psychology. *With an Introduction to recent findings from the fields of Anthropology, Physiology, Medicine, Psychometrics and Sociometry. 288 pp.*

● The Social Psychology of Education: *An Introduction and Guide to Its Study. 136 pp.*

Linton, Ralph. The Cultural Background of Personality. *132 pp.*

● **Mayo, Elton.** The Social Problems of an Industrial Civilization. *With an Appendix on the Political Problem. 180 pp.*

Ottaway, A. K. C. Learning Through Group Experience. *176 pp.*

Plummer, Ken. Sexual Stigma. *An Interactionist Account. 254 pp.*

● **Rose, Arnold M.** (Ed.) Human Behaviour and Social Processes: *an Interactionist Approach. Contributions by Arnold M. Rose, Ralph H. Turner, Anselm Strauss, Everett C. Hughes, E. Franklin Frazier, Howard S. Becker et al. 696 pp.*

Smelser, Neil J. Theory of Collective Behaviour. *448 pp.*

Stephenson, Geoffrey M. The Development of Conscience. *128 pp.*

Young, Kimball. Handbook of Social Psychology. *658 pp. 16 figures. 10 tables.*

SOCIOLOGY OF THE FAMILY

Bell, Colin R. Middle Class Families: *Social and Geographical Mobility. 224 pp.*
Burton, Lindy. Vulnerable Children. *272 pp.*
Gavron, Hannah. The Captive Wife: *Conflicts of Household Mothers. 190 pp.*
George, Victor and **Wilding, Paul.** Motherless Families. *248 pp.*
Klein, Josephine. Samples from English Cultures.
   1. Three Preliminary Studies and Aspects of Adult Life in England. *447 pp.*
   2. Child-Rearing Practices and Index. *247 pp.*
Klein, Viola. The Feminine Character. *History of an Ideology. 244 pp.*
McWhinnie, Alexina M. Adopted Children. *How They Grow Up. 304 pp.*
● **Morgan, D. H. J.** Social Theory and the Family. *About 320 pp.*
● **Myrdal, Alva** and **Klein, Viola.** Women's Two Roles: *Home and Work. 238 pp.*
   27 tables.
Parsons, Talcott and **Bales, Robert F.** Family: Socialization and Interaction Process.
   In collaboration with James Olds, Morris Zelditch and Philip E. Slater. 456 pp.
   50 figures and tables.

SOCIAL SERVICES

Bastide, Roger. The Sociology of Mental Disorder. *Translated from the French by Jean McNeil. 260 pp.*
Carlebach, Julius. Caring For Children in Trouble. *266 pp.*
George, Victor. Foster Care. *Theory and Practice. 234 pp.*
   Social Security: *Beveridge and After. 258 pp.*
George, V. and **Wilding, P.** Motherless Families. *248 pp.*
● **Goetschius, George W.** Working with Community Groups. *256 pp.*
Goetschius, George W. and **Tash, Joan.** Working with Unattached Youth. *416 pp.*
Heywood, Jean S. Children in Care. *The Development of the Service for the Deprived Child. Third revised edition. 284 pp.*
King, Roy D., Ranes, Norma V. and **Tizard, Jack.** Patterns of Residential Care. *356 pp.*
Leigh, John. Young People and Leisure. *256 pp.*
● **Mays, John.** (Ed.) Penelope Hall's Social Services of England and Wales. *368 pp.*
Morris, Mary. Voluntary Work and the Welfare State. *300 pp.*
Nokes, P. L. The Professional Task in Welfare Practice. *152 pp.*
Timms, Noel. Psychiatric Social Work in Great Britain (1939–1962). *280 pp.*
●   Social Casework: *Principles and Practice. 256 pp.*

SOCIOLOGY OF EDUCATION

Banks, Olive. Parity and Prestige in English Secondary Education: a Study in Educational Sociology. *272 pp.*
● **Blyth, W. A. L.** English Primary Education. *A Sociological Description.*
   2. Background. *168 pp.*
Collier, K. G. The Social Purposes of Education: *Personal and Social Values in Education. 268 pp.*
Evans, K. M. Sociometry and Education. *158 pp.*
● **Ford, Julienne.** Social Class and the Comprehensive School. *192 pp.*
Foster, P. J. Education and Social Change in Ghana. *336 pp. 3 maps.*
Fraser, W. R. Education and Society in Modern France. *150 pp.*
Grace, Gerald R. Role Conflict and the Teacher. *150 pp.*
Hans, Nicholas. New Trends in Education in the Eighteenth Century. *278 pp. 19 tables.*
●   Comparative Education: *A Study of Educational Factors and Traditions. 360 pp.*
● **Hargreaves, David.** Interpersonal Relations and Education. *432 pp.*
●   Social Relations in a Secondary School. *240 pp.*
   School Organization and Pupil Involvement. *A Study of Secondary Schools.*

- **Mannheim, Karl** and **Stewart, W. A. C.** An Introduction to the Sociology of Education. *206 pp.*
- **Musgrove, F.** Youth and the Social Order. *176 pp.*
- **Ottaway, A. K. C.** Education and Society: An Introduction to the Sociology of Education. *With an Introduction by W. O. Lester Smith. 212 pp.*

Peers, Robert. Adult Education: *A Comparative Study. Revised edition. 398 pp.*

Stratta, Erica. The Education of Borstal Boys. *A Study of their Educational Experiences prior to, and during, Borstal Training. 256 pp.*

- **Taylor, P. H., Reid, W. A.** and **Holley, B. J.** The English Sixth Form. *A Case Study in Curriculum Research. 198 pp.*

SOCIOLOGY OF CULTURE

Eppel, E. M. and **M.** Adolescents and Morality: *A Study of some Moral Values and Dilemmas of Working Adolescents in the Context of a changing Climate of Opinion. Foreword by W. J. H. Sprott. 268 pp. 39 tables.*

- **Fromm, Erich.** The Fear of Freedom. *286 pp.*
- The Sane Society. *400 pp.*

Johnson, L. The Cultural Critics. *From Matthew Arnold to Raymond Williams. 233 pp.*

Mannheim, Karl. Essays on the Sociology of Culture. *Edited by Ernst Mannheim in co-operation with Paul Kecskemeti. Editorial Note by Adolph Lowe. 280 pp.*

Merquior, J. G. The Veil and the Mask. *Essays on Culture and Ideology. Foreword by Ernest Gellner. 140 pp.*

Zijderfeld, A. C. On Clichés. *The Supersedure of Meaning by Function in Modernity. 150 pp.*

SOCIOLOGY OF RELIGION

Argyle, Michael and **Beit-Hallahmi, Benjamin.** The Social Psychology of Religion. *256 pp.*

Glasner, Peter E. The Sociology of Secularisation. *A Critique of a Concept. 146 pp.*

Hall, J. R. The Ways Out. *Utopian Communal Groups in an Age of Babylon. 280 pp.*

Ranson, S., Hinings, B. and **Bryman, A.** Clergy, Ministers and Priests. *216 pp.*

Stark, Werner. The Sociology of Religion. *A Study of Christendom.*

Volume II. *Sectarian Religion. 368 pp.*

Volume III. *The Universal Church. 464 pp.*

Volume IV. *Types of Religious Man. 352 pp.*

Volume V. *Types of Religious Culture. 464 pp.*

Turner, B. S. Weber and Islam. *216 pp.*

Watt, W. Montgomery. Islam and the Integration of Society. *320 pp.*

SOCIOLOGY OF ART AND LITERATURE

Jarvie, Ian C. Towards a Sociology of the Cinema. *A Comparative Essay on the Structure and Functioning of a Major Entertainment Industry. 405 pp.*

Rust, Frances S. Dance in Society. *An Analysis of the Relationships between the Social Dance and Society in England from the Middle Ages to the Present Day. 256 pp. 8 pp. of plates.*

Schücking, L. L. The Sociology of Literary Taste. *112 pp.*

Wolff, Janet. Hermeneutic Philosophy and the Sociology of Art. *150 pp.*

SOCIOLOGY OF KNOWLEDGE

Diesing, P. Patterns of Discovery in the Social Sciences. *262 pp.*

7

- **Douglas, J. D.** (Ed.) Understanding Everyday Life. *370 pp.*
- **Hamilton, P.** Knowledge and Social Structure. *174 pp.*

Jarvie, I. C. Concepts and Society. *232 pp.*

Mannheim, Karl. Essays on the Sociology of Knowledge. *Edited by Paul Kecskemeti. Editorial Note by Adolph Lowe. 353 pp.*

Remmling, Gunter W. The Sociology of Karl Mannheim. *With a Bibliographical Guide to the Sociology of Knowledge, Ideological Analysis, and Social Planning. 255 pp.*

Remmling, Gunter W. (Ed.) Towards the Sociology of Knowledge. *Origin and Development of a Sociological Thought Style. 463 pp.*

Scheler, M. Problems of a Sociology of Knowledge. *Trans. by M. S. Frings. Edited and with an Introduction by K. Stikkers. 232 pp.*

URBAN SOCIOLOGY

Aldridge, M. The British New Towns. *A Programme Without a Policy. 232 pp.*

Ashworth, William. The Genesis of Modern British Town Planning: *A Study in Economic and Social History of the Nineteenth and Twentieth Centuries. 288 pp.*

Brittan, A. The Privatised World. *196 pp.*

Cullingworth, J. B. Housing Needs and Planning Policy: *A Restatement of the Problems of Housing Need and 'Overspill' in England and Wales. 232 pp. 44 tables. 8 maps.*

Dickinson, Robert E. City and Region: *A Geographical Interpretation. 608 pp. 125 figures.*

The West European City: *A Geographical Interpretation. 600 pp. 129 maps. 29 plates.*

Humphreys, Alexander J. New Dubliners: *Urbanization and the Irish Family. Foreword by George C. Homans. 304 pp.*

Jackson, Brian. Working Class Community: *Some General Notions raised by a Series of Studies in Northern England. 192 pp.*

- **Mann, P. H.** An Approach to Urban Sociology. *240 pp.*

Mellor, J. R. Urban Sociology in an Urbanized Society. *326 pp.*

Morris, R. N. and **Mogey, J.** The Sociology of Housing. *Studies at Berinsfield. 232 pp. 4 pp. plates.*

Mullan, R. Stevenage Ltd. *About 250 pp.*

Rex, J. and **Tomlinson, S.** Colonial Immigrants in a British City. *A Class Analysis. 368 pp.*

Rosser, C. and **Harris, C.** The Family and Social Change. *A Study of Family and Kinship in a South Wales Town. 352 pp. 8 maps.*

- **Stacey, Margaret, Batsone, Eric, Bell, Colin** and **Thurcott, Anne.** Power, Persistence and Change. *A Second Study of Banbury. 196 pp.*

RURAL SOCIOLOGY

Mayer, Adrian C. Peasants in the Pacific. *A Study of Fiji Indian Rural Society. 248 pp. 20 plates.*

Williams, W. M. The Sociology of an English Village: *Gosforth. 272 pp. 12 figures. 13 tables.*

SOCIOLOGY OF INDUSTRY AND DISTRIBUTION

Dunkerley, David. The Foreman. *Aspects of Task and Structure. 192 pp.*

Eldridge, J. E. T. Industrial Disputes. *Essays in the Sociology of Industrial Relations. 288 pp.*

Hollowell, Peter G. The Lorry Driver. *272 pp.*

- **Oxaal, I., Barnett, T.** and **Booth, D.** (Eds) Beyond the Sociology of Development.

Economy and Society in Latin America and Africa. 295 pp.

Smelser, Neil J. Social Change in the Industrial Revolution: *An Application of Theory to the Lancashire Cotton Industry, 1770–1840. 468 pp. 12 figures. 14 tables.*

Watson, T. J. The Personnel Managers. *A Study in the Sociology of Work and Employment, 262 pp.*

ANTHROPOLOGY

Brandel-Syrier, Mia. Reeftown Elite. *A Study of Social Mobility in a Modern African Community on the Reef. 376 pp.*

Dickie-Clark, H. F. The Marginal Situation. *A Sociological Study of a Coloured Group. 236 pp.*

Dube, S. C. Indian Village. *Foreword by Morris Edward Opler. 276 pp. 4 plates.*
India's Changing Villages: *Human Factors in Community Development. 260 pp. 8 plates. 1 map.*

Fei, H.-T. Peasant Life in China. *A Field Study of Country Life in the Yangtze Valley. With a foreword by Bronislaw Malinowski. 328 pp. 16 pp. plates.*

Firth, Raymond. Malay Fishermen. *Their Peasant Economy. 420 pp. 17 pp. plates.*

Gulliver, P. H. Social Control in an African Society: a Study of the Arusha, Agricultural Masai of Northern Tanganyika. *320 pp. 8 plates. 10 figures.*
Family Herds. *288 pp.*

Jarvie, Ian C. The Revolution in Anthropology. *268 pp.*

Little, Kenneth L. Mende of Sierra Leone. *308 pp. and folder.*
Negroes in Britain. *With a New Introduction and Contemporary Study by Leonard Bloom. 320 pp.*

Tambs-Lyche, H. London Patidars. *About 180 pp.*

Madan, G. R. Western Sociologists on Indian Society. *Marx, Spencer, Weber, Durkheim, Pareto. 384 pp.*

Mayer, A. C. Peasants in the Pacific. *A Study of Fiji Indian Rural Society. 248 pp.*

Meer, Fatima. Race and Suicide in South Africa. *325 pp.*

Smith, Raymond T. The Negro Family in British Guiana: *Family Structure and Social Status in the Villages. With a Foreword by Meyer Fortes. 314 pp. 8 plates. 1 figure. 4 maps.*

SOCIOLOGY AND PHILOSOPHY

Adriaansens, H. Talcott Parsons and the Conceptual Dilemma. *About 224 pp.*

Barnsley, John H. The Social Reality of Ethics. *A Comparative Analysis of Moral Codes. 448 pp.*

Diesing, Paul. Patterns of Discovery in the Social Sciences. *362 pp.*

● **Douglas, Jack D.** (Ed.) Understanding Everyday Life. *Toward the Reconstruction of Sociological Knowledge. Contributions by Alan F. Blum, Aaron W. Cicourel, Norman K. Denzin, Jack D. Douglas, John Heeren, Peter McHugh, Peter K. Manning, Melvin Power, Matthew Speier, Roy Turner, D. Lawrence Wieder, Thomas P. Wilson and Don H. Zimmerman. 370 pp.*

Gorman, Robert A. The Dual Vision. *Alfred Schutz and the Myth of Phenomenological Social Science. 240 pp.*

Jarvie, Ian C. Concepts and Society. *216 pp.*

Kilminster, R. Praxis and Method. *A Sociological Dialogue with Lukács, Gramsci and the Early Frankfurt School. 334 pp.*

● **Pelz, Werner.** The Scope of Understanding in Sociology. *Towards a More Radical Reorientation in the Social Humanistic Sciences. 283 pp.*

Roche, Maurice. Phenomenology, Language and the Social Sciences. *371 pp.*

Sahay, Arun. Sociological Analysis. *212 pp.*

● **Slater, P.** Origin and Significance of the Frankfurt School. *A Marxist Perspective. 185 pp.*

Spurling, L. Phenomenology and the Social World. *The Philosophy of Merleau-Ponty and its Relation to the Social Sciences. 222 pp.*

Wilson, H. T. The American Ideology. *Science, Technology and Organization as Modes of Rationality. 368 pp.*

International Library of Anthropology
General Editor Adam Kuper

● Ahmed, A. S. Millennium and Charisma Among Pathans. *A Critical Essay in Social Anthropology. 192 pp.*
  Pukhtun Economy and Society. *Traditional Structure and Economic Development. About 360 pp.*

Barth, F. Selected Essays. *Volume I. About 250 pp.* Selected Essays. *Volume II. About 250 pp.*

Brown, Paula. The Chimbu. *A Study of Change in the New Guinea Highlands. 151 pp.*

Foner, N. Jamaica Farewell. *200 pp.*

Gudeman, Stephen. Relationships, Residence and the Individual. *A Rural Panamanian Community. 288 pp. 11 plates, 5 figures, 2 maps, 10 tables.*
  The Demise of a Rural Economy. *From Subsistence to Capitalism in a Latin American Village. 160 pp.*

Hamnett, Ian. Chieftainship and Legitimacy. *An Anthropological Study of Executive Law in Lesotho. 163 pp.*

Hanson, F. Allan. Meaning in Culture. *127 pp.*

Hazan, H. The Limbo People. *A Study of the Constitution of the Time Universe Among the Aged. About 192 pp.*

Humphreys, S. C. Anthropology and the Greeks. *288 pp.*

Karp, I. Fields of Change Among the Iteso of Kenya. *140 pp.*

Lloyd, P. C. Power and Independence. *Urban Africans' Perception of Social Inequality. 264 pp.*

Parry, J. P. Caste and Kinship in Kangra. *352 pp. Illustrated.*

Pettigrew, Joyce. Robber Noblemen. *A Study of the Political System of the Sikh Jats. 284 pp.*

Street, Brian V. The Savage in Literature. *Representations of 'Primitive' Society in English Fiction, 1858–1920. 207 pp.*

Van Den Berghe, Pierre L. Power and Privilege at an African University. *278 pp.*

International Library of Phenomenology and Moral Sciences
General Editor John O'Neill

Apel, K.-O. Towards a Transformation of Philosophy. *308 pp.*

Bologh, R. W. Dialectical Phenomenology. *Marx's Method. 287 pp.*

Fekete, J. The Critical Twilight. *Explorations in the Ideology of Anglo-American Literary Theory from Eliot to McLuhan. 300 pp.*

Medina, A. Reflection, Time and the Novel. *Towards a Communicative Theory of Literature. 143 pp.*

International Library of Social Policy
General Editor Kathleen Jones

Bayley, M. Mental Handicap and Community Care. *426 pp.*

Bottoms, A. E. and McClean, J. D. Defendants in the Criminal Process. *284 pp.*

Bradshaw, J. The Family Fund. *An Initiative in Social Policy. About 224 pp.*

Butler, J. R. Family Doctors and Public Policy. *208 pp.*
Davies, Martin. Prisoners of Society. *Attitudes and Aftercare. 204 pp.*
Gittus, Elizabeth. Flats, Families and the Under-Fives. *285 pp.*
Holman, Robert. Trading in Children. *A Study of Private Fostering. 355 pp.*
Jeffs, A. Young People and the Youth Service. *160 pp.*
Jones, Howard and Cornes, Paul. Open Prisons. *288 pp.*
Jones, Kathleen. History of the Mental Health Service. *428 pp.*
Jones, Kathleen with **Brown, John, Cunningham, W. J., Roberts, Julian** and
    Williams, Peter. Opening the Door. *A Study of New Policies for the Mentally
    Handicapped. 278 pp.*
Karn, Valerie. Retiring to the Seaside. *400 pp. 2 maps. Numerous tables.*
King, R. D. and **Elliot, K. W.** Albany: Birth of a Prison—End of an Era. *394 pp.*
Thomas, J. E. The English Prison Officer since 1850: *A Study in Conflict. 258 pp.*
Walton, R. G. Women in Social Work. *303 pp.*
● **Woodward, J.** To Do the Sick No Harm. *A Study of the British Voluntary Hospital
    System to 1875. 234 pp.*

International Library of Welfare and Philosophy
General Editors   Noel Timms and David Watson

● **McDermott, F. E.** (Ed.) Self-Determination in Social Work. *A Collection of Essays
    on Self-determination and Related Concepts by Philosophers and Social Work
    Theorists. Contributors: F. P. Biestek, S. Bernstein, A. Keith-Lucas, D. Sayer,
    H. H. Perelman, C. Whittington, R. F. Stalley, F. E. McDermott, I. Berlin, H. J.
    McCloskey, H. L. A. Hart, J. Wilson, A. I. Melden, S. I. Benn. 254 pp.*
● **Plant, Raymond.** Community and Ideology. *104 pp.*
Ragg, Nicholas M. People Not Cases. *A Philosophical Approach to Social Work.
    168 pp.*
● **Timms, Noel** and **Watson, David.** (Eds) Talking About Welfare. *Readings in
    Philosophy and Social Policy. Contributors: T. H. Marshall, R. B. Brandt, G. H.
    von Wright, K. Nielsen, M. Cranston, R. M. Titmuss, R. S. Downie, E. Telfer, D.
    Donnison, J. Benson, P. Leonard, A. Keith-Lucas, D. Walsh, I. T. Ramsey.
    320 pp.*
● Philosophy in Social Work. *250 pp.*
● **Weale, A.** Equality and Social Policy. *164 pp.*

Library of Social Work
General Editor   Noel Timms

● **Baldock, Peter.** Community Work and Social Work. *140 pp.*
○ **Beedell, Christopher.** Residential Life with Children. *210 pp. Crown 8vo.*
● **Berry, Juliet.** Daily Experience in Residential Life. *A Study of Children and their
    Care-givers. 202 pp.*
○ Social Work with Children. *190 pp. Crown 8vo.*
● **Brearley, C. Paul.** Residential Work with the Elderly. *116 pp.*
● Social Work, Ageing and Society. *126 pp.*
● **Cheetham, Juliet.** Social Work with Immigrants. *240 pp. Crown 8vo.*
● **Cross, Crispin P.** (Ed.) Interviewing and Communication in Social Work.
    *Contributions by C. P. Cross, D. Laurenson, B. Strutt, S. Raven. 192 pp. Crown
    8vo.*

● **Curnock, Kathleen** and **Hardiker, Pauline.** Towards Practice Theory. *Skills and Methods in Social Assessments. 208 pp.*

● **Davies, Bernard.** The Use of Groups in Social Work Practice. *158 pp.*

● **Davies, Martin.** Support Systems in Social Work. *144 pp.*

Ellis, June. (Ed.) West African Families in Britain. *A Meeting of Two Cultures. Contributions by Pat Stapleton, Vivien Biggs. 150 pp. 1 Map.*

● **Hart, John.** Social Work and Sexual Conduct. *230 pp.*

● **Hutten, Joan M.** Short-Term Contracts in Social Work. *Contributions by Stella M. Hall, Elsie Osborne, Mannie Sher, Eva Sternberg, Elizabeth Tuters. 134 pp.*

Jackson, Michael P. and **Valencia, B. Michael.** Financial Aid Through Social Work. *140 pp.*

● **Jones, Howard.** The Residential Community. *A Setting for Social Work. 150 pp.*

● (Ed.) Towards a New Social Work. *Contributions by Howard Jones, D. A. Fowler, J. R. Cypher, R. G. Walton, Geoffrey Mungham, Philip Priestley, Ian Shaw, M. Bartley, R. Deacon, Irwin Epstein, Geoffrey Pearson. 184 pp.*

Jones, Ray and **Pritchard, Colin.** (Eds) Social Work With Adolescents. *Contributions by Ray Jones, Colin Pritchard, Jack Dunham, Florence Rossetti, Andrew Kerslake, John Burns, William Gregory, Graham Templeman, Kenneth E. Reid, Audrey Taylor. About 170 pp.*

○ **Jordon, William.** The Social Worker in Family Situations. *160 pp. Crown 8vo.*

● **Laycock, A. L.** Adolescents and Social Work. *128 pp. Crown 8vo.*

● **Lees, Ray.** Politics and Social Work. *128 pp. Crown 8vo.*

● Research Strategies for Social Welfare. *112 pp. Tables.*

○ **McCullough, M. K.** and **Ely, Peter J.** Social Work with Groups. *127 pp. Crown 8vo.*

● **Moffett, Jonathan.** Concepts in Casework Treatment. *128 pp. Crown 8vo.*

Parsloe, Phyllida. Juvenile Justice in Britain and the United States. *The Balance of Needs and Rights. 336 pp.*

● **Plant, Raymond.** Social and Moral Theory in Casework. *112 pp. Crown 8vo.*

Priestley, Philip, Fears, Denise and **Fuller, Roger.** Justice for Juveniles. *The 1969 Children and Young Persons Act: A Case for Reform? 128 pp.*

● **Pritchard, Colin** and **Taylor, Richard.** Social Work: Reform or Revolution? *170 pp.*

○ **Pugh, Elisabeth.** Social Work in Child Care. *128 pp. Crown 8vo.*

● **Robinson, Margaret.** Schools and Social Work. *282 pp.*

○ **Ruddock, Ralph.** Roles and Relationships. *128 pp. Crown 8vo.*

● **Sainsbury, Eric.** Social Diagnosis in Casework. *118 pp. Crown 8vo.*

● Social Work with Families. *Perceptions of Social Casework among Clients of a Family Service. 188 pp.*

Seed, Philip. The Expansion of Social Work in Britain. *128 pp. Crown 8vo.*

● **Shaw, John.** The Self in Social Work. *124 pp.*

Smale, Gerald G. Prophecy, Behaviour and Change. *An Examination of Self-fulfilling Prophecies in Helping Relationships. 116 pp. Crown 8vo.*

Smith, Gilbert. Social Need. *Policy, Practice and Research. 155 pp.*

● Social Work and the Sociology of Organisations. *124 pp. Revised edition.*

● **Sutton, Carole.** Psychology for Social Workers and Counsellors. *An Introduction. 248 pp.*

● **Timms, Noel.** Language of Social Casework. *122 pp. Crown 8vo.*

● Recording in Social Work. *124 pp. Crown 8vo.*

● **Todd, F. Joan.** Social Work with the Mentally Subnormal. *96 pp. Crown 8vo.*

● **Walrond-Skinner, Sue.** Family Therapy. *The Treatment of Natural Systems. 172 pp.*

● **Warham, Joyce.** An Introduction to Administration for Social Workers. *Revised edition. 112 pp.*

● An Open Case. *The Organisational Context of Social Work. 172 pp.*

○ **Wittenberg, Isca Salzberger.** Psycho-Analytic Insight and Relationships. *A Kleinian Approach. 196 pp. Crown 8vo.*

Primary Socialization, Language and Education
General Editor   Basil Bernstein

Adlam, Diana S., *with the assistance of Geoffrey Turner and Lesley Lineker.* Code in *Context. 272 pp.*
Bernstein, Basil. Class, Codes and Control. *3 volumes.*
●   1. *Theoretical Studies Towards a Sociology of Language. 254 pp.*
    2. *Applied Studies Towards a Sociology of Language. 377 pp.*
●   3. *Towards a Theory of Educational Transmission. 167 pp.*
Brandis, W. and **Bernstein, B.** Selection and Control. *176 pp.*
Brandis, Walter and **Henderson, Dorothy.** Social Class, Language and Communication. *288 pp.*
Cook-Gumperz, Jenny. Social Control and Socialization. *A Study of Class Differences in the Language of Maternal Control. 290 pp.*
● **Gahagan, D. M.** and **G. A.** Talk Reform. *Exploration in Language for Infant School Children. 160 pp.*
Hawkins, P. R. Social Class, the Nominal Group and Verbal Strategies. *About 220 pp.*
Robinson, W. P. and **Rackstraw, Susan D. A.** A Question of Answers. *2 volumes. 192 pp. and 180 pp.*
Turner, Geoffrey J. and **Mohan, Bernard A.** A Linguistic Description and Computer Programme for Children's Speech. *208 pp.*

Reports of the Institute of Community Studies

Baker, J. The Neighbourhood Advice Centre. A Community Project in Camden. *320 pp.*
● **Cartwright, Ann.** Patients and their Doctors. *A Study of General Practice. 304 pp.*
Dench, Geoff. Maltese in London. *A Case-study in the Erosion of Ethnic Consciousness. 302 pp.*
Jackson, Brian and **Marsden, Dennis.** Education and the Working Class: *Some General Themes Raised by a Study of 88 Working-class Children in a Northern Industrial City. 268 pp. 2 folders.*
Marris, Peter. The Experience of Higher Education. *232 pp. 27 tables.*
●   Loss and Change. *192 pp.*
Marris, Peter and **Rein, Martin.** Dilemmas of Social Reform. *Poverty and Community Action in the United States. 256 pp.*
Marris, Peter and **Somerset, Anthony.** African Businessmen. *A Study of Entrepreneurship and Development in Kenya. 256 pp.*
Mills, Richard. Young Outsiders: *a Study in Alternative Communities. 216 pp.*
Runciman, W. G. Relative Deprivation and Social Justice. *A Study of Attitudes to Social Inequality in Twentieth-Century England. 352 pp.*
Willmott, Peter. Adolescent Boys in East London. *230 pp.*
Willmott, Peter and **Young, Michael.** Family and Class in a London Suburb. *202 pp. 47 tables.*
Young, Michael and **McGeeney, Patrick.** Learning Begins at Home. *A Study of a Junior School and its Parents. 128 pp.*
Young, Michael and **Willmott, Peter.** Family and Kinship in East London. *Foreword by Richard M. Titmuss. 252 pp. 39 tables.*
  The Symmetrical Family. *410 pp.*

Reports of the Institute for Social Studies in Medical Care

Cartwright, Ann, Hockey, Lisbeth and **Anderson, John J.** Life Before Death. *310 pp.*
Dunnell, Karen and **Cartwright, Ann.** Medicine Takers, Prescribers and Hoarders. *190 pp.*
Farrell, C. My Mother Said. . . *A Study of the Way Young People Learned About Sex and Birth Control. 288 pp.*

Medicine, Illness and Society
General Editor   W. M. Williams

Hall, David J. Social Relations & Innovation. *Changing the State of Play in Hospitals. 232 pp.*
Hall, David J. and **Stacey, M.** (Eds) Beyond Separation. *234 pp.*
Robinson, David. The Process of Becoming Ill. *142 pp.*
Stacey, Margaret *et al.* Hospitals, Children and Their Families. *The Report of a Pilot Study. 202 pp.*
Stimson, G. V. and **Webb, B.** Going to See the Doctor. *The Consultation Process in General Practice. 155 pp.*

Monographs in Social Theory
General Editor   Arthur Brittan

● **Barnes, B.** Scientific Knowledge and Sociological Theory. *192 pp.*
Bauman, Zygmunt. Culture as Praxis. *204 pp.*
● **Dixon, Keith.** Sociological Theory. *Pretence and Possibility. 142 pp.*
The Sociology of Belief. *Fallacy and Foundation. About 160 pp.*
Goff, T. W. Marx and Mead. *Contributions to a Sociology of Knowledge. 176 pp.*
Meltzer, B. N., Petras, J. W. and **Reynolds, L. T.** Symbolic Interactionism. *Genesis, Varieties and Criticisms. 144 pp.*
● **Smith, Anthony D.** The Concept of Social Change. *A Critique of the Functionalist Theory of Social Change. 208 pp.*

Routledge Social Science Journals

The British Journal of Sociology. *Editor – Angus Stewart; Associate Editor – Leslie Sklair. Vol. 1, No. 1 – March 1950 and Quarterly. Roy. 8vo. All back issues available. An international journal publishing original papers in the field of sociology and related areas.*
Community Work. *Edited by David Jones and Marjorie Mayo. 1973. Published annually.*
Economy and Society. *Vol. 1, No. 1. February 1972 and Quarterly. Metric Roy. 8vo. A journal for all social scientists covering sociology, philosophy, anthropology, economics and history. All back numbers available.*

Ethnic and Racial Studies. *Editor – John Stone. Vol. 1 – 1978. Published quarterly.*
Religion. Journal of Religion and Religions. *Chairman of Editorial Board, Ninian Smart. Vol. 1, No. 1, Spring 1971. A journal with an inter-disciplinary approach to the study of the phenomena of religion. All back numbers available.*
Sociology of Health and Illness. *A Journal of Medical Sociology. Editor – Alan Davies; Associate Editor – Ray Jobling. Vol. 1, Spring 1979. Published 3 times per annum.*
Year Book of Social Policy in Britain. *Edited by Kathleen Jones. 1971. Published annually.*

Social and Psychological Aspects of Medical Practice
Editor Trevor Silverstone

Lader, Malcolm. Psychophysiology of Mental Illness. *280 pp.*
● **Silverstone, Trevor** and **Turner, Paul.** Drug Treatment in Psychiatry. *Revised edition. 256 pp.*
Whiteley, J. S. and **Gordon, J.** Group Approaches in Psychiatry. *240 pp.*